THE CRASH OF
TWA FLIGHT 260

The Crash of TWA Flight 260

Charles M. Williams

University of New Mexico Press
Albuquerque

Library of Congress Cataloging-in-Publication Data
Williams, Charles M., 1931–
  The crash of TWA flight 260 / Charles M. Williams.
    p. cm.
  Includes bibliographical references.
  ISBN 978-0-8263-4807-4 (pbk. : alk. paper)
  1. Aircraft accidents—New Mexico—Albuquerque Region. I.
Title.
  TL553.525.N6W55 2010
  363.12'40978961--dc22
                                        2010005555

Dedicated to the victims of TWA Flight 260; to TWA Captain Larry DeCelles, who devoted himself to setting things right; and to the Family Assistance Foundation, whose worldwide mission is empowering disaster victims.

Contents

Illustrations

path as conjectured by the Civil Aeronautics Board.   *26*

Figure 17 View of the wreckage from a helicopter shortly after it was found atop the smoke-blackened pinnacle; the Rio Grande is in the background.   *31*

Figure 18 Close-up of the tail section of the aircraft hanging over the edge of the cliff. The east face of the pinnacle buttress plunges down beneath the tail. The sun-bathed rock to the right is evidence of the presence of the precipitous south face.   *32*

Figure 19 Sherman Marsh fires up his Primus stove for the weary rescuers who had endured the frigid night on the mountain below the crash site.   *42*

Figure 20 Frank Powers, parishioner of Rev. Davis, enjoys his breakfast out of a can, the East Mesa in the background far below.   *43*

Figure 21 The author gingerly steps over the rubble atop the pinnacle. The left horizontal stabilizer seventy-five feet down the sloping top of the buttress has the appearance of a wing looming up in front of him, the vertical stabilizer jutting out over the east cliff.   *45*

Figure 22 George Hankins (rope over shoulder) follows Sherman Marsh (carabiner on belt) uphill through crash debris.   *46*

Figure 23 Rubble everywhere. The tail section from another angle.   *47*

Figure 24 The crash pinnacle from TWA Canyon. Bodies of four victims fell onto the snowbank at the base of the shadowed near-vertical north cliff. Our path to the notch of the wreck pinnacle—hidden from view by the intervening Mizar spire—traverses right and upward from the snowbank.   *48*

Figure 25 The vertical stabilizer of the tail section projecting back over the cliff in 1955.   *48*

Figure 26 Dr. Szerlip examines remains while George Hankins takes notes.   *49*

Figure 27 Wreckage remains in a once-shredded tree to this day, but the tree is now luxuriant with foliage.   *50*

Figure 28 This "WORL" photo provided the author with crucial evidence for his analysis of the crash. Albuquerque KOB-TV photographer Dick Kent—burdened with a heavy 16mmTV-news camera—examines a large piece of fuselage emblazoned with a portion of the TWA logo above a window port. The Alioth and Mizar spires are visible in the background. 54

Figure 29 TWA transportation agent Gil Buvens examines the "WORL" wreckage from another angle. 54

Figure 30 TWA mechanic Norman McIntosh examines the right propeller hub remaining atop the pinnacle. The left engine and its propeller hub had fallen to its base. 55

Figure 31 TWA Capt. Larry DeCelles at the time he investigated the TWA Flight 260 accident in 1955. 84

Figure 32 Upper regions of Echo Canyon, where granite cliffs merge with lighter limestone layers above. The Kiwanis Cabin appears as a light dot atop the limestone sloping to its right. Below it, the silhouetted Alioth and Mizar spires tower like tombstones above crash pinnacle rising a short distance above its notch and saddle. 138

Figure 33 The crash pinnacle from the southeast. When the tail was cut free of its control cables, it fell from the tail ledge to the shrub shaped like a Christmas tree, then into the narrow cleft. The left wing fell to the base of the south face of the buttress upon impact with the cliff. Alkaid rises to the left of the pinnacle and Mizar, beyond it, to its right. 139

Figure 34 View from TWA Canyon of the crash pinnacle, Mizar, and Alioth. The ledge on which the tail section rested and the "Christmas tree" below it are visible here. A tall tree in shadow stands in the V-shaped defile between the Mizar and Alioth spires. Further to the right, a small cairn lies atop a sunlit chimney-shaped rock, placed there by climbers. The desert floor and Albuquerque lie in the remote distance. 141

Figure 35 October 8, 2005, photo from the same clearing as in Figure 25, the former taken a half century earlier. The foliage on the canyon floor is far more abundant now, but trees on the skyline are little changed. Falling rock splintered the tree in the foreground. 142

Figure 36 Wreckage jammed beneath a giant block of granite

Preface

This is the heartwarming tale of a tragedy: the crash of Trans World Airlines Flight 260 onto the upper slopes of Sandia Mountain near Albuquerque, New Mexico, on February 19, 1955.

It is a topsy-turvy tale of the events concerning the crash of an airliner in which facts and their apparent contradictions are both true; and well-considered conclusions, turned round, become the basis for comprehending the realities.

It is a tale of days, minutes, and seconds spread out over the span of half a century; a dramatic adventure story of days spent upon a beautiful, spectacular, treacherous mountain; a mystery story of the last few minutes of the aircraft as it approached its end and of its last few seconds before it crashed upon a magnificent granite spire.

Acknowledgments

This book would not have been possible without the diligence of Hugh Prather, who devoted a considerable portion of his life to searching for information concerning the crash of TWA Flight 260, tracked down knowledgeable individuals who knew something about the subject, and somehow managed to convince municipal authorities that it would be a good idea to establish a memorial to the flight at the Albuquerque Sunport a full fifty years after the disaster.

His contact with TWA Captain Larry DeCelles was a godsend to me, for Larry's meticulous records and his gift for eloquent, logical, and no-nonsense descriptions of the airliner takeoff and his efforts to vindicate the pilots provided me with invaluable insight into why the crash occurred in the first place and how the subsequent congressional investigation went awry. In short, Larry provided me with vivid accounts of the demise of the plane and his investigations, which succeeded in making a congressional committee change its collective mind.

And tops in this millennium were the efforts of Dr. Ginny Campbell, who, having lost her father and maternal grandparents

Figure 1. TWA Flight 260: Skyliner Binghamton at Louisville, Kentucky, in 1953. (Edward Peck Photo/John Proctor Collection.)

aboard the airliner, contacted me a short while after she had trekked to the crash site with Hugh Prather—supplying me with a bounteous horde of visual imagery that she, her brother Bill, and their cousin, Bill Pearson, had collected. Ginny then became my mentor when I began disentangling the newspaper accounts of what had happened a half century ago.

And later on I was blessed to have Dr. Carolyn V. Coarsey, PhD, get me on target about matters concerning the personal grief that assails the families of disaster victims. She's the brains behind the chapter entitled "Compassion" and the fascinating story about how the concept of Disaster Family Assistance came to be a world calling.

And there were fellow search-and-rescuers—Sherm Marsh, Dick Heim, Bill Lucas, A. S. "Governor" Rodgers, Steve Lagomarsino, and Gil Buvens—and rescuer family members—George Ann Hankins, Hazel and Michael Thornton, Janet Szerlip Harris—who supplied me with photos, evidence, and anecdotes about 1955 experiences as well as wondrous tales of their own adventures and successes afterward.

Victim family members Jana Creason Childers, Dan Collier, Gary Creason, Lester Davis, Leroy Doyel, Mary Balk Fink, Colleen Hamilton, Sandy Nicholl Hoch, Joe Horvat, Clark Nicholl, Anne Schoonmaker

Pearson, Peggy Collier Peters, Lynn and Judy Schoening, Barbara Schoonmaker, and Bob Tips provided me with invaluable insights into the lives and doings of their loved ones.

Chris Clark set me straight on the early history of aviation, Bob Evelyth and Jane Love put me on track with geological matters, and Catherine Baudoin supplied me with Hibben memorabilia and the photo of him with his artistic apes.

The insightful help that editor Clark Whitehorn and reviewer Bob Julyan have given me on this project was top-notch from start to finish. Karen Mazur did a great job with the book design, and copy editor Diana Rico patched up my awkward phrasing and detected "minor" errors that would have disgraced me in the eyes of a careful reader. Linda Muse and Robin Dent of Georgia State University helped immensely with putting the early manuscript into a form that I could send to UNM Press.

And last, but certainly not least, I am grateful for the support of my wife, Stanley, and the rest of my family, who bore well the travails of three years of writing.

Figure 2. Passenger waiting room in the Albuquerque terminal, circa 1950. The Pop Chalee (Merina Lujan) buffalo murals above the TWA ticket counter are still on display at the Albuquerque Sunport. (By permission of the Albuquerque History Museum.)

1
Flight Prelude

Prelude

The story begins at the Albuquerque airport terminal in the early hours of a frigid Saturday morning in February 1955. Completed in 1939, the Old Airport Terminal was—and still is—a noteworthy place. Carefully designed and constructed of adobe bricks made at the site and of wood and flagstone from the mountain forests near the city, it blends in with the surrounding desert landscape. The City of Albuquerque Web site eloquently describes its picturesque interior features "high ceilings with herringbone latillas, rough-hewn beams, heavy wood columns with corbel brackets, rough-plastered walls, recessed bays with ornate wooden screens, tin chandeliers, flagstone floors, and even a corner fireplace."

Albuquerque had been an important stopover point from the earliest days of transcontinental commercial aviation. Modern navigational systems, weather prediction technologies, and reliable radios hadn't been developed then; and pilots followed railroad tracks and highways to wend their ways over the barren desert landscapes. Eastward flights from San Francisco were directed south through Los Angeles because the Sierra Nevada Mountains blocked the direct route for low-altitude aircraft. Short hops were in vogue because of unpredictable weather conditions and limited flying ranges. Night flying was out of the question because of all of the above.

The development of sophisticated electronic technology, weather prediction systems, and systematic approaches to navigation were greatly accelerated by World War II, but were still in their infancy in 1955—they were not widely understood, accepted, or implemented in either commercial or private aviation.

The *Skyliner Binghamton*

One of the victims in this saga was the *Skyliner Binghamton*, a Martin 404 that was endowed with an improbably prominent tail that towered almost twenty-nine feet above the tarmac and some five feet higher than the Lockheed Constellation, the largest passenger liner flying at that time.

That incongruous tail will loom large throughout this saga.

Its wingspan of ninety-three feet and length of seventy-five made it a large plane, but its passenger capacity was less than half that of the Constellation. Its cruising range of one thousand miles matched that of the far smaller Douglas DC-3, the dominant airliner of that time. Passengers boarded the *Skyliner Binghamton* (identified by the number on its tail) using the retractable stairs, shown in Figure 1, that were built into the plane itself, thus permitting it to serve out-of-the-way airports that could ill afford special boarding stairs.

Friday, February 18

Trans World Airlines Flight 260 began its trip eastward from San Francisco, flew directly to Las Vegas, Nevada, and then proceeded to Albuquerque for an overnight stay. The plan was to continue on to Baltimore, Maryland, the next day. It could fly over the Sierras because the Martin 404 aircraft—with a pressurized cabin and altitude ceiling of twenty-nine thousand feet—had the capacity for topping the summit of Mount Everest. Its flying range of one thousand miles, however, dictated landing for fuel every four hours.

An overnight stay in a comfortable hotel in downtown Albuquerque would break up the flight. The crew for the first leg of Flight 260 would not continue eastward, as they were based in either San Francisco or Albuquerque—alternating between the two cities being less fatiguing for them and more economical for the airline.

Flight Hostess Kathleen Kadas would remain in her home in Albuquerque that night. She would long remember Flight 260.

Her replacement, Sharon Schoening, would not.

Saturday, February 19 | The Passengers

Early the next morning, the thirteen passengers for Flight 260 were checking in at the ticket counter.

Alfred and Dorothy Schoonmaker, the oldest among them, were from Sausalito, California. They had taken the flight from San Francisco to Albuquerque the evening before to meet their son-in-law, William R. Campbell, who had been summoned at the last moment from Tenafly, New Jersey. The three would make the short hop that morning to Santa Fe, where the men would explore the possibility of setting up an extension of their company. As her children were all grown, Mrs. Schoonmaker was enjoying the opportunity for traveling with her husband and visiting her niece at Los Alamos. Campbell's wife, Alice, would have enjoyed the trip too, but remained in New Jersey with the travails of early pregnancy.

Figure 3. Passenger Alfred G. Schoonmaker. (Courtesy of Barbara Schoonmaker.)

Mr. Schoonmaker was a diesel man—a remanufacturer of diesel engines. He bought used engines (sometimes sold to him as junk) disassembled them, repaired or replaced worn-out or obsolete components, then reassembled them for customers, who were buying functionally new machines at bargain prices.

Figure 4. Passenger Dorothy Schoonmaker. (Courtesy of Barbara Schoonmaker.)

His father had founded the A. G. Schoonmaker Company in 1898 in New Jersey and opened a New York office in 1918 at 25 Church Street, the future site of the World Trade Center. The firm marketed heavy equipment, buying used cranes and earthmovers and reselling them in Latin America. They established a London office and a yard in Jersey City, where he stored purchases and consignments to be shipped to foreign buyers.

Upon the death of his father in 1932, he assumed control of the company and discovered that it was bankrupt. The depth of the Great Depression was hardly a propitious time to start afresh, but he succeeded in redirecting the company's efforts toward the diesel engines that were beginning to come into prominent use and were destined to become the company mainstay. Diesel engines would become the primary power source for military equipment on the ground and at sea during World War II.

Immediately after the war, the company became engaged in the postwar dismantling of Navy ships, buying destroyer escorts, submarines, landing ship mediums (LSMs), and landing ship tanks (LSTs) from the government; keeping their diesel engines; and converting the rest to scrap. They set up operations in Sausalito near San Francisco and San Carlos near San Diego. Schoonmaker Point, Schoonmaker Marina, and the Schoonmaker Building remain in Marin County, across the bay from San Francisco, to this day.

Electrical power came into its own after the war, and the company found ready markets for power-generating units for industries, utilities, and municipalities in regions throughout the world, including Brazil, England, Ceylon, India, Chile, and East Africa.

Figure 5. Passenger William R. Campbell. (Courtesy of Ginny Campbell.)

William R. Campbell, vice president of A. G. Schoonmaker, was ideal for the job. Prematurely bald at the age of twenty-nine, Bill Campbell looked far older, and company clients liked and trusted him as a man who knew his business. His father-in-law had asked him to travel to Albuquerque at the last minute because he needed his expertise at the business meeting scheduled in Santa Fe.

Robert Balk, an eminent geologist at the New Mexico Bureau of Mines, was traveling eastward to attend a meeting of the scholarship committee of the National Science Foundation. He was carrying a recently completed geological map of the Precambrian formations of the Tres Hermanas Mountains of New Mexico. He had chosen TWA Flight 260 so that he could have a brief visit with his daughter Mary. She was a student at Stephens College in Columbia, Missouri.

Born in 1899 in Reval, Estonia, Balk attended geology lectures at Breslau University in Poland to pass his oral exam for the PhD, which he earned summa cum laude in 1923. Facing the problem of how to earn a living amid the monetary inflation years of the postwar Depression, he gladly accepted a ticket from an uncle living in New York to come and see the geology of the Hudson River Valley. He supported himself as an assistant in the geology department at Columbia University and as a part-time waiter.

Figure 6. Passenger Robert Balk. (Courtesy of the Geological Society of America.)

He did so well at the latter that in six months' time he was offered the position of headwaiter, but instead accepted the lower salaried position of instructor at Hunter College in New York City. There he remained until 1935, when he ascended to the chairmanship of the geology department at Mount Holyoke College in Massachusetts.

The studies that gained Balk national prominence in geological circles were done largely at his own expense on weekends and in his spare time. He declined an oil company offer so that he could focus his energies on the investigations that he loved. Though igneous rock would never prove as lucrative as oil-bearing shale, his life's work would be devoted to it.

He married in 1946 and a year later leaped at the opportunity to teach at the University of Chicago, where he could concentrate on scientific research. Though he loved teaching at Mount Holyoke, he longed to do more research and have students who desired to apply their lives to his field. The Mount Holyoke College administration and his colleagues recognized his achievements, but their purpose was to educate well-rounded women citizens who would take their places in society—not in geology—after graduation.

The move to Chicago proved fruitful in that regard, but his remoteness from the field began to vex him. He was a superb teacher but was dedicated to fieldwork and was happiest next to an outcrop—be it under the blazing sun, the gray, cloudy skies of New England, or the snows of the Adirondacks.

He accepted an offer to join the New Mexico Bureau of Mines at Socorro, New Mexico, in 1952 as principal geologist. The geological landscape there entranced him, as did the good weather for fieldwork and a highly congenial atmosphere. Balk was happy and enjoyed his work as never before.

He was president of the tectonophysics section of the Geophysical Union, and his participation in activities of the National Research Council brought him east at least once a year.

Precambrian geology was his passion. And it was Precambrian granite that felled him.

Harold E. Tips, like Robert Balk, was associated with geology—not as a scientist, but as an accountant. As the vice president and land man for the Helmerich Payne Oil & Gas Drilling & Exploration Company, he had been searching land records in Santa Fe the day before the crash and had boarded a plane to return to his home in Tulsa, Oklahoma. When the flight turned back because of bad weather, he remained in Albuquerque to have dinner with longtime friends—the DeWitt Blacks, formerly of Pecos, Texas.

Figure 7. Passenger Harold E. Tips. (Courtesy of Robert Tips.)

During his visit with the Blacks that evening, he showed them a demitasse cup he had purchased that day for his wife. After the cup was lost in the ensuing crash, Mr. Black bought and delivered a duplicate cup to the surviving family during his stay in Tulsa for his friend's funeral.

Just before ending his visit, Tips played several songs on the piano, ending with the gospel hymn "In the Garden."

In the Garden
John 20:18

I come to the garden alone,
While the dew is still on the roses;
And the voice I hear, falling on my ear,
The Son of God discloses.

And he walks with me, and he talks with me,
And he tells me I am his own;

And the joy we share as we tarry there,
None other has ever known.

He speaks, and the sound of his voice
Is so sweet, the birds hush their singing,
And the melody that he gave to me,
Within my heart is ringing.

I'd stay in the garden with him,
Though the night around me be falling,
But he bids me go; through the voice of woe,
His voice to me is calling.

Harold Tips was born in 1905 in Runge, Texas; his uncle became its first mayor when the town was later incorporated in 1912. Like Robert Balk, the Tips family had emigrated—though far earlier, in 1849, from Germany. Harold attended San Marcos State College, then graduated from the University of Texas with a bachelor's degree in accounting and began employment in accounting firms in San Angelo and Fort Worth. In 1937 he became manager of the Eppenauer Drilling Company as well as of several of Mr. Eppenauer's farms near Pecos, Texas. He was made an officer and manager of Texas Cotton Industries, a cotton gin cooperative, in 1943; then moved to San Angelo in 1945 to be the manager of Cardinal Oil Company. The firm was acquired by Helmerick & Payne in 1949, necessitating a move to Tulsa, Oklahoma, his home when he boarded Flight 260.

Six feet tall and weighing 190 pounds, Tips was a robust and active man, deacon in the Presbyterian Church, avid fisherman, hunter, golfer, champion tennis player in his early adult life, and Boy Scout Troop committeeman.

The Reverend Earl Frederick Davis was a newcomer to Albuquerque when he boarded Flight 260. Three weeks earlier, he and his wife, Jessie, had traveled from their former church near Modesto, California, to assume their duties as the new pastors of the First Assembly of God Church.

Upon receiving word that his brother Walter had died of a heart attack on February 18, the day before the crash, he immediately made plans to attend the funeral in Oklahoma City. That evening, members and friends of the First Assembly of God Church gave the Davises a welcoming reception—perhaps at the same time that Harold Tips was playing "In the Garden" on the piano for his friends.

Figure 8. Passenger Rev. Earl F. Davis (on the far right, behind his wife, Jessie) at the July 1936 Seminole (Oklahoma) District Camp for the Assemblies of God. (Courtesy of the Flower Pentecostal Heritage Center, Springfield, Missouri.)

Earl Davis was born in 1903 in Fort Smith, Arkansas, and eighteen years later married Jessie Barger in Purcell, Oklahoma. In 1925 he accepted Christ as his Savior, entering the ministry as an evangelist in 1927 and being ordained in 1929, four days after the stock market crash that heralded the arrival of the Great Depression.

Most of the rest of his life was spent in full-time ministry, pastoring, and evangelism. Between all but two of his pastorates he spent time as an evangelist in the field.

He pastored at picturesquely named towns: Hichita, Henryetta, Gracemont, Chickasha, El Reno, Oklahoma City, and Tulsa, Oklahoma; Tulare, Stockton, Alameda, and Ceres in California; and El Dorado in Arkansas.

He also served as Christ's ambassador president and Sunday school director of the Oklahoma district for two years and, while pastoring, was a sectional presbyter in both Oklahoma and California.

Lois Dean, a farmer's daughter turned schoolteacher, was born in 1913 in Hollis, Oklahoma. The fourth of five daughters of Thomas and Kate Dean, she also had four half siblings from her mother's previous marriage. After her mother's death in 1925 and her father's in 1932, Lois and her sisters lived with a half sister and her husband for the next two years.

Their life during the Great Depression was Spartan. Spending money was scarce. Though it was also the dust bowl era, they had sufficient water to grow food for the family on their own farm. Her family had remained in Hollis, but most of the highway travel then was headed west, where folks hoped to find work.

Having obtained her teaching credentials from Southwestern State Teachers College, she was teaching first grade in McLoud, near Oklahoma City, when World War II broke out. Her sister Jessie Doyel moved nearby with her two children and husband, Marvin, who would commute to work in the Douglas plant that opened at Tinker Air Force Base in 1943 to build C-47 aircraft.

Figure 9. Passenger Lois Dean as a first grade teacher at the Lew Wallace School in Albuquerque. (Courtesy of Leroy Doyel.)

According to her nephew, Leroy Doyel, Lois headed west about 1947 and continued teaching in public schools, becoming so enthralled with Albuquerque and New Mexico in general that she convinced Jessie to visit her with her two sons and consider moving there. The three arrived in 1950 accompanied by Lois's older half sister, Gracie, and her husband, Estel, who had never been farther than fifty miles from Hollis. Jessie and her sons remained in Albuquerque, but the others returned to Oklahoma.

Lois was a pillar of strength, a mentor, and an inspiration to Jessie as well as to others who knew her—especially her nieces and nephews, whom she adored. She was active in the First Baptist Church of Albuquerque, teaching Sunday school, visiting parishioners, performing benevolence work, and helping young people.

Although she was highly satisfied and happy as a first grade teacher at Lew Wallace School in Albuquerque, Lois's horizons broadened and she was seriously considering employment with the U.S. government teaching military dependents overseas in Japan. Applicant interviews were being conducted at the regional office in Oklahoma City.

As Lois had never flown and thought it would be a good experience, she booked her ticket aboard TWA Flight 260.

Dan A. Collier was president of the Dan Cohen Shoe Company (reputedly the first shoe chain in the USA), headquartered in Cincinnati and consisting of roughly a hundred retail stores, primarily in Ohio, Kentucky, and the southeastern United States. (Some of the stores operated under the name of Cohen were changed to Collier to reflect the family name.) The reason for his ill-fated trip to Albuquerque was that the company had recently opened a store there. He was on his

Figure 10. Passenger Dan A. Collier as a lieutenant commander during World War II. His youthful appearance was much the same in 1955. (Courtesy of Dan A. Collier Jr.)

Figure 11. Passenger Worth H. Nicholl. Photo taken at the Boy Scout banquet for Governor Simms shortly before the crash. (Courtesy of Mary Hoch.)

way to Little Rock, Arkansas, and expected to return home to Cincinnati to celebrate his fiftieth birthday on the following Friday.

A 1927 graduate of the University of Michigan, he obtained a master's degree from the University of Chicago, then attended Harvard Law School and graduated from the College of Law at the University of Cincinnati. He served as a lieutenant in the U.S. Navy during World War II. Though he had a law degree, he never practiced law.

His family included his wife, Betty, and two children, Dan Jr. and Peggy, who described him as a very nice, soft-spoken man—a man who loved to play the harmonica, had a passion for flying, and owned a small plane.

Worth H. Nicholl, a professional engineer and assistant to the executive vice president of the Public Service Company of New Mexico, was looking forward to rejoining his family in Amarillo, Texas, and celebrating his son Larry's fourteenth birthday on February 22. A council commissioner for the Northern New Mexico Boy Scouts, he had been master of ceremonies at a scout leader banquet in Santa Fe the week before, in which council leaders had given Governor John F. Simms a report on the progress of scouting during the year.

Born in 1911 in Plainview, Texas, he grew up in Tulia. He delivered milk before and after school for his dairyman father, who, having only an eighth-grade education, sent his sons to Texas A&M College in the worst of the Great Depression. Worth earned a degree in mechanical engineering, and his brothers became veterinarians.

Married in 1935, living in Paris, Texas, and earning his livelihood as a salesman, he moved later to Amarillo to work for the Public Service Company of Texas. A lieutenant commander in the Naval Reserve during World War II, he volunteered for service in the Seabees, but was called back as his services were far more valuable at home. After the war he worked for the U.S. Bureau of Reclamations, developing significant transmission line and power plant innovations at Elephant Butte Dam in New Mexico and Hoover Dam in Nevada. A frequent testifier at congressional hearings in Washington, he was also an established procrastinator—his staff learned to line up at the airport to snare his signature on documents.

The Public Service Company of New Mexico hired him in 1954, after they tired of having him as an opponent. While maintaining his residence in Amarillo, where some of his children were in school, he lived at the Elks Club in Albuquerque and also served as scoutmaster of Troop 142, sponsored by the Saint Francis Xavier Catholic Church. He was an avid weight lifter and a large man even by today's standards; he worked out at the YMCA three days a week. He had also run cross-country at Texas A&M.

Nicholl was also an accomplished musician who had learned to play the tuba in high school, played in the marching band at Texas A&M, and later established himself with the Amarillo Symphony. He encouraged his children to play musical instruments and sing in choral groups.

I knew him slightly and have never forgotten the classy way that he had first introduced himself to me at Boy Scout camporee in the fall of 1954: "I'm Worth Nicholl—but some folks say I'm not even worth a nickel."

He was looking forward to moving his family to Albuquerque in the summer.

Robert S. Nyeland and **Harry M. Shuth**, professional engineers, had boarded Flight 260 in Las Vegas, Nevada, to return home to Kansas City. They were production supervisors for Bendix Corporation and had traveled west the previous Sunday as an observation team to witness nearby atomic bomb tests.

Homer Bray, an Albuquerque insurance and real estate operator, was en route to Topeka, Kansas, on business.

Robert B. Reilly, a highly respected regional engineer for the American Institute of Steel Construction (AISC) and a 1926 graduate of Texas A&M College, was returning to his home in Dallas, Texas.

AISC continues to this day as a not-for-profit technical institute and trade association for the use of structural steel in the construction industry.

Figure 12. TWA Captain Ivan Spong. (Courtesy of Larry DeCelles.)

The Crew

The crew for the second leg of Flight 260, from Albuquerque to Kansas City, had flown into Albuquerque from Kansas City the night before.

Captain Ivan Spong was born on a farm west of Chanute, Kansas, in 1910, and had learned to shoulder responsibilities early in life. His father had contracted the flu during the great pandemic of 1918 and had suffered from weakened lungs until his death in 1926. As the oldest male, Ivan worked after school, on weekends, and in the summers to help support his family. He had little free time in high school, but still did well in math, science, and shop classes and in basketball and track. With the family's financial constraints, he never had a chance to attend college, delivering ice and working in the oil fields instead.

Spong showed an interest in flying at an early age and loved to hang around the Chanute airport—perhaps inspired by the Kansas sky that dominated the landscape or by the airplane manufacturing plants in nearby Wichita. He received formal flight training in Chanute through a Depression-era program while picking up knowledge about airplane mechanics, navigation, and instrument flying on his own. When he found a badly wrecked airplane, he used his mechanical skills to repair it with salvaged parts. His landing strip was the farm where one of his sisters lived; an old barn served as a hangar.

He began his professional flying career in Wichita as a test pilot for Cessna Aircraft, earned extra cash as a local flight instructor, and later flew bombers to Canada for a U.S. aircraft company before being accepted for training as a TWA pilot in 1942. During World War II, he made over one hundred trips to Europe, flying large transport planes for the Air Transport Command; he carried supplies and payroll on his way over and returned with injured U.S. soldiers or German prisoners-of-war. When returning to New York with the latter, he made a point of flying by the Statue of Liberty to give them a vivid reminder of why our country was in the war.

Spong rose to the rank of captain with TWA after the war, and he and his wife, Jean, adopted a son, Michael, in 1950, providing Ivan with a new focus and a chance to pass on the many things he had learned about life. He was doing well in business with investments in oil leases around Chanute and a partnership interest in an airplane; and he continued to play a strong role in supporting his mother.

He was known among his fellow pilots as a quiet but firm captain— one who flew by the book. When a cousin asked him whether he was ever afraid while flying, he replied that he wasn't, but that the route between Albuquerque and Santa Fe gave him concern when he had to fly under poor visibility.

Captain Spong was now a veteran pilot who had just completed his twelfth year for the airline at the age of forty-four. He had logged nearly thirteen thousand hours—at least fifteen hundred of them flying instruments in the clouds—and more than one hundred trips over the Atlantic, to London, Paris, Lisbon, Rome, Athens, and Cairo. He had flown the route from Albuquerque to Santa Fe many times, in all kinds of weather; this trip would be his twelfth in the current month. A week earlier he had flown it under the watchful eye of a company check pilot.

First Officer Jesse James Creason Jr. was born in 1925 in Datto, a small farming community in the pancake-flat cotton fields of northeastern Arkansas. Known as "Junior" as a youngster, he disliked the nickname, and as an adult used "J. J." on business correspondence, although his family and friends called him "Jim."

He and two older sisters spent their early years helping their parents on a family farm in the poverty-stricken rural South during the Great Depression. An elder brother had died at a young age after being kicked by a horse. Junior's feet may have been in the dirt, but his thoughts were in the skies; he dreamed of things far beyond what a small town in Arkansas had to offer. He quit school after the ninth grade and left home at the age of eighteen to work for Bendix Aircraft Corporation in Wayne, Michigan, where he learned to inspect aircraft carburetors and read specification

Figure 13. TWA First Officer J. J. Creason Jr. (Courtesy of Gary Creason.)

blueprints. He had an aptitude for mechanical work and a talent for drawing, and he loved airplanes.

For a gifted young man of limited means, World War II would offer opportunity as well as danger and adventure. He was inducted into the army in Detroit in October 1943, and, as the nation desperately needed pilots and crews to man U.S. Army Air Corps bomber squadrons, his lack of formal schooling did not stand in the way. The army stood ready to provide the necessary training, and he seized the opportunity. Initially trained as an aircraft engine mechanic and crew chief, he shifted to be an aerial gunner and bombardier, ending up as a flight engineer on B-17s. The war ended before he was deployed into combat, and Sergeant Creason was honorably discharged in April 1946.

While home on leave during the war, he met a young woman named Tommie King from a nearby farm in Arkansas. They were married soon after he was discharged from the army and spent their first few years together in such places as Pocahontas, Arkansas; Malden, Missouri; and St. Louis, Missouri.

Like many returning World War II soldiers, Creason used the G.I. Bill to maximum advantage, taking civilian flying lessons and embarking on a career as a pilot. By age twenty-four, in 1949, he had become an accomplished aviator, earning licenses as private pilot, commercial pilot, and flight instructor while studying for a General Education Diploma (GED). He received his GED in early 1950, only a few days before earning a flight examiner license.

He had also accumulated an impressive number of flight hours crop dusting (a delicate and hazardous occupation), conducting flight instruction, and flying U.S. Forest Service personnel over fire-ravaged areas for aerial photography. During those years, he managed to buy several airplanes, including a Stearman, a legendary open-cockpit biplane.

Like many young pilots of that era, Creason loved fast cars and spent much of his spare time building and tinkering with them. This was a time when state-of-the-art automotive technology was accessible to a car enthusiast working in a home garage. By the time of his death, Creason had painstakingly converted a black 1950 Ford V-8 convertible into a gleaming hot rod, complete with delicately tuned chrome-plated dual carburetors, chrome-plated dual exhausts, and a growling glass-pack muffler system.

Jim Creason quickly embraced fatherhood when a son, Gary, was born in 1950. By the age of two, Gary regularly accompanied his father everywhere around North Kansas City, Missouri, where they now lived—to automotive garages, an occasional tavern, and the local pool hall.

Creason's airline career began with TWA in 1951 in Kansas City, when he first met his soon-to-be close friend, TWA Captain Al Gettings, in a room full of other hopeful job applicants. About ten minutes before closing time at 5:00 p.m., frustrated Jim Creason rose to leave, muttering words to the effect that he was an experienced pilot, and if TWA wasn't interested, he could find a good flying job elsewhere. Gettings, by then the only other applicant still waiting, stopped Creason and persuaded him to wait just a little longer. Moments later, an exhausted interviewer entered the room and hired them on the spot.

By February 1955, at age twenty-nine, First Officer Creason had been piloting for TWA for more than three years and had amassed nearly four thousand flying hours. He had flown the Albuquerque route some thirty-two times and was well acquainted with its hazardous features.

He and Tommie had recently bought their first house. A second child, an eleven-month-old daughter named Jana, had her father wrapped around her finger. He would never see his third child, Jill, who would be born exactly five months after his final day in the air.

Flight hostess Sharon Schoening was born May 3, 1931, the daughter of Mr. and Mrs. Delbert Schoening, in Spencer, Iowa—the home of Iowa's largest county fair and the seat of Clay County at the confluence of the Sioux and Ocheyedan Rivers in the northwest corner of the state.

Nicknamed Shari, she and her twin brother, Dean, were raised there and graduated from the high school in the class of 1949. She was then employed by the Equitable of Iowa Life Insurance Company, serving there for two years before venturing forth to Kansas City, Missouri, for a year and a half of training at the TWA flight school. After completing her training she worked as a hostess for the airline for twenty months prior to her death.

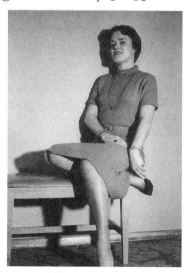

Figure 14. TWA flight hostess Sharon Schoening. Photo taken shortly before her death. (Courtesy of Lynn Schoening.)

Flight hostesses of that era were proud of the title. To them, *hostess* implied distinction. *Flight attendant* was a pedestrian term—its initials also stood for *fat ass*.

Flight toward Santa Fe

TWA Captain Larry DeCelles is the source for the following narrative. He was not in Albuquerque that day, but his descriptions of the aircraft crew's flight preparation and takeoff were derived from official records and from his own professional experiences. He will play a major role in this saga, but I'll introduce him more properly later.

The *Skyliner Binghamton* was parked on the tarmac near the terminal—an air-conditioner truck pumping heated air into its frigid cabin, while a ground-power unit was supplying its electricity. Baggage handlers were busy too, loading the cargo bins, while commissary men carried aboard thermoses full of hot coffee and containers with ham and scrambled eggs.

A fuel truck pulled up and parked under the nose of the ship. The ground service helper climbed out of the truck and walked into the airport restaurant, where he found the captain and the first officer sipping coffee with the flight hostess as she finished her breakfast. The men were planning to have their breakfasts on board the plane after departing from Santa Fe, just twenty-six minutes' flying time from Albuquerque.

The ground service helper asked the captain whether he was satisfied with the amount of fuel specified in the dispatcher's release message. When the captain confirmed the amount, he returned to his truck.

The elevation of Albuquerque is one mile above sea level, while Santa Fe, a thousand feet higher, lies just forty-five miles away on a straight-line course to the northeast. Directly between them, Sandia Mountain rises a precipitous vertical mile above the Rio Grande Valley floor to a height of nearly eleven thousand feet. Originating at a point southeast of Albuquerque, the mountain ridge extends to the north-northwest, passing ten miles east of the airport and terminating at a point approximately twenty miles north-northeast of the city. Though the minimum safe altitude for the straight-line course from Albuquerque to Santa Fe was thirteen thousand feet, airport officials never authorized instrument-guided flights over it.

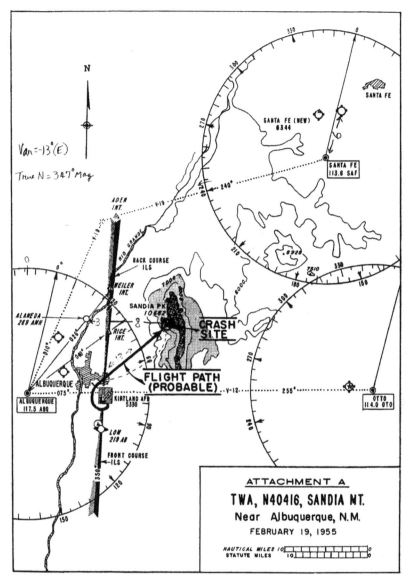

Figure 15. Probable path of TWA Flight 260 as conjectured by the Civil Aeronautics Board. The path deduced by the Air Line Pilots Association is the dashed line below it.

The approved air route was only nine miles longer than the straight-line course—a dogleg running north-northwest from Albuquerque, then east-northeast into Santa Fe. The minimum prescribed altitude for instrument flight along this route is nine thousand feet above sea level. It was along this route and at this altitude that Spong and Creason had planned their flight. The trip would take twenty-six minutes.

An air force colonel was having breakfast in the kitchen of his home a mile and a half northeast of the airport terminal building. He had planned a hunting trip in the Sandias, and his companions were to pick him up at 7:00 a.m. Looking out the window, he noted the snowstorm in the mountain area.

TWA Flight 371—a Constellation bound for Los Angeles with stops at Albuquerque and Phoenix—had encountered snow on its approach to Albuquerque from the south. Directly over Albuquerque, its pilot saw the airport and started his landing approach in the clear, heading north and making a right turn for a south landing at 6:40 a.m. He noticed that the view of the dogleg airway to Santa Fe was blocked by a storm cloud and falling snow.

The pilots deplaned and were about to enter the operations office when Captain Spong and First Officer Creason emerged to board their flight. The four pilots exchanged greetings and briefly discussed the weather—the copilot of the Constellation walking a short distance with the Martin pilots to view the snowstorm. Looking toward Sandia Ridge fourteen miles northeast, they could see only the foothills. From the air, even those would not have been visible.

By 6:45, Spong and Creason were in their cockpit, positioning the controls and checking the radios and navigational equipment in accordance with their checklist.

By 6:59, the engines were started, the ground service helper directed Flight 260 to depart from the ramp, and Spong asked the airport control tower for taxi clearance.

At 7:00, exactly on schedule, Flight 260 rolled away from the Albuquerque terminal and taxied the short distance to the run-up block for runway eleven where the crew began its before-takeoff check—the first item requiring the pilot to erect the gyro used to stabilize the fluxgate compass—an instrument that will play a center stage role in what follows.

The voice of the tower came in clearly over the static-free radio channel: "Airways Traffic Control clears TWA Flight 260 for an approach to the Santa Fe airport. Cruise nine thousand feet by way of Victor airway number nineteen. Climb northbound on the back course of the Albuquerque ILS localizer." Although an instrument landing system, or ILS, is designed to allow a pilot to land at an airport in cloudy conditions or at night using "localizer" radio beams, it can also be used during flight in the opposite direction on the "back course" (details to be discussed in a later chapter). In brief, the pilot is being instructed to fly from Albuquerque to Santa Fe using the route designed for flying on instruments from Santa Fe to Albuquerque.

This instrument flight clearance conformed to Spong's flight plan in every respect except for the departure routing that specified using the back course of the Albuquerque ILS localizer. To comply with the clearance, Flight 260 would take off from runway eleven toward the southeast and then make a right turn—away from the mountain—to attain a northerly heading and follow a radio course line (the "back course of the Albuquerque ILS localizer") north from Kirtland Air Field until it intersected another radio course line ("Victor airway nineteen") extending northeast to Santa Fe. The radio course lines would be displayed to the pilots by means of "course-deviation indicators" on the instrument panel.

In keeping with TWA practice, Captain Spong recorded the clearance into his flight log and read it back to the tower. The response came: "Roger, report passing Weiler intersection to Approach Control, please."

"Weiler intersection?" asked Spong. He was looking at the current departure procedure chart contained in the navigation kit, and it did not show a checkpoint by that name.

"That's correct," replied the tower operator, "zero-two-six degree radial and the back course."

A "radial" is a course line that radiates from a radio transmitter as a spoke radiates from the hub of a bicycle wheel. Spong and Creason would understand that the Weiler intersection was the point where the north course of the Albuquerque runway localizer would cross the course line radiating twenty-six degrees from the Albuquerque omni-directional radio station west of the airport.

At 7:04, having completed their pretakeoff check, the pilots of Flight 260 called the tower and requested takeoff clearance. The tower operator replied, "TWA 260, wind south, one-zero, cleared for takeoff, runway one-one."

First Officer Creason would fly the airplane to Santa Fe. Spong was handling the radio and wanted to be doubly certain about the Weiler intersection. He asked the tower to confirm his understanding that it was the point where the localizer crossed the twenty-six-degree radial of the Albuquerque omnidirectional radio station. The tower replied, "Zero-two-six degree radial from the Albuquerque omni. The old Alameda intersection, it's been renamed."

Flight 260 taxied onto the runway, and Creason shoved the throttles forward. The engines roared and the airplane moved down the concrete strip—the nose wheel lifting first—and when the airspeed was one hundred knots, the main wheels broke ground. Five seconds later, the landing gear had been retracted, and Creason was making the first of a standard series of power reductions.

The time was 7:05. The sixteen persons on board had eight minutes to live.

At 7:06, Spong requested Tower permission to make a right turn. The tower replied: "TWA 260 cleared to make right turn."

The tower operator last noticed the flight in a normal right turn south of the field. Then his attention was directed elsewhere.

At 7:08, the ground service helper looked up from his duties and saw Flight 260 about half a mile due north of the terminal building. The flight was rolling out of its right turn, but instead of heading north as the ground service helper had seen other flights do, Flight 260 was headed east-northeast—directly toward Sandia Mountain.

The ground service helper, L. E. Olsen, was busy, but he stopped to watch the flight fly toward the clouds until it was five or six miles away—appearing as a small object against the somber backdrop of the storm cloud that now obscured the Rio Grande Valley to the north and the entire mountain range to its east. He could barely make out the lower parts of the foothills at the base of the mountains.

The air force colonel was standing in front of his home a mile and a half north-northeast of the airport, waiting for his hunting companions, binoculars slung over his shoulder. He noticed Flight 260 approaching from the direction of the west edge of the airport. As it passed overhead, a thought occurred to the colonel: "If he's eastbound, he's too low; if he's northbound, he's off course."

At 7:09, the weather observer came out of the weather bureau office on the northeast side of the passenger terminal for another routine check of the weather conditions. Flight 260 had just disappeared into the clouds, headed for Sandia Ridge.

Three-quarters of an hour had elapsed since his earlier observation. During the interval the clouds over the airport had lifted and thinned somewhat; the wind had shifted slightly and was now blowing from the south-southeast at six knots. The snowstorm obscuring the mountains to the east had developed northward. The television antennas on Sandia Crest, which he had seen at the time of his earlier observation, were now hidden by the storm. Only the foot of the mountain was visible.

The observer time-stamped the record of his observations at 7:12 a.m.

At 7:09, First Officer Creason readied the plane for cruising at nine thousand feet. He closed the cowl flaps and the oil cooler shutters, consulted the power table, pulled the throttles back to the setting prescribed in the table, and toggled the propellers down to cruise rpm.

He had already turned on the anti-icing equipment. The wing heaters were pouring hot air through the leading edge of the wing to prevent ice formation, and a steady flow of alcohol was coursing down the leading edge of each propeller blade. Electricity flowing through the heating element on the intake for the airspeed indicator was keeping that vital channel open; and hot air from the cabin heaters was being channeled between the thermopanes of the windshield.

Since rolling out of the long right turn that had begun shortly after takeoff, Spong and Creason had been flying by instruments. The snow cloud, obscuring the valley and the mountain, had left them no horizontal reference except that of the "artificial horizon" presented by their flight instruments.

They had entered the cloud at 7:09. Cruising now at a speed of approximately two hundred thirty miles per hour, they were waiting for the Weiler intersection to appear on Spong's course-deviation indicator. Spong had just finished noting the takeoff time on the navigational log sheet and was now making the customary entries in the engine and aircraft log book.

At 7:11, having finished his log entries, Spong was trying to raise the Albuquerque company radio operator to give him the takeoff time. Because of the snow, there was a great deal of static on the line, and Spong was unable to get through. He decided to use the static-free radio that was still tuned to the tower.

At 7:12, Spong was in the act of changing radio frequencies when the terrain-warning bell suddenly sounded its alarm. Instinctively, both pilots looked out the window. Nothing but gray cloud, but then, flashing through a weak spot in the cloud just beyond the right wingtip, they saw the sheer cliffside of Sandia Crest—an appalling shock, for they should have been ten miles from the mountain.

Reacting instantly, they rolled the airplane steeply to the left and pulled its nose up. The heading indicator spun rapidly. When it was indicating a westerly heading, they started to level the wings. This was their final act. Hidden by the dense cloud, another cliffside lay directly ahead. When they struck it, they were still in a left bank, nose high. The airplane exploded. The time was 7:13.

At 7:12, the Albuquerque tower received a radio call from Pioneer Air Lines Flight 62, requesting clearance to taxi out for takeoff. Like TWA 260, Pioneer's destination was also Santa Fe.

The tower replied, "Pioneer 62, cleared to runway seventeen or eleven, wind south at eight knots, altimeter twenty-nine point eighty-one, time zero-seven-one-two."

As Pioneer 62 rolled away from the ramp, the tower operator started to phone Airways Traffic Control (ATC) to request en route clearance for the flight, but interrupted himself, realizing ATC would first want the position of TWA 260. Reaching for the microphone instead of the telephone, he called: "TWA 260, are you northbound on the back course yet?"

There was no reply. In the clouds, approaching Sandia Ridge, Captain Spong was in the act of changing to the company radio frequency to transmit the time of takeoff—an act he never completed.

After several fruitless attempts to contact TWA 260, the Tower secured and issued an ATC clearance to the Pioneer flight to proceed to Santa Fe at an altitude of ten thousand feet, one thousand feet above the level at which TWA 260 had been cleared.

Pioneer 62 took off and made a long, slow, climbing turn south of the airport. Looking north and northeast, the Pioneer pilots noted that the weather would require instrument flight. The mountains and the valley to the north along the airway were completely obscured by the snowstorm. The snowfall was heavy. It appeared as a solid wall, just a few minutes' flying time north of the airport. They climbed to the top of the cloud and proceeded to Santa Fe. At ten thousand feet they were just skimming through the tops of the cloud and, when they were north of the mountain, made the turn in the dogleg course to break out into the clear. While descending to land at Santa Fe, they learned that TWA 260 was unreported and overdue.

The hunting companions of the air force colonel arrived, and they drove off toward the mountains. The colonel couldn't get that airplane off his mind. "Very strange," he mused.

The tower operator called repeatedly: "TWA 260, Albuquerque Approach Control; over. TWA 260, Albuquerque Approach Control; over." But there was only silence. (Approach Control is a radar facility associated with an airport.)

The pilots of the Constellation took off for Phoenix, the sound of the Tower's plaintive call echoing chillingly in their ears. They, too, took up the call. Even after changing to the radio frequency used by TWA flight operations, they kept up the hopeless refrain.

With the departure of the Phoenix flight, the ground service helper was able to relax for a moment and was having a cigarette when he heard that Flight 260 was overdue at Santa Fe.

Norman, Oklahoma

Bob Tips—whose father, Harold, had played "In the Garden" for his friends in Albuquerque—woke with a start about 7:13 a.m. in a fraternity house dorm. He looked out the window to see that it was sleeting outside, then hopped back into his bunk and pulled the covers over his head to go back to sleep—it was Saturday morning, and he could sleep late. His mother would phone him later that morning to tell him that his father's plane was missing, and a fraternity buddy would drive him all the way to Tulsa so that he wouldn't have to take the bus.

An ROTC student at the University of Oklahoma, Bob Tips had last seen his dad four days earlier, when he had marched out of the armory. He remembered his father leaning against a tree, grinning at him.

Santa Fe

Eleanor Weddell and her husband, Larry, waited in vain at the Santa Fe airport for the arrival of her aunt and uncle, the Schoonmakers. They had waited for hours when a man with the Civil Air Patrol (CAP) asked them why they were there. When they explained, the CAP man told them that no one knew where the plane was. "It had just disappeared. We know the plane is down, for they only had enough fuel to stay in the air until noon."

Larry stayed in Santa Fe until that evening. Heavily involved with ham radios, he was a main source of communication for the CAP during the search. He was thus one of the first to get the news on Sunday that the plane had been found.

The sense of the futility and emptiness of that day would remain with Eleanor Weddell for over half a century.

Columbia, Missouri

Mary Balk's parents were divorced when she was three. She grew up knowing that her father was a famous geologist, but he saw her only occasionally, visiting her for an hour or two on his way to a professional meeting every few years or so, or from time to time sending her beautifully written letters (some with exquisitely drawn sketches) portraying the wonders of the countryside he was investigating.

Plans had been made for her to visit him in New Mexico a year later, during the summer of 1956. She hoped that she would get to know him better then. But that would never happen now.

2
Search

The Sandias

The Sandia Mountains, as seen from Albuquerque, shine a vivid red in the alpine glow of sunset—the name (which means "watermelon" in Spanish) being an apt description of the color. The Sangre de Cristo (blood of Christ) Mountains rising above Santa Fe are so named for the same reason.

As mountains go, the Sandias are far too small to be plural, and yet they are referred to both in the singular and the plural—with Sandia Peak, Sandias, mountain, and mountains all in common use.

The Sandias rise a full mile above Albuquerque to an altitude of 10,678 feet. They are part of a fault block, a portion of the earth's crust that was fractured and began tilting upward seventeen million years ago, creating a split in the earth's crust now known as the Rio Grande Rift. The land to the west of the fault subsided into the trench, now marked by the Rio Grande that extends all the way to Colorado. The Rio Grande Valley was thus created by a fractured earth rather than river erosion. The eastern and northern sides of the Sandias slope gradually to the crest; their surfaces, reasonably smooth and forested, are ideal for skiing once snow arrives.

The precipitous western and southern faces are evidence of the fracture itself. Their immense granite cliffs are of the Precambrian era, capped by a layer of Pennsylvania limestone that was deposited at the bottom of a shallow sea about three hundred million years ago. It was exposed when thousands of feet of sedimentary deposits were eroded off the eastern slopes. The same layer of rocks that are seen atop the crest lie buried twenty thousand feet beneath Albuquerque—a dislocation of some five miles that makes the Rio Grande Rift one of the most impressive on earth.

The size of the cliffs is not readily apparent from town, and a viewer can have the false impression of a two-dimensional surface devoid of depth. In actuality, the face has a complex topography abundant with narrow canyons, knife ridges, and isolated spires—all hidden from sight—that have a propensity for illogically changing their appearances when viewed from different angles.

A telescopic view of the west face of the wreck pinnacle reveals that it is part of a ridge with a massive face and spires rising above it—best viewed at sunset, when shadows delineate their features, but

Figure 16. Sandia Mountain at sunset, the silhouetted face of the crash pinnacle in the center. Shadowed outlines of the spires near the wreck pinnacle magically appear above it at dusk each day, the sunlit spires themselves visible to the left and higher. The dotted line shows the flight path as conjectured by the Civil Aeronautics Board. (Courtesy of Hugh Prather.)

there is no hint of the pinnacle's own spirelike qualities, which are more clearly evident from the slopes beneath it. Seen end on, the pinnacle reveals that it is indeed a narrow, finlike ridge.

The plane struck the pinnacle's eastern face out of sight of Albuquerque—its western face readily visible from town. The plane came to rest on the sloping top of a buttress of the pinnacle on its eastern side. Though Flight 260 was heading west toward Albuquerque when it struck the pinnacle, the wreckage could not be seen from town.

A Hike up the Sandias

That morning, Ken Shaw and I were up early to go climbing up the La Luz Trail. Albuquerque was sunny, but the Sandias were enshrouded in clouds—they looked cold. From my room at the Bachelor Officers' Quarters at Kirtland Air Force Base, I observed two planes waiting for takeoff on the Kirtland runway. One of them, I learned later, was TWA Flight 260, bound for Santa Fe and Baltimore. I remember seeing a glint of white through one of the passenger windows—perhaps someone waving a handkerchief at me. I like to think that it was Lois Dean.

I had arrived in Albuquerque in late August as a raw air force second lieutenant, stationed at Kirtland as a physicist doing research and development in the Air Force Special Weapons Command. I had joined the air force in tribute to my uncle, Lieutenant Charles L. Williams, who died when his aircraft stalled and fell into the sea off Oahu, Hawaii, in 1927. Williams Air Force Base (now Phoenix-Mesa Gateway Airport) in Arizona was named in his honor. During its fifty-two years as a military facility, more than 26,500 men and women earned their wings at "Willie," which graduated more student pilots and instructors than any other base in the country and supplied 25 percent of the Air Force's pilots annually.

Ken was an air force captain—a large, quiet, slow-talking, methodical kind of man who had the deceptive appearance of being better suited for inactive life than mountaineering. Ken was a person you could count on, a genius for conjuring up the perfect solution for whatever arose.

We had breakfast and then picked up Sherman Marsh, a nineteen-year-old geology major at the University of New Mexico. I would later do the bulk of my rock climbing in the Sandias with Sherman. He was a delightful guy, a fine climber and companion. We made a good team, for he was left-handed; I could lead climbing pitches requiring right-handed piton hammer skills, and he could lead the lefts.

We drove east up Central Avenue and then north on Juan Tabo—a graded dirt road beyond the outskirts of town—and turned up the side road that winds its way a thousand feet up to the foot of the trail. It was extremely cold and the clouds were full of powdery snow, but up the La Luz we went. I remember being irritated by a small, pernicious cloud behind the Thumb that persistently blocked the warming rays from the morning sun. It had a distinctive appearance, being dark and relatively immovable; its lighter neighbors were in constant motion, driven by the unceasing winds.

We climbed upward and about noon reached a small cave near the base of the Thumb, where we had a leisurely lunch by a nice warm fire. We started down early and were thinking of the rather pleasant, easy day's outing when we heard the sound of dogs barking on the trail below. The dogs soon appeared, followed by horses and then men, who informed us of the disappearance of a TWA airplane. They suggested that we could help in the search by reversing our steps and going back up the La Luz all the way to Sandia Crest. They would follow the alternate trail in the adjacent canyon to the north, and we planned to meet in the TV transmitting tower station at the summit. The time was 12:30.

So back we went past the cave, and then upward across the talus pile at the base of the Thumb at an altitude of about ninety-two hundred feet, when Ken remarked that the extreme cold and heavy drifts were slowing us down considerably. If we chose to look along the Crest Trail on top of the rim as well, we wouldn't get back down before dark. He volunteered to return to his car, drive it around to the other side of the mountain, then up to Sandia Crest so that we could all ride home in style from there.

Ken went down alone, and Sherman and I proceeded to battle our way up through the drifts. The extreme cold and cutting wind took their toll, exhausting us so that we took a full three more hours to reach the top, a total of five hours' hike from the bottom. We had seen nothing of the missing aircraft. We had forgotten the dark cloud that had obscured the sun a few hours earlier—perhaps smoke rising from the burning airplane that had crashed onto a hidden pinnacle some three-quarters of a mile beyond the Thumb.

The men manning the TV station had just finished their weather measurements when we arrived at the Crest—the temperature had topped out at half degree below zero. New Mexico State Police Patrolman Bill Lucas drove up to the station soon afterward and offered us a lift. We readily accepted, hopped into his car, and proceeded down the road until we encountered Ken Shaw driving up. Patrolman Lucas evidently didn't think much of his explanation for doing so, for he proceeded to write Ken a ticket for breaking a state law prohibiting uphill traffic after 3:30 p.m. Fortunately, Ken was able to talk him out of it.

Search

State Patrolman Steve Lagomarsino was in his squad car atop nine-mile hill on the West Mesa when he received word that the TWA plane had failed to arrive in Santa Fe. He would always remember the way the mountains appeared that early morning: the clouds hugging the slopes like a sugarloaf, a beautiful, tranquil scene that gave no hint of the ravaging torrents of air that coursed beneath the cloud cover's canopy.

The massive search for the plane began at noon, when it became obvious that it could no longer be airborne. Upwards of fifty planes and hundreds of men combed an area seventy-five by seventy-five miles for signs of it. The Helmerick & Payne Oil Company sent a company plane to Albuquerque to join them, hoping they would find Harold Tips, their vice-president.

All were called in at nightfall except for one plane that would search for flares or campfires indicating the possible presence of survivors of a forced landing. Despite bitter cold, many searchers maintained vigils on the ground throughout the night to check out the reported sightings.

Dr. Christina Balk, an eminent geologist in her own right, was part of group of thirty-eight research staff and students from the New Mexico Institute of Mining and Technology who arrived at 6:45 p.m. in thirteen cars in hopes that they might find her husband and beloved colleague, Dr. Robert Balk. They were well suited for the task, for geology field trips had long conditioned them to night travel on primitive roads across rugged landscapes.

Also at hand were fifty members of the Civil Air Patrol (CAP) who had formed into twenty-five two-man teams. Their search-and-rescue missions had well-coordinated air and ground mobile units, accustomed to working night and day in all types of weather. Their efforts were supported by four hundred members of the Bernalillo County Citizens Unit, who moved out and camped in the hills northeast and northwest of Albuquerque.

It was a busy night. Fires or flares were reported from a multitude of desolate and sometimes virtually inaccessible sites north and northwest of Albuquerque and southeast of Santa Fe, such places as Rowe Mesa, San Ysidro, Valle Grande, Cabezon Peak, Las Vegas, Clayton, and Clines Corners.

Sunday, February 20

Assembling for the search at 4:00 a.m. the next day were four hundred Explorer Scouts and Boy Scout executives, motivated by the fact that Worth Nicholl was aboard the plane. Those participating in the search were told to be prepared for extreme cold and heavy snow. The party was equipped with one weasel, ten Jeeps, eight trucks, and fifty pairs of snowshoes.

Scheduled for takeoff at daybreak were more than nineteen planes from the Albuquerque CAP, and more from Santa Fe; ten air force planes from Kirtland; naval reserve planes flown by TWA pilots from Kansas City; two planes and a helicopter from Clovis Air Force Base; three planes from Amarillo Air Force Base; and TWA officials' rented planes for their own use. All told, some fifty planes were flying from Albuquerque and other northern New Mexico cities, each assigned to a specific sector of the area seventy-five by seventy-five miles square.

A massive search over an immense geography, but the plane wreckage was finally found high up on Sandia Mountain only ten miles from town by James R. Bixler, chief pilot for the Carco Air Service. An *Albuquerque Journal* article told his story.

On scheduled shuttle flights between Albuquerque and Los Alamos, he had repeatedly flown his plane over an area of the Sandias where he thought the plane might be. A little early on his run to Los Alamos that morning, he had turned south to work his way into a cove he hadn't been in before, noticing something that didn't seem quite right, "a little piece that didn't seem to be metal or rock, tree or snow. I pulled up, eased into the cove—and there it was.

"I had felt the plane was in that area throughout the search, although I had flown by it not less than fifteen times without seeing it.

"I started my last pass at about ten thousand five hundred feet and let the plane down into the cove. I dropped down to about ninety-three hundred feet and gauged the wreck's altitude at about nine thousand feet.

"I saw only the tail section. You can't see anything else from the air, and I was lucky to see it when I did."

It was if he had been searching for a lost golf ball in the rough, giving up and walking away, only to step upon it inadvertently.

Within minutes after Bixler's report, an umbrella of military and Civil Air Patrol craft rushed to inspect the area, necessitating air force officials to order all planes to stay west of the Rio Grande. Colonel Gibson, commander of the 44th Air Rescue Squadron from Lowry Air Force Base in Denver, then flew to the pinnacle in a helicopter and hovered within fifty feet of the wreckage, saying it "definitely was the missing aircraft and there was no possibility any survived." Flying in a helicopter over the site, State Patrolman Bill Lucas—who had given us a lift down the mountain the day before—reported to Captain White of the New Mexico State Police that "it really doesn't look as if there's much hurry" about getting to the wreckage.

Figure 17. View of the wreckage from a helicopter shortly after it was found atop the smoke-blackened pinnacle; the Rio Grande is in the background. Wire photo transmission errors probably caused the break in the image. (Courtesy of Steve Lagomarsino.)

Bob Shumway, a *Journal* photographer, rode over the scene in the helicopter later in the afternoon: "They had to make four passes before I could see anything, and then it was just a tiny piece of the plane's tail."

Figure 18. Close-up of the tail section of the aircraft hanging over the edge of the cliff. The east face of the pinnacle buttress plunges down beneath the tail. The sun-bathed rock to the right is evidence of the presence of the precipitous south face.

Captain Joseph Cosgrove, commander of an Air Rescue Service from Lowry, described the crash scene as "a splotch of black. It appears the plane had blown up and blackened the surrounding rocks jet black." The area was a series of perpendicular spires with the tail section impaled on one.

The *Skyliner Binghamton* had been a good-sized airplane, yet an aerial photo of the crash site revealed that most of it had vanished. All but the tail had been reduced to insignificant rubble by the impact with solid granite—its only recognizable feature being the tail section, which looked minuscule in comparison with the immense cliffs dominating it. The smoke-blackened wreck pinnacle, not the tail section of the wreckage, may have been the anomaly that first attracted Bixler's attention.

The searchers had been looking for an airplane. They found scorched rock instead.

And even more surprisingly, the photo also showed that the plane was heading west when it struck the sloping top of a buttress that jutted out eastward from the pinnacle—the wreckage hidden from view from Albuquerque by the pinnacle itself. How had the pilot managed to get behind that spire and turn the plane around in such a constrained area?

In summary, here are the significant facts concerning the crash:

1. The plane was flying from Albuquerque to Santa Fe.
2. Santa Fe is northeast of Albuquerque.
3. Sandia Crest is northeast of Albuquerque.
4. The plane took off to the southeast, then looped around to head north past Sandia Crest, then northeast to Santa Fe.
5. The plane was last seen heading directly toward Sandia Crest.
6. The plane struck a pinnacle on the western side of Sandia Crest.
7. The pinnacle is visible from Albuquerque.
8. The plane was headed west when it crashed into the eastern side of the pinnacle.
9. The crash site is not visible from Albuquerque.

Without knowledge of the topology of Sandia Crest, the last two facts might appear to be in contradiction to the others. And some of the others seem unimportant for understanding what had happened.

The preponderance of evidence signified that the plane was traveling northeast while, indeed, it was heading due west when it crashed—contradictory facts that would soon be forgotten, as they muddled comprehension.

"The plane was flying northeast to Santa Fe and was last seen heading toward the prominent western face of Sandia Crest, where it crashed onto a pinnacle" is what the public learned and came to understand—and a lot of officials too.

It would cause considerable grief for people who didn't deserve it.

A Harrowing Climb

From the time it was discovered until almost noon, a period of about two hours, the state police made efforts to get a fix on the crash site from the ground, using a high-powered, tripod-mounted telescope to pinpoint the area by watching the hovering helicopter above it. This failed when the helicopter disappeared behind a ridge. Bill Lucas told me fifty years later that high winds were swirling so badly above the site that the helicopter couldn't hold its position.

Lucas obtained enough landmarks on his helicopter ride over the crash site to find the scene in the telescope. About 3:00 p.m. he and three others left the rescue base on Juan Tabo Road and headed across the desert in a Jeep toward the mountain to begin their climb toward the crash site. They were able to drive an estimated three miles, but had to hike after that. (Bill told me that he landed on a cactus when he hopped out of the Jeep and had to suffer those wounds throughout the harrowing ordeal that was to follow.)

Other ground parties also began trekking across the desert: Master Sergeant Cecil Gray, heading the 44th Air Rescue Unit from Lowry Air Force Base, and Sheriff's Captain A. S. "Governor" Rodgers with District Attorney Paul Tackett of Bernalillo County; Dr. Eugene Szerlip, a member of a Civil Air Patrol ground team; TWA and army personnel; as well as others with no official status.

The hike upward was arduous. Members of the various parties began to drop out from fatigue and retrace their steps to the base camp in the desert. The groups began to coalesce, and other individuals joined them—unknown volunteers who wanted to help. Bill Lucas had no way of knowing who those strangers were, nor their motivations. He was concerned about maintaining security of the crash scene and wanted them to turn back.

Sheriff's Captain Rodgers, however, was concerned about their safety if they did so. It was fast approaching nightfall, and they might lose their way or fall and injure themselves, suffering a frigid death in the ensuing dark. Sending them back might prove to be a death sentence for which he would be responsible.

Accordingly, the amalgamated groups stayed together and inched their way upward, arriving below the western cliff of the pinnacle, perhaps six hundred yards from the notch. It was some four hours after they had begun their journey, and they had no food or warm clothing to sustain them over the long night that would soon follow.

A plane attempted an airdrop of bedrolls, blankets, and food about dusk, but the supplies disappeared into another canyon. The pilot "reported a bright light on top of the pinnacle opposite the tail piece" as well as "two fires at the foot of the pinnacle and another some two hundred fifty feet below where a second party camped."

They had lit the two fires before nightfall, but "we didn't have enough wood to keep the fires going," Lucas later told a reporter. "Then it got dark and we were afraid to move." He used a walkie-talkie—a twenty-five-pound portable radio transmitter—to alert the base camp of their plight; and the state police beamed huge searchlights on them from Juan Tabo Road so that they could forage for wood. He said the night spent in the mountains by his party was "miserable." The temperature dropped to twenty degrees below zero.

Dr. Clay T. Smith, a geology professor at New Mexico Tech and close associate of Robert Balk, was also in his party. He was hoping to find Robert Balk's geology map, said to be worth five thousand dollars by the *Albuquerque Journal*, but to no avail. In the party at the campfire hundreds of feet below them were nine airmen, seven TWA men, and four CAP members.

Sheriff's Captain Rodgers also spoke of almost freezing. "We had two fires, but they didn't do much good, and we couldn't get enough fuel. Every minute seemed like hours until daylight." They had to stay awake to stay alive.

Dr. Szerlip told an *Albuquerque Journal Magazine* reporter a quarter century later: "We tried green aspens to build two fires in rows. We had a few sandwiches, some tea, candy, and apples, but nothing to sleep in. We stood up all night. There was no place to sleep anywhere. We were on a ledge."

The food he mentioned was probably from his own voluminous knapsack in which he stuffed medical supplies and other sundries. Sheriff's Captain Rodgers remembers that Szerlip stood with him by the fire that night and proffered him a draft of scotch to ward off the cold. Though not a drinking man, he was pleased to accept the offer.

It still astonishes me that both Sheriff's Captain Rodgers and State Patrolman Lucas had been wearing only their leather uniform jackets. The campfire scorched Lucas's trousers, and he was still suffering from his earlier impalement by the cactus plant.

A paramedical team from Lowry Air Force Base was also on the mountain, but failed to get near the crash site that evening. Their story was reported in the *Albuquerque Tribune* by Bill Richardson, bureau chief of Associated Press in Albuquerque (and no relation to the New Mexico governor), who accompanied their group. As his descriptions of the terrain match those of Echo Canyon, I'll proceed with the assumption that that's where they were—but first, a little background information that may explain why they ended up off target.

Travelers in such terrain are rarely afforded views that give them a sense of their position on the mountainside or where they are headed. Cardinal directions don't count for much—directions being limited to up, down, left and right. And *south* is an especially ambiguous term in this context: the wreck site is considered south of Echo Canyon when one is viewing the west face of the Sandias from Albuquerque, whereas, compass-wise, it is actually east.

The youthful airmen may have inadvertently strayed into Echo Canyon because they had not had benefited from observing the terrain from the air as had Lucas, who knew that the entrance to the mountain was Domingo Baca Canyon and that Echo Canyon was an offshoot from it. The problem for the airmen was that the merge of these two canyons was well disguised—the obvious path (to Echo Canyon) lying straight ahead up the creek bed that they had been following and the path to the crash site up Domingo Baca Canyon, inexplicably accessed by an ill-defined trail abruptly up an escarpment to the right.

That murky intersection of canyons plagues hikers to this day.

In addition to the Associated Press's Bill Richardson, the airmen were accompanied by four civilians: Frank Busch, director and future vice president of TWA operations; Ray Dunn, director of TWA engineering and maintenance and future vice president of TWA technical services; Phillip Goldstein, air safety investigator for the Civil Aeronautics Board (CAB); and Jack Asire, safety representative for the Air Line Pilots Association (ALPA).

In modern management practices, corporate executives would delegate such responsibilities to subordinates, but executives of the world's largest airline in 1955 thought otherwise.

The group encountered sheer drops, frozen waterfalls, and bitter cold on their way up the mountain, but by nightfall had still seen no wreckage. Out of radio contact with the other search teams because of the narrow canyon, they signaled an SA16 rescue plane and asked for clues to the location of the wreck site—being suitably appalled when a red and white Carco Bonanza circled a spot many miles south of where they were clinging to the mountainside.

The SA16 circled back and dropped parachutes with sleeping bags, food, clothing, and water, but they missed the narrow canyon. This was a modest tragedy for the airmen, who had lugged sleeping bags in heavy packs up the mountain face, but the civilians, alerted to come at a moment's notice, were wearing clothing suitable only for a cool evening.

The airmen readily shared their limited rations with the out-of-condition civilians, but no one expected them to give up their bedrolls.

There wasn't room to lie down on the ledge where they started their fire, so they stood shoulder-to-shoulder toward the warmth. As one side got warm—or rather baked and smoked—the other side quickly froze in the below-zero breeze off the snow-covered heights. They hunched on their ledge for some fourteen hours—from 4:30 p.m., when light began to fail, until 6:30 a.m., when it was light enough to see their way down.

They talked of the crash, the scene of which was then brightly illuminated nearly directly to their right—but miles away by foot—by the two searchlights at the foot of the mountain. And they speculated as to why the crash had happened.

"He could have just reversed his compass and instrument readings when he took off," TWA's Frank Busch said. "That has happened, and it would have put him in about here," in the general vicinity of where they were standing, only a short distance from the airport.

Someone ventured his opinions about the probable condition of the wreckage. "When you hit a rock wall like that at a hundred and fifty miles an hour, a plane just explodes. There aren't any big pieces left." Both the TWA and safety officials agreed it probably would never be known what caused the airliner to plow into the mountain.

Finally, after 6 a.m., the first light touched the sky, and the civilians could make out the airmen sleeping on the ledge below them. Far across the canyon, the other half of the paramedic team lit fires. The civilians awakened one of the airmen, thanked him, returned the hatchet he had loaned them, and hoofed it out of the wilderness. They knew the toughest part of the climb lay ahead. It would be an estimated two more days before the paramedics returned.

At base camp, State Police Captain White gave them their first news that a New Mexico State Police party had reached the crash scene some time before, using a simpler route.

Albuquerque Carpenters to the Scene

The first to reach wreckage from the downed aircraft were two Albuquerque carpenters, Frank Powers and George Boatman, who had heard about the crash in church Sunday morning. Their account was not reported until twenty-five years later, in an *Albuquerque Journal Magazine* article.

The two men had rushed to the entrance of Bear Canyon on Juan Tabo Road, but the police would not let them through their barricade until they explained that Rev. Davis was their preacher and that Powers had done some remodeling on the home of Homer Bray, the Albuquerque insurance and real estate man on the flight.

They reached wreckage at the eastern base of the crash pinnacle in early afternoon to find some of the debris still smoking. The two carpenters then returned home with a still-oily valve assembly from one of the plane's cylinders to prove they had been there. They may have told fellow parishioners that there were no survivors, but they apparently did not report their findings to the authorities.

I woke up Sunday morning feeling sore—apparently my feet had become partially frozen on Saturday—but the symptoms abated after an hour's walk. Ken Shaw, Sherman Marsh, and I had decided to take a short hike near the base of the Shield to see what we could from there. The plane hadn't been found.

At about ten o'clock George Hankins, the oldest member of the New Mexico Mountain Club, listening on the police band, heard the official radio report to all search parties that the plane had been sighted high up above Bear Canyon in the Sandias. George promptly phoned the New Mexico State Police, the Civil Air Patrol, and Kirtland to offer our services, explaining that the club members knew the country well, were in good physical shape, and had climbing abilities. The police told him to stand by and get his men together. Sherman, Ken, Paul Stewart, and I ended up at George's house about noon.

We called the police again and were told to come to police headquarters, where we would be issued passes to get us to the police base camp near Juan Tabo Road at the foot of the mountain; it had been cordoned off to facilitate speedy access for important vehicles. We arrived and again offered our services. Captain Archie White of the New Mexico State Police thanked us, but said that a crew of experienced mountaineers was well on its way up. He explained that officials needed to remove high-security information from the airship before others could be permitted in.

He referred us to the air force personnel at Kirtland and, before shoving us off, thanked us again and showed us the approximate location of the wreck. It was apparently very high up; and we suggested that perhaps a party coming down from the top might more easily reach it than one from the bottom. He replied that this might be possible, but the experts had decided to go up from the base of the mountain.

Returning to George's house, we began making phone calls. Someone at Kirtland told us that there was no security material on the aircraft and that, in his opinion, the more rescuers who showed up, the better. He referred us to TWA representatives, who weren't in charge of the search at all—apparently they weren't interested. They referred us to the Civil Aviation Authority (CAA), but the CAA folks said that, while CAA might actually be technically in control, there were experts in the field from other organizations; they would call us later if we were needed. The CAP proved to be no better; they were no longer involved once the crash had been located. A Major Perry of their organization, however, asked whether we would like to join their group sometime to form a rescue patrol.

We called it quits and went home.

That evening reports came streaming in. The experts were on the mountain, but the tail was five hundred vertical feet above them, and they were having trouble; they realized at about six o'clock that they had no food or sleeping bags. The failed attempt to airdrop food and sleeping bags around dusk was mentioned.

Then came radio news about a forest ranger, a Mr. Hicks, who arrived in town initially alleging that he had just returned from the wreck, but eventually changing his story to say he had been two hundred and fifty yards away, separated by a canyon with unclimbable cliffs. Nevertheless, his description of the crash site in the next day's paper—apparently viewed from Sandia Crest—was very creditable.

He said the plane plowed right into a sheer wall.

"On top," he said, "a piece of something that looked like rags whipped in the wind. The tail was still smoking.

"Farther down, on a sort of shelf, lay what looked like part of the fuselage. Pieces were scattered over small rock ledges all the way down the cliff.

"There was a passage between the pinnacle and the main cliff about seventy-five feet wide. I don't think the pilot could have made it through there, but if he'd been a hundred feet higher he would have cleared it."

Hicks also contended, however, that only a party from the bottom could reach the wreck—causing us to blow our tops and drive to the New Mexico State Police headquarters, where a paratroop colonel was explaining how he could parachute down to the wreck. I told him that his parachute wouldn't be of much help in the thin air of ten thousand feet and that he would not be able to negotiate the winds. I didn't claim to know much about parachutes, but I had had plenty of experience with the winds.

We informed the police that we were going to attempt a rescue from the top in the morning. We had yet to find a cliff in the Sandias that couldn't be rappelled, and we could resort to that if need be. We were going up on our own, would take care of ourselves, but would be glad to help in any way possible.

We left.

An hour later, George Hankins received a call that the police would furnish us an escort to the Crest if we would meet them at the station in town early in the morning.

3
The Crash Site

Monday, February 21. We arrived at police headquarters at six o'clock in the morning and proceeded up to the Crest with State Police Patrolmen Arnold "Rocky" Payne and Maurice Cordova following in their squad car. Ken Shaw was a slow driver, and we had to put on chains halfway up, but we finally arrived at the Crest. Mr. Hicks, the forest ranger who was to act as guide, was nowhere in sight at the TV towers where he was supposed to meet us. We got our group together anyhow and hiked down to the Kiwanis Cabin, following Hicks's tracks apparently made the previous day. From a point on the far side of the cabin we came to the end of his tracks and looked down the canyon. Patrolman Payne spotted the tail section, and I looked at it through binoculars.

It was stuck high up on a pinnacle and was the only piece of the wreckage visible. The familiar red TWA markings distinguishing it from the natural terrain were vertical and gave me the impression that the plane had struck the pinnacle while heading eastward, leaving its tail section on top.

Sherman Marsh and I did a reconnaissance to determine a feasible path to the crash site. The best route appeared to be straight down what is now called the TWA Canyon to the base of the pinnacle, then up to its notch, then to the top from the notch. There were no cliffs that would require a rappel on the way to the pinnacle, though we might need a rope to access the tail from its top. This pinnacle was unknown to us—only George Hankins remembered having seen it before.

Wreck Pinnacle

The TWA wreck pinnacle is a rock ridge that ascends about eight hundred feet northward from its base at an eighty-six-hundred-foot elevation. Its top, at ninety-four hundred feet, is about forty feet higher than its notch, and its eastern face is hidden from Albuquerque. Its name, the Dragon Tooth, aptly describes its shape.

Our party—Ken Shaw, George Hankins, Sherman Marsh, Patrolmen Maurice Cordova, Arnold "Rocky" Payne, an unknown air force lieutenant, and me—started down into the canyon. George was the official head of the group. He, at the age of fifty-seven, was the original paradigm for my belief that old age doesn't have much to do with aging. We didn't slow down for him, though he may have slowed

Figure 19. Sherman Marsh fires up his Primus stove for the weary rescuers who had endured the frigid night on the mountain below the crash site. (Courtesy of Sherman Marsh.)

for us. A machinist by trade, he enjoyed tinkering in the machine shop in his garage, where he was perfecting a mechanical calculator that he had invented.

I was the leader for the climb to the notch—a dirt slope covered with snow—with no ropes needed. We reached the notch to find a fire and the advance party. Two men were at the wreckage on top, having climbed there in the morning after receiving word that ropes were coming. So up we went and arrived at the crash site. The final climb to the top was on rock, but it wasn't bad going. We left fixed ropes for others to use, however.

Figure 20. Frank Powers, parishioner of Rev. Davis, enjoys his breakfast out of a can, the East Mesa in the background far below. (Courtesy of Sherman Marsh.)

It had taken us three hours from the state police station in town, including an hour and a quarter of driving time, reconnaissance, and a descent slowed somewhat by the inexperienced policemen.

We were surprised to see State Patrolman Bill Lucas at the notch—we had not heard about his helicopter travels or that he was a member of the advanced party. Sherman cooked him his first meal in twenty-one hours.

We were also not aware that Dr. Frank C. Hibben from the University of New Mexico had left for the Sandias at three o'clock that morning to travel alone to the crash site. "Erroneous directions sent him into Pino Canyon," the *Albuquerque Journal* reported, "but from there he traveled northward across several headers and found the wreckage on the north side of Tabac Canyon." (Perhaps this was a misprint: the pinnacle is not on the north side of any canyon, and to this day no one knows where Tabac Canyon is.)

Hibben later climbed down to the base of the pinnacle, where he found four bodies—Homer Bray, a close friend of his, among them. Hibben had volunteered for the venture because he knew three of the victims; the pilot, Ivan Spong, and first officer, J. J. Creason, had attended his evening archeology class the previous fall. Hibben was an internationally known archeologist, author, and big game hunter. He had killed a mountain lion not one hundred yards from the pinnacle and described the terrain as "the roughest in New Mexico."

The Wreck Scene

We found twelve bodies atop the pinnacle, with the four that were down below the three-hundred-foot north face of the pinnacle buttress making sixteen in all. An explosion had hurled them and some wreckage down to the dirt and talus slopes below.

Or so we thought.

There was very little wreckage visible from the summit of the pinnacle, but lighter debris was strewn everywhere—some of it in the top branches of the taller pines. About three trees were burned lower down, and several others had been cut off sharply at the ground.

I had envisioned a wreck site filled with fragmented, crushed, but still recognizable sections of an airplane—the wings broken off perhaps, with the fuselage split in two. A *Denver Post* photo (Figure 21) of me at the crash site seemed to corroborate those expectations, for it clearly showed a wing rising up in front of me.

But pictures can be deceiving. What looked like the wing tip was actually part of the tail assembly, the only recognizable major component of the airplane. The winglike object shown sticking up was not part of the main wing at all, but was instead the tip of the right horizontal stabilizer—one of the small wings that stick out sidewise beneath the vertical stabilizer (or sail). They provide lift to the rear end of the aircraft and help keep it level in flight.

The photo showed the bottom surface of the horizontal stabilizer—a view that would normally have been obtained by pointing the camera straight up while the plane was flying overhead. The vertical stabilizer was still attached to the tail, projecting horizontally behind it over the lip of the cliff; its horizontal red stripes were vertical now. The edge of the vertical stabilizer was also visible, but difficult to discern. The tail section wasn't pointing eastward over the lip of the cliff, as I had initially thought. It had instead been rotated backward and was now balanced precariously on the edge. Cables to its control surfaces were all that kept it from going over, anchored by something buried in the debris above.

Figure 21. The author gingerly steps over the rubble atop the pinnacle. The left horizontal stabilizer seventy-five feet down the sloping top of the buttress has the appearance of a wing looming up in front of him, the vertical stabilizer jutting out over the east cliff. (Courtesy of Steve Lagomarsino.)

The remains of the fuselage and wings also appeared in the picture. I was gingerly stepping over what had been reduced to rubble—a trash dump composed of shattered, twisted, and generally unrecognizable fragments of metal. A few small sections of the fuselage, containing passenger windows, were evident; but the wings were gone, disintegrated by exploding fuel tanks. The preponderance of the wreckage remained atop the pinnacle—the tail, engines, propellers, and wheel assemblies the only readily recognizable components from what had been a handsome airplane.

The body of the hostess was lying near the tail assembly on the ledge above the eastern cliff, inaccessible because of the intervening wreckage that threatened to career downhill off the sloping summit of the buttress.

The wreckage made no sense to me—everything was backwards. The tail section was intact because it had never reached the edge of the pinnacle at all. The fuselage in front of it had disintegrated, and the vertical sail of the aircraft had rotated backwards over the cliff under the force of gravity alone. The airplane could not have been traveling east! It was traveling west instead.

Or was it?

Illogically, it was headed west, directly toward Albuquerque, when it smashed head-on into the upper section of the eastern face of the

Figure 22. George Hankins (rope over shoulder) follows Sherman Marsh (carabiner on belt) uphill through crash debris. (Courtesy of Steve Lagomarsino.)

pinnacle. Had it been flying slightly higher it would have cleared the top, only to fly head-on into the eastern face of another wall of a neighboring pinnacle towering some four hundred feet above it. In either case the wreckage of the plane would not have been visible from town, for it lay on the far side of solid granite. The plane was probably flying northward directly toward Santa Fe when a break in the clouds revealed the Crest rising sharply above it. The pilot then made a sharp turn to the left, putting full power to the engines and attaining more than ninety degrees of rotation before striking the pinnacle. The canyon is, at most, half a mile in width at that point.

Figure 23. Rubble everywhere. The tail section from another angle. (Courtesy of Sherman Marsh.)

The Victims

The human victims had also been subjected to crash, fire, and explosion. The sudden deceleration caused by the crash smashed their skulls, so that death was instantaneous; and many of their bodies were dismembered. We found isolated torsos, arms, legs, feet—some burned, but none gory, because they had been frozen solid. The fire and subsequent extreme cold had made the crash site a somber place but not unbearable. The corpses were headless in the sense that their heads were formless—skull bones having been pulverized by the initial impact so that they no longer supported recognizable facial features. The body parts tended to be whole entities, encased in the original clothing that had been ripped apart at the seams rather than being torn asunder by sharp objects.

Most of the bodies were in a small, elongated area in the shattered remains of the fuselage; some were ejected over the north edge of the cliff by exploding fuel tanks. Only five were reasonably complete, including the hostess and the pilot, who were identifiable by their blue uniforms, and Mrs. Schoonmaker, who was found lying facedown on the dirt slopes above the other wreckage next to a man whom I had presumed to be her husband, but later proved to be Rev. Earl F. Davis. They had somehow been propelled through the fuselage and up the mountainside to land forward of the impact area. They made a

Figure 24. The crash pinnacle from TWA Canyon. Bodies of four victims fell onto the snowbank at the base of the shadowed near-vertical north cliff. Our path to the notch of the wreck pinnacle—hidden from view by the intervening Mizar spire—traverses right and upward from the snowbank. (Courtesy of Steve Lagomarsino.)

poignant sight that I will never forget.

As Dr. Szerlip, the CAP medical doctor, wanted to visit the wreckage, I engineered a rope elevator for him and hauled him up.

"It was a gruesome sight," Szerlip told an *Albuquerque Journal* reporter twenty-five years later. "The whole scene was eerily preserved, like in a giant icebox."

He described the top of the pinnacle as cup shaped and was particularly impressed with the amount of broken crockery strewn up slope of the wreckage. He mistakenly attributed it to the hostess's having been about to serve breakfast, but she was in the back of the plane when it struck the mountain.

Figure 25. The vertical stabilizer of the tail section projecting back over the cliff in 1955. (Photo by Gil Buvens.)

Figure 26. Dr. Szerlip examines remains while George Hankins takes notes. (Courtesy of Sherman Marsh.)

George Hankins Crash Scene Notes

Dr. Szerlip then proceeded with body identification while George Hankins took notes. They were found in George's diary by his grandson, Mike Thornton, in July 2006. Mike lives in his grandfather's old house in Albuquerque.

The first sequence of entries describing the passengers appears to have been written while the men were traversing from south to north above the impact area.

Earl Frederick Davis PO box 961 Santa Cruz CA

Mrs. Schoonmaker was lying next to Reverend Davis.

Gray-haired woman two Diamond, one simple Gold ring, blue suit with jacket, wool gabardine

Brown overcoat with zipped in lining, detachable, fine linen handkerchief

The next entry probably describes the first body that I encountered while descending from atop the pinnacle. (Because of events that will be described later, I now believe it was that of Mr. Schoonmaker.)

Male body with no ring on left-hand—no clothes. Gray trousers with narrow leather belt—fuzzy deep blue coat

The next entry probably describes the body shown in Figure 26, with George taking notes.

Figure 27. Wreckage remains in a once-shredded tree to this day, but the tree is now luxuriant with foliage. (Courtesy of Steve Lagomarsino.)

Body—dark blue suit, might be uniform, finely with initials R, and more light brown gloves not hand made

The note taker now apparently reverses his path to proceed lower down nearer the bulk of the wreckage, traversing from north to south.

Brown overcoat—Clipper Craft tailored for Emory Bird Thayer of Kansas city—pair of pigskin gloves, Clipper—long 11342—40, tailored shoulders, large pinstripe

Man's gray trousers Red and blue line, lines about an inch apart, bits of flesh attached

The hostess near the tail can be seen from a distance.

Long hair—light brown—light blue uniform down in tail

Man's arm with ring on left third finger—heavy gold—oval black stone in black stone gold emblem: sheaf, sword, thorns and ribbon under

White rayon shirt, light blue tweed suit

Body—right hand—ring, right forth, square stone been knocked out

Body—left-hand—no ring on left-hand

Body—tweed suit—probably Brown—left-hand simple gold wedding band left-hand fourth finger

Body, Retina 2A camera

The notes below seem to pertain to the southern extent of the upper part of the debris field, traversing from south to north. The pilot is mentioned, but not described. Captain Spong was lying on top of the wreckage at the southern edge of the top of the debris field; First Officer Creason was found the next day, lying next to and north of him.

He may have been under a section of fuselage and therefore out of sight when the notes were taken.

letter from Louis Borrego general delivery Espanola, near pilots body

Body—right hand, No marks

Apparently, George kept notes of personal effects separate from those about the victims. This note sequence repeats that used in describing the victims above.

Bible in black case—contains letter—Mrs. Earl F. Davis— associated with body of long gray hair lady with rings

Blue cloth pocketbook with prescription—Mrs. Dorothy Schoonmaker 437853—4th February 55 Dr. Miller, Martinez pharmacy of Hackensack NJ

gray felt hat Royal Stetson stratoliner 71/8 sold by Plato's of Modesto CA

Revere stereo camera associated with unidentifiable body

Lee black sable hat—brown felt sold at La Porte IN, no size, no initial

The Bible mentioned above belonged to the Reverend Davis, not Mrs. Schoonmaker. His parishioner Frank Powers described seeing it that day: "The pages were ruffling in the wind." He started to pick it up to return it to Davis's widow, but the authorities wouldn't let him.

Powers had returned to the pinnacle alone, as his buddy George Boatman had to go to work. I do not remember seeing him on the pinnacle, but it is obvious that he was there that day.

Retreat

Our mountain club group and Patrolman Rocky Payne then went down from the notch to the base of the north cliff, where Payne pointed out Homer Bray's shirtless body lying face down in a snowbank. He was identified by his wallet, which Payne carried back to the police station.

Further down we encountered the lead group of experienced climbers from Kirtland on their way up.

We then retraced our steps back up to the Crest, and the others retreated down their longer path to the base camp on the mesa.

I drove back to town with Patrolman Payne. He was thoroughly bushed by the expedition and asked me to drive while he took a short nap. I did so, being amazed by the paucity of faster drivers willing to pass a slow-moving state police cruiser going well below the speed limit.

Reporters interviewed us at the police station, and the paper quoted George Hankins as saying that he saw at least "a dozen people at the crash site," adding that he didn't know who they all were, but they were all "working hard."

Youthful Harry Moskos at the *Albuquerque Tribune* began sending out photos of the crash site on the United Press International (UPI) telephoto machine. He had been hired for the job two years earlier, at the end of his junior year at Albuquerque High.

He would remember those pictures for over half a century.

Late that afternoon we began planning for the recovery of the bodies the following day. George was asked for his opinion, which resulted in the plan for bringing all men to the Crest in the morning and having them drop down to the wreck, get the bodies, and carry them down the mountain to a place where horses could relieve them of their burdens.

Captain White then asked George whether the mountain club members would help out in these proceedings. George said that we would rather not—certainly some of the people in the assemblage could furnish men for the task? When Captain White said he would prefer us, we agreed to guide the expedition in, string ropes, and help in any climbing operations that became necessary.

We were an incongruous lot to be chosen for this mission. None of us had had previous mountain rescue experience. George, at age fifty-seven, was obviously well past his prime. I was a youthful second lieutenant who had first encountered rock climbing barely a year and a half before. Sherman was a teenager, and Ken Shaw didn't have the looks of a mountaineer. We were eager for the task, however, and might somehow muddle our way through the ordeal.

4
Recovery

Tuesday, February 22. We arrived at police headquarters at 5:00 a.m. and went up to the Crest in 6X6 army trucks. With us were the leader of the expedition, Dr. Frank Hibben, PhD; Dr. W. B. Mitchell, MD, of Sandia Base (now part of Kirtland); Patrolman Bill Lucas; and mountain club members: Ken Shaw, George Hankins, Sherman Marsh, Hank Tendall, and Dick Heim. The men for the work were volunteers from the army mountain troops (a fine outfit), air intelligence people, and thirty-four men from Manzano Base, a nuclear weapons storage facility. Also in the party were a Mr. R. B. Riordon, district sales superintendent of TWA, and some of his subordinates—all volunteers—including transportation agents Gil Buvens, Dean Johnson, and Roger Burns and mechanics Gordon Oakley and Norman McIntosh. Gil Buvens, who later became the editor of the *TWA Skyliner* magazine, was the photographer for Figures 25 and 30.

I was surprised to see Patrolman Bill Lucas here after his harrowing ordeal Sunday night; a good night's sleep, and he was back on the

TOP: Figure 28. This "WORL" photo provided the author with crucial evidence for his analysis of the crash. Albuquerque KOB-TV photographer Dick Kent—burdened with a heavy 16mm TV-news camera—examines a large piece of fuselage emblazoned with a portion of the TWA logo above a window port. The Alioth and Mizar spires are visible in the background. (Courtesy of Steve Lagomarsino.)

BOTTOM: Figure 29. TWA transportation agent Gil Buvens examines the "WORL" wreckage from another angle. (Courtesy of Gil Buvens.)

job again. His mission today was to search for and retrieve mail sacks from the wreckage.

Dr. Hibben assembled the group at the top of TWA Canyon and told me to lead away. I took off and broke a trail downward, staying out of the iced-over old one. I made the going comparatively slow in an attempt to keep the entire party together. The strategy worked, and we reached the crash scene at 9:30 a.m. I scrambled up the pinnacle, checked the ropes that were already in place—put there after we had left on Monday by Lieutenant John Hawkins of Kirtland—then placed one of my own higher up and rigged a belay for every man to use coming up.

Figure 30. TWA mechanic Norman McIntosh examines the right propeller hub remaining atop the pinnacle. The left engine and its propeller hub had fallen to its base. (Photo by Gil Buvens.)

Mountaineering Terminology

We used a body rappel in those days. One end of a climbing rope was attached to a tree and the other, tossed over the cliff. You faced uphill, straddling the rope, which was looped across your back, over your right shoulder, across your chest, under your left arm, and across your back again, to be held by your right hand. You then backed down the cliff using your left arm to keep from falling backwards and your right hand to brake your progress, the friction of the rope around your body keeping you in place. You slid down the rope by relaxing the gentle pressure of your right hand, thereby permitting the rope to slip around your body. Leather patches on the left leg and right shoulder prevented rope burns and torn clothing.

You can also climb a rappel rope by prussiking up it. Two small loops of hemp rope called *slings* are wound, one above the other, around the rappel rope. Downward tension on a prussik sling crimps the rappel rope and creates friction that holds them fast together. Moving upward is reasonably simple. First, you step into and shift all your weight onto the lower sling, thereby releasing tension on the upper sling that can easily be slipped upward on the rappel rope. You then step upward into it and reach down to slip the lower sling upward to a position just below the upper, repeating the process until you get to the top. No strength is required for either rappelling or prussiking—rope friction does all the work.

Clothing

As artificial fiber wasn't commonly available in 1955, we kept warm with multiple layers of ordinary apparel, using trapped air as natural insulation. I wore a fishnet shirt next to my body, covered with a cotton T-shirt, covered with a cotton long-john underwear shirt, covered with a long-sleeve cotton shirt, covered with a long-sleeve wool shirt, covered with a Levi's denim jacket. My lower body was covered with cotton underwear shorts, covered by cotton long-john underwear pants, covered with an outer layer of Levi's denim pants. Layers could be added or deleted to suit temperature and wind conditions.

My feet were covered with wool socks and Vibram rubber-soled climbing boots. Some climbers wore cotton socks under the wool ones, but I found that they tended to bunch up and become uncomfortable. I wore a wool stocking cap to keep my ears from freezing and ski mitts to protect my hands, shunning fingered gloves as they cut off blood circulation. Good blood circulation throughout the body was a major factor in keeping us warm, and, accordingly, experienced climbers kept moving and covered up when they weren't.

Frigid temperatures in the Sandias were readily tolerable in calm conditions because of the low humidity and low air densities at higher altitudes. Protection from the wind was our main concern, as air moving across bare skin could rapidly lead to frostbite.

Recovery of the Hostess

Recovery of the body of Sharon Schoening near the tail section was the biggest problem of the day. We had spotted it the day before and discovered that rope work would be needed. I selected a tree and tied a half-inch manila rope to it for a rappel. Then George Hankins found a good belay spot and tossed me a seven-sixteenths-inch nylon for a belay. If the twisted metal cut one rope, we hoped the other would hold. Down I went over the metal and landed on a ledge. She was there all right, and apparently intact—draped over the ledge and frozen tightly to the rock. So I went off rappel and onto the tension of my belay rope (the rope from me to George, taut), tied the rappel rope to her arm, and hauled. She came free of the rock, but not free from the ledge. She was wedged under part of the old fuselage. I reached down and tried to move her and after much hauling and pushing finally got her off. But she slipped backward and disappeared over the cliff—dangling below the ledge, but still tied to the rappel rope.

Hollywood would have shown me hauling her body up with the rope itself, but those kind of theatrics don't play well in practice. I had to get her back to the ledge in stages. First, I went over the cliff so that I was slightly above her, the belay rope around my waist kept taut so that I could bend over to lift her to the level of my waist. This created slack in the rope attached to her, which was taken up by people above. I then used her rope to haul myself up a step, creating slack in my rope that was taken up by George. About ten minutes of this and she was up to the ledge again, where I attempted to get the body bag over her, but failed, as I couldn't do it alone. This necessitated more tedious hauling to a safer place, where Hank Tendall could get down to me to help out. We finally succeeded, and she was secure at last.

Descent

Meanwhile others devised a system of rope elevators, and all the remains atop the pinnacle were shunted down to the notch. We were ready to quit the pinnacle then, the major party descending down the west gulley, while others went down from the notch to the east gulley to pick up the bodies beneath the north cliff. We were now free of the treacherous slopes of the pinnacle and began what we trusted would be an uneventful descent of the relatively gentle slopes of the canyon floor.

It proved instead to be a continuous fight with vegetation, rocks, and weights much too heavy for the few men we had. There should have been at least six men per body bag, but we didn't have that many available. The light canvas body bags began to tear apart under the onslaught of brush, sharp rocks, and wayward tree limbs; the bodies inside contributed to the mayhem as they were still frozen, hard and unyielding. We patched the bags as best we could and took more care in our downward progress—slipping and falling nevertheless, but with less frequency.

We atop the pinnacle had become inured to the sight of human remains, wreckage, and utter carnage; but the future bearers of body bags had remained below—witnessing neither remains, wreckage, nor carnage and becoming inured only to the spectacular mountain scenery. It must have been a horrifying jolt for them when those bag-draped remains first began to emerge from their fragile shrouds.

An interesting interlude occurred when we discovered a freshly killed deer in a pleasant glade near the small creek flowing intermittently down the base of the canyon. Dr. Hibben showed us the footprint of the mountain lion that had killed it; it was to be my closest encounter with a cougar in eight years of climbing in the Sandias. Widely recognized as a mountain lion hunter, he told us that his master's thesis in zoology on the big cats had gained him instant fame as an expert. He had since been called all over the Southwest whenever anyone wanted one of the critters removed.

We finally arrived at the mouth of the canyon about six. The body bags were then put on the backs of horses so that they could be carried the final half-mile to waiting trucks and members of the press.

Thousands of persons had gathered near the base of operations on Juan Tabo Road as the bodies were being brought down, making necessary special precautions for crowd control.

I told the news reporters that the plane had turned around and had crashed while heading directly toward Albuquerque. Although that bizarre fact appeared in the newspapers the next day, it attracted little attention and was soon forgotten.

The job had required a terrific amount of work, and the mountain club received recognition from all quarters. Captain White told us we would be called first in any emergency—he and the CAP wanted us to form a mountain rescue organization especially for this type of work. TWA would get us new ropes and replace any equipment that was lost. The post office department wanted us to go back up to find mail that was still lost in the wreckage.

At the start of the day we were devoid of rescue expertise, we had defective equipment, and we were woefully short of personnel. Our work would challenge us; it would be physically exhausting; it would be thrilling; and it would be immensely difficult. The terrain would prove unfriendly; it would be relentlessly treacherous; and it would be spectacular and beautiful. But at the end of the day, we had somehow muddled our way through to success—immensely tired but unscathed. We had not known what we were doing, but we had done it very well.

Fortunately, no rescuer died or was injured because our mountain club team wasn't believed at first.

The plane and its passengers had not fared as well. It was obvious that the pilot had done a remarkable job in horsing his aircraft around to make his escape from the mountain, but he had no business being there in the first place. The only logical conclusion was that he had tried a short cut to Santa Fe and had aimed too low—flying into the mountain rather than over it.

Or so we believed.

George Hankins received plaudits from the press and all the organizations involved, deserving them all. He had kept the pressure up when everyone else insisted we weren't needed; he was the most persistent of us all. Added to that, he did two days of terrific labor in spite of being fifty-seven years old. I think he especially enjoyed being called "Pop" by the Manzano men. We got cooperation when we needed it. The state police had proved to be a fine organization, giving us all the help we wanted, as well as a free rein.

I later learned that because we lacked sufficient manpower, one of the bodies had been left on the mountainside to be retrieved the next day. Perhaps the captain of the airship had remained behind on the mountain until his charges were safely down.

When Dr. Hibben returned to town, he reported to his associate, Jack Campbell, that the crash site had attracted numerous birds. The carrion eaters of the Sandia slopes were not vultures or crows, or the goraks of Everest, but piñon jays that meticulously cleansed the sullied pinnacle. The mountain was beginning to mend itself.

Searching for Mail

Saturday, March 5. The post office department asked us to go up to the wreck scene again and attempt to find mail for them. The only scraps of mail that had been recovered had come from the bag for Santa Fe; there had been no trace of mail from the other two bags destined for other places. They hoped that only one bag had been burned and the others were intact somewhere.

George Hankins's diary entries were especially valuable in describing what follows because he recorded both the date and the weather conditions.

George, Sherman, Paul Stewart, and I drove up to the TV towers and descended to the pinnacle by the route we had pioneered earlier. Today was cold and blustery, and frozen, iced-over areas made travel especially challenging. As we lacked authorization to move debris, we found only four letters among the rubble, but discovered a large amount of debris on a shelf about a hundred and twenty feet down in the chimney to the south.

Sherman belayed me while I rappelled off the eastern cliff and found a passenger's briefcase sitting on a ledge a short way down, sheltered by the tail hanging over the cliff. Intact and none the worse for wear, it only got scratched when we hauled it up. I also found the pilot's personal diary—somewhat battered, but readable.

I then saw human remains that touched off another expedition—two unrecognizable torsos on ledges near the tail above the north cliff, and one complete body atop the pinnacle that was still strapped to his seat by a safety belt. This last was Worth Nicholl, whose acquaintance I had made at a Boy Scout campoeree the previous fall. He was probably uncovered when a gust of wind lifted the debris concealing him, for his body was in plain sight, easily accessed when we found it. As severed body parts do not necessarily imply deaths, the torsos—inaccessible without rope—would provide unassailable evidence of fatalities aboard the plane.

We promptly returned to the police station and reported our findings to Captain White, who immediately got in touch with TWA.

George soon learned that the state police were planning an expedition of some kind, probably during the week.

Monday night, George and I went to the Alvarado Hotel in Albuquerque, where we met Mr. Greenman, a prominent TWA official in the home office; another Bill Williams, an official of the local TWA office; and a Dr. Mitchell of Sandia Laboratories.

We learned from these people that only thirteen bodies had been identified before; the relatives of the other three passengers were told that the caskets they were burying were essentially empty—the terrain and crash had made recovery impossible.

Our plan of attack was the same as before. We were to come down from the Crest again on Wednesday with a total of nineteen men specially selected for the job. There was to be absolute secrecy to avoid publicity about the operation. The mountain club was again to have control, and I was to be in charge of the climbing.

George had already obtained permission from the CAB to cut the tail section free of the pinnacle.

Second Recovery

Wednesday, March 9. Our mountain club party, consisting of Ken Shaw, Paul Stewart, George Hankins, Sherman Marsh, and me, reported to the state police station at 5:00 a.m. and started up the Crest in airport taxis. We ended our trip by walking the last quarter mile, as the 170-horsepower engines under their hoods were inconveniently shackled by speed governors. We started our trek down the canyon and made the wreck by 9:00 a.m., our descent being slowed by ice on the rocks and the absence of cushioning snow. The weather was pleasant.

Up on top, we got the body in the safety belt first—two-hundred-plus pounds. I then rappelled down and got the two remains near the tail section, Dr. Mitchell helping me hoist them up. Meanwhile, Sherman, George, and Paul were setting up an aerial tramway that provided us with a highly efficient means for getting engine parts of interest to the CAB as well as the bodies off the top while maintaining safety in all of our operations. It was rigged with two hundred sixty feet of half-inch manila rope. Our rope supply for the entire operation consisted of five hundred feet of half-inch manila, five hundred feet of three-eighths-inch manila, two three-eighths-inch hundred-twenty-foot nylons, and one eighty-foot nylon.

The Tail Section

Next came the fun of the day—the task of getting the tail section off the cliff. It was still prominently visible from the Crest and was a potential menace to the safety of curious visitors who would inevitably be attracted to the site in the spring. Dr. Mitchell of Sandia Base and I used fire axes to cut the control cables holding it to the pinnacle, but it didn't move downward as we had hoped.

We then began throwing rocks at the section, finally knocking it loose when all of us heaved a five-hundred-pound boulder until it slid free, tumbled down the slope, and walloped the tail—which obligingly fell, but became entangled with a tree fifteen feet further down. So I went down to the edge of the cliff and tried another hundred-pound rock on its tip; this merely broke off the horizontal stabilizer. We resumed our original boulder-rolling escapades and at last hit it with another five-hundred-pounder; the tail disappeared from sight with a thunderous roar and plummeted the final two hundred and fifty feet to the canyon floor. Dust and papers were blown skyward by the inrush of air chasing the descending wreckage and remained aloft for ten minutes afterwards.

The tail section—the largest piece of identifiable wreckage on the top of the pinnacle—now lay at its base, where it would later be identified by hikers as the "wing." And where are the wings and fuselage now? The larger pieces now lie in the canyon, but a multitude of twisted metal fragments remain scattered atop the pinnacle where they first fell a half century ago.

After the commotion ended, I rappelled down, retrieved an engine part I was looking for, and then prussicked back up. We began our exit to the mesa below.

Exit to the Mesa

We were encumbered with heavy packs on the way down: our climbing equipment and physical evidence that we had collected. My load consisted of my own gear, two ropes, an empty body bag, a distributor, and some other engine parts—a weight of nearly fifty pounds.

The trek down was arduous but uneventful, as the new body bags proved to be excellent. They had been constructed especially for the occasion of heavy rubberized canvas, costing about a hundred dollars apiece.

We encountered an unattended campfire a short distance up the canyon from the horses that would bear our heavy loads to the mesa below. As Paul and Ken had remained to fight the fire, George, Sherman, and I returned to them to help put it out. We worked at it for half an hour, but found that it had a life of its own, flames springing up in out-of-the-way places every time the wind gusted. George and Ken stayed to fight the blaze while the rest of us retraced our steps to guide the rest of the party downward.

Dr. Mitchell, Mr. Greenman, Paul, Sherman, and I ended up on foot walking together, while the others accompanied the laden horses downward. Near the entrance to the canyon we came upon two saddleless horses ranging around the top of a hill—they had escaped from Sheriff's Captain A. S. "Governor" Rodgers, who was acting as their wrangler. Deciding to outnumber the beasts, Dr. Mitchell and Mr. Greenman joined him as wranglers while Sherman and I acted as guides to herd them off the hill. They were the first rock-climbing horses that I had encountered, but we got them down with everything intact.

We returned to the police station via taxi, grabbed my car, and Paul and I drove back to pick up George and Ken—we were to report any remaining fire activity to the forest service. We had walked a mile back up the trail when we met the other two. They had succeeded in stopping the blaze by isolating the active coals and beating them out individually. We never discovered how the fire was started.

We arrived home at eleven o'clock, nineteen hours after beginning our ventures, totally bushed.

We were proud of the entire proceedings, at least from the safety angle. Our only casualties occurred on the second expedition, when one of the men carrying the two-hundred-pound body injured his knee on a rock, though not seriously. A Dr. Dye, head medico for TWA, however, suffered pulled ligaments in his knee on the way down to the wreck. This might have proven to be serious, but he made so little fuss about it that I never knew a thing was wrong until we got to the horse camp, and he rode horseback from there down.

All families now had official confirmation that their relatives had perished in the crash; estates and insurance claims could be settled without further ado. We had brought down everything of interest; and Mr. Greenman believed that the CAB would be finished with the crash site now, as all of the pertinent wreckage had been recovered.

Bill Campbell's Key Case

Saturday, March 12. George Hankins, Sherman Marsh, Paul Stewart, a Bandelier National Monument forest ranger named John Mohlhenrich, and I returned to the wreck. Traveling up Domingo Baca Canyon, this time from the East Mesa—rather than down from the Crest—we would avoid the complexities of motoring up and down the back slopes of the mountain.

Finding no trace of mail at the base of the pinnacle, Sherman, John, and I became interested in a parachute lying on top of a rock ridge on the eastern side of the canyon. We decided to investigate by climbing the rock cliffs beneath it while George and Paul remained at the pinnacle.

When our ascent was blocked by a rock overhang, we sat down underneath it to eat our lunches, thoroughly enjoying ourselves until we were dismayed by the sound of rocks falling above us. We were also surprised to hear clear conversations between George and Paul, as we believed they had remained at the wreck site. We yelled at them to be more careful—they were dumping rocks onto our heads. They made no reply. The sound of falling rocks continued, but then ceased. We made a hasty rappel off of the rock, then turned around to look up the ridge, but couldn't see any evidence of our companions.

Greatly mystified, we returned to the wreck site to find them atop the pinnacle. They had been there the whole time and had not heard our shouts. The canyon walls had created an echo chamber in which sounds of rock falls and human conversations from atop the wreck pinnacle seemed to emanate from the cliffs above us. Though George and Paul couldn't hear us at all, we heard them clearly—but from the wrong direction.

They had covered the lower part of the canyons and various shelves before going up to the top, where they found a key case with a hundred dollars in it belonging to Bill Campbell. They turned it over to the state police.

The next day, George, Sherman, and I went back up and easily reached the parachute from the rocks above it, Sherman rappelling down to retrieve the pitons and carabiners we had left the day before.

We donated the silk parachute to George's daughter Jo, hoping that she could make a dress from it. (Her sister, George Ann, told me in March 2008 that she had made a blouse of it instead. George Ann was delighted to learn of the origin of the parachute. Believing for fifty years that it had come from the airliner, she could not imagine why a parachute would have been aboard the plane.)

The contents of the air-dropped food package that we recovered that day is noteworthy for its lack of nutritional balance. Able-bodied men of that era craved meat, sweets, stomach-filling foods, and cigarettes; and that's what they got. These fares were wonderful antidotes for weary days spent in the wilderness, but they and inactive lives led to habits that felled men before age fifty.

> 1 can salted peanuts
> 1 can strawberry jam
> 1 can tomatoes
> 1 can tomato ketchup
> 1 can cherry jam
> 1 can fig pudding
> 1 can solid (condensed) milk
> 2 cans hamburgers and gravy
> 3 cans bread-type biscuits
> 1 can roast beef
> 1 can pears
> 1 can potatoes
> 1 can chopped ham and eggs
> 1 moisture-proof package of candy, gum, cigarettes, sugar. and other useful items

A Diamond Ring

Saturday, March 19. My friend Nicoll Galbraith and his brother Whitney drove down from Colorado Springs for a visit to the pinnacle. Nicoll, having sent me a front-page *Denver Post* photo of me "approaching" the tail (Figure 21), was interested in seeing the wreck firsthand.

We encountered especially strong and bitter north winds on the Crest that day, but hoped for better conditions at the pinnacle on the lee side of the mountain. We found no mail, but Paul discovered a man's diamond ring on a hand attached to an arm pinned under a rock at the base of the north cliff. We also discovered passenger Homer Bray's overcoat with some business cards and gloves in the pocket. Reportedly valued at fifteen hundred dollars, the ring also belonged to Homer Bray, whose son Charles sent George a gracious letter thanking him for its return.

George's diary noted that when he returned home that evening, he found a five hundred dollar check from TWA made out to the mountain club for our rescue and recovery efforts. He had been overly chilled that day, but felt much better the next morning, when it was bright and sunny in Albuquerque—in sharp contrast to the mountain, which looked gloomy and cold.

CAB Investigator Phil Goldstein

Thursday, March 31. George, Ken, and I were asked to guide a party of investigators to the crash site on a day that appeared ill suited for climbing. Severe winds that began assaulting Albuquerque the day before continued during the night and all through the day while we were on the mountain. The pinnacle—apparently above the storm—was warm and sunny.

The party included CAB Investigator Phil Goldstein, four TWA personnel, and George's daughter Jo. Goldstein and the TWA men searched the more level areas, while the rest of us explored cliff shelves and ledges.

We climbers found key cases belonging to passengers Robert Reilly from Dallas and the geologist Robert Balk, as well as several more body parts, two of which were about thirty pounds each; a piece of skull bone; and six human feet still encased in their shoes.

A majority of the passenger victims were footless—a fact that I attribute to the use of metal footrests in the passenger cabin. Passengers had the choice of placing their feet on top of the rests or beneath them. Had I been aboard that plane, I would have chosen the latter, and my feet would have remained there while my body traveled elsewhere from the force of the crash. Metal footrests disappeared from airliner cabins a few years later.

On the trek down to the crash site, Phil Goldstein told us about one of his experiences while investigating another airplane crash that had resulted in three badly charred corpses. As the flight plan specified only two crew members, he suspected murder, and requested that all three bodies be embalmed—only to find that one had already been! The plane had been carrying a corpse in a casket that had been consumed by the fire, leaving the intact body behind. Foul play had not been the cause of the accident.

Tuesday, April 19. Chief mechanic Gordon Oakley of TWA had called George the evening before to ask if he would accompany him and a man named Reece to the crash site. They left at 5:00 a.m., made good time to the Crest, and arrived at the wreck only forty-five minutes later. It took them an additional hour to get the required piece out of the tail section; and they then searched for instruments on shelves and ledges until 12:30, but found nothing noteworthy. The weather at the crash site that day had been remarkably inconsistent. The strong wind accompanied by considerable dust had been blowing up the canyon when they reached the wreckage, making them cold and miserable. Yet the day turned decidedly pleasant when the wind slackened at 10:00 a.m., and the sun felt nice and warm.

Sunday, May 1. George reported that a man named Merkel (probably from TWA) had asked him to outline the search of the various shelves at the wreck scene, for Merkel would be leading a four-day expedition to investigate the wreck on Tuesday. It sounded like a big production, but George was not invited to participate. He was glad for the opportunity to get back to work full force on his calculator.

The Plane's Compass

Saturday, May 14. To avoid any possible discovery by visitors to the site during the summer months, we decided to pick up and bury all the human remains still left atop the pinnacle. We collected and buried over one hundred and fifty pounds of body parts in a grave just to the north and slightly above the point where the plane impacted the pinnacle, covering them with a foot of soil and piling rocks on top for a measure of protection. As the remains were still in reasonably good condition, it was not a terrible job, and we were rewarded by the feeling that we had done a good service.

Then we discovered the plane's compass in a portion of the South Chimney off of the hundred-twenty-foot shelf—a significant discovery, as the plane's compass would provide valuable information in subsequent investigations. The plane's two fluxgate compasses were mounted in the left wingtip. The other wreckage in the chimney was also from the left wing that had sheared off when the plane struck the pinnacle. Only the fuselage and right wing were atop the pinnacle.

Sunday, July 24. This was George's twelfth—and my last—visit to the wreck site. It was the rainy season for the Sandias, and the vegetation seemed more luxuriant than we had remembered it. George found seven miniature vacuum tubes for a radio. The fragile tubes were functional; the demolished radio was not.

Memories

All of us who visited the crash scene in 1955 knew full well that we wanted no contact with family members of the victims. We wouldn't know what to say to them; and we had no desire to refresh the very memories that we were trying to forget of what we had witnessed atop the spire. Family members should never be told of what we saw. They should remember their loved ones as they treasured them, not as what they had become at the last instant of their lives.

Nor did we rescuers discuss those scenes among ourselves. We wanted them to vanish from our minds. Sherman Marsh told me not long ago that he had initially suffered nightmares. I had none myself, but the only mementoes that I collected from the site were a droplet of melted aluminum shaped like a chocolate kiss and a passenger-seat placard with the plastic liner bubbled by the heat. I kept the aluminum as a curiosity, but later discarded the placard because it reminded me of the victims.

We grieved for those victims, but it was best to forget them along with the appalling sights that we had seen.

Or so we believed.

The Albuquerque Mountain Rescue Council

Later that year, in November, our mountain club group rescued Albuquerque architect Jason Moore and his son Jon, who were bow hunting in the Sandias. Funds contributed by Jason Moore and TWA to the mountain club were later used to found the Albuquerque Mountain Rescue Council, which is still going strong today.

5
Victim Families

The travails of the rescuers may have been over, but the families of the victims would be plagued by both the business practices of that era and the ineptness of the New Mexico bureaucracy.

Restitution

Insurance claims for the passengers would be paid by the airline, but payments were limited to ten thousand dollars per victim by New Mexico law. There were no provisions for suits against the airline for negligence.

Ironically, a bill that provided for such suits had already been passed by the New Mexico legislature during the latter days of Governor Edwin L. Mechem's administration. Three months later—at time of the crash—the bill was still languishing, unsigned on the desk of the newly elected Governor John F. Simms.

A costly suit by the Schoonmaker family would ensue, but to no avail.

Travails of the Campbell Family

Other travails that inflicted the victims' kin are typified by those of the Campbell and Schoonmaker families.

First, there was no official mechanism for informing families that an airliner had disappeared or a crash had occurred. They learned about the tragedy through rumors or haphazard news releases.

I have already described how the Schoonmakers' niece Eleanor Weddell and her husband had waited for hours at the Santa Fe airport for the arrival of Flight 260 before they learned that it was missing. The public had been alerted to its disappearance by radio and television news reports, but there was no such announcement at the airport.

Bill Campbell's widow, Alice, would receive news by radio that a TWA plane was missing in New Mexico. She had been lying in bed with morning sickness while a neighbor went to the grocery store for her. When her neighbor returned, she found Alice looking pale as a ghost.

Her brother would receive the news via a newspaper two days later, when he saw headlines while paying for gas on his way to Florida for a vacation with his family. The vacation was abruptly canceled, and they returned to New Jersey.

The families had heard nothing from TWA, nor would they in the near future.

The newspapers hounded Alice Campbell until she gave them pictures of their dead (her husband, Bill, and parents Alfred and Dorothy Schoonmaker). The Campbells in Tenafly were fortunate that their neighbors became an extended family, enveloping them and their relatives in a cocoon, with their church congregation a safety net. The children were sent across the street to stay with friends to avoid the chaos until her husband's parents traveled from Pennsylvania to be with them. It was a terrible time for all.

A few days later, Alice was even more devastated when a postcard from her husband arrived, written on his flight to New Mexico and mailed on the stopover in Chicago the day before the accident.

Her brother-in-law, Bud Pearson, had to drive to the New York airport to claim the three urns and take them to the funeral home in Hackensack. TWA did not help with funeral arrangements or transportation of the remains.

The children did not attend the funerals, which were paid for by the Schoonmaker Company. Alice had lost her husband and her mother and father. She was left with two little girls, a twenty-one-month-old and a four-year-old.

The next shocker came in the form of a lurid article in the tabloid *Stag* magazine that appeared at the newsstands in September 1955. It had photos of the crash site and descriptions of headless bodies and mangled flesh—hardly welcome news for grieving families who chanced upon the material.

And matters were seriously compounded a month later when the CAB report came out on October 12, concluding that the accident was, indeed, due to pilot error. That was not in itself surprising, but the board also used unfortunate phrasing: "The direct course [into the mountain] taken by the flight was intentional." This was interpreted by some to mean that the pilots had committed suicide and had thus murdered the passengers.

The Civil Aeronautics Board had thereby unwittingly committed an appalling blunder, inflicting grieving families with the additional wounding possibility that their loved ones had been murdered.

The CAB report was announced the day Alice gave birth to William Richard Campbell Jr.—a wonderful blessing, but the CAB findings were decidedly not. Alice's younger daughter, Ginny, could not imagine the additional grief that her mother must have experienced at that time and how she got out of bed every day with her newborn child.

Although the airline was at fault for the crash, there was no way to collect damages that could pay for things her husband would have been able to provide for the family as an executive of a multi-million-dollar company. The only thing she received from TWA was a condolence letter from the president of the company.

Providentially, her husband had had the wisdom to make the first two monthly payments on his life insurance policy. He had been traveling extensively for the company and had the forethought, at the age of twenty-nine, to ensure financial care for his family in case of his demise. Alice told Ginny that she didn't know how she would have managed without that policy.

Years later, Alice's aunt told her that her older daughter had said to her soon after the funeral, "Do you know that my Daddy isn't coming home because he doesn't love me anymore?" Her aunt's explanation for not telling Alice at the time was that she didn't want to upset her.

Ginny's sister was never the same after the accident, and Ginny would be the focus of her anger years later. Her mother spent a fortune to get her sister help, but the anger grew deeper and deeper.

The family rift continues to this day. Perhaps Ginny's sister would have been able to resolve her grief if someone had realized she needed help right away.

Perhaps she would have been able to resolve her grief had she been allowed to attend her father's funeral.

We know today that small children readily accept the reality of death if they are told about it. Death is a natural consequence of living. Daddy won't be coming home anymore—he's in a box under the ground.

As Bill Campbell had been an only child, his parents were particularly devastated by his death. His father—described as a happy-go-lucky man until the crash—became embittered. When his wife was diagnosed with terminal cancer and her pain grew unbearable, they committed suicide in their car on the Bucknell College football field, attaching a hose to the tailpipe the day after Ginny's fifth birthday. She would not learn the truth of her grandparents' "car accident" until she was in college; she found out from a neighbor who thought Ginny already knew.

Secrets come out with time.

Sandy Nicholl

Memories were far clearer for Worth Nicholl's ten-year-old daughter, Sandy Nicholl. Someone had fetched her from a friend's house to tell her that her dad's plane had crashed and that he was dead. At the same time, her friend's parakeet had escaped its cage and had attacked her face. She hasn't liked house birds since.

As Sandy recalls, "Other memories of the week that followed were of things important to a ten-year-old. Quiet-talking Mom crying for the first time ever, brothers not teasing me, a chocolate pie made for me by a neighbor, lots of people coming in and out of the house, relatives arriving, lots of hugs and 'It'll be all right.' The funeral was huge, a church filled with people, following the casket with Mom holding my hand.

"Classmates have told me about the change Daddy's death made in their lives: the wondering if death changes those around it; would I look or sound different.

"And I did change. I didn't talk at school for a long time. My style of writing changed to a small script that tried to disappear from the paper. Being with Mom was more important than going places; needing to be alone in the backyard, where I would swing for hours, going as high as I could to reach where he was; going to the closet to feel and hold his tuba."

Christina Lochman-Balk

The death of her husband, Dr. Robert Balk, abruptly changed Dr. Christina Balk's life in far different ways. "Among other things, the crash sent me back to work," she told a reporter in 1980. "I'd been a housewife before that." As nepotism rules had prevented her from obtaining faculty status at the same institution as her husband, she had been constrained to lecturer positions at both the University of Chicago and New Mexico Tech. Like the legendary phoenix, her professional career would now rise from its ashes.

She was an eminent geologist in her own right, but the rocks she studied contained evidence left by once-living creatures. She was a paleontologist—a studier of "old beings." Her Cambrian rocks had fossils in them from the ancient beds of shallow seas. Her husband's Precambrian rocks contained no such signs of life, as they originated from molten magma far beneath the earth's crust.

Receiving a PhD in paleontology from Johns Hopkins in Baltimore in 1933, she had signed on as instructor of geology at Mount Holyoke. After her research gained her national recognition, she was appointed to serve on the subcommittee on nomenclature for the National Research Council in the late 1930s. Though she was still an instructor at Mount Holyoke, her fellow committee members were nationally prominent. In 1940 she was promoted to the rank of assistant professor and a year later was elected Fellow of the Geological Society of America—the twentieth woman in fifty-three years to be so honored.

New Mexico Tech

After her husband's death, she joined the New Mexico Bureau of Mines as a stratigraphic geologist, and two years later, in 1957, became a professor of geology at New Mexico Tech. According to her colleague Clay T. Smith—a veteran of that frigid night upon the mountain—her arrival in the department enhanced its stature almost instantaneously.

"In addition to being a world-famous paleontologist, she could teach any course offered in the department, including optical mineralogy if necessary."

And—as the only woman faculty member at the time—she also served as the first dean of women at New Mexico Tech. Though minuscule, the number of women students was growing steadily—today they constitute nearly 40 percent of the student body, thanks largely to her efforts.

She even influenced education outside of geology by introducing the first biology courses in the college—recognizing the need for a biology background for sedimentary geologists at a time when the biology department had yet to come into existence. Her influence enabled the geology department to increase its graduate offerings to a PhD in earth sciences.

Robert Balk Fellowship

In 1964, in memory of her husband, Christina established the Robert Balk Fellowship to support research in geology. Following her retirement in 1972, in 1986 she created the Christina Lochman-Balk Fellowship in stratigraphy, sedimentary geology, and paleontology to provide financial support for graduate students pursuing MS and PhD degrees.

Ten years later, in 1996, she was awarded the President's Citation from the Paleontological Society for her distinguished accomplishments.

She died in 2006 at the age of 98.

Betty S. Collier

Betty Collier, widow of Dan Collier, did not fare as well. An active, athletic woman who was an avid bridge player and could complete the *New York Times* crossword puzzle without the aid of help books, she was only thirty-nine at the time of the crash. Afterward, she continued as an accomplished golfer, won some local championships, traveled some, had lots of friends—both old and new—and tried to deal with the pressures of raising two children on her own.

But according to her daughter, Peggy, "The shock of the air crash precipitated a rapid deterioration in her health." She suffered a heart attack on the golf course five years after the crash, then a paralyzing stroke at age forty-six; later she developed breast cancer. According to her son, Dan Jr., "She had nurses round the clock from the time of the stroke until her death in 1977 at age sixty-one. It is remarkable, with this terrible family history, that Peggy and I have enjoyed reasonably good health."

Robert S. Nyeland and Harry M. Shuth

The names Nyeland and Shuth are well known to employees of the National Nuclear Security Administration's Kansas City plant, for in 1958 members of the Bendix Corporation's management club had endorsed a scholarship fund in their memory. The company is now managed and operated by Honeywell Federal Manufacturing & Technology, LLC, but Nyeland-Shuth college scholarships continue as one of the most direct means for the plant to support education.

Based on academic achievement and school and community involvement, they are bestowed annually on Education Day to graduating high school seniors who are children of Honeywell employees and retirees. Over the years, the employees' club has provided nearly $100,000 to help employees' children pay for college.

Crew Families

The families of the crew victims were assailed by additional burdens, for hourly compensation for the crew ceased at the time of the accident. There were no provisions for insurance, burial costs, or severance pay. Once the crew members were dead, the airline had no concern about the welfare of their families. Though harsh by today's standards, such practices were common in 1955. Personal insurance in that era tended to be a private matter, not a corporate one.

Worse yet, hate would also be directed at Jean Spong, the pilot's widow. Cranks were prone to phoning widows of airline captains—especially when pilot error was suspected—but this time they had specific things to talk about.

A woman would call Jean at various hours of the night to ask, "Is this where the TWA pilot lives that got killed?" Then she would laugh and hang up when Jean responded. Jean would also answer early morning calls to hear nothing but heavy breathing.

Her mail increased and came from perfect strangers. One letter contained nothing but a piece of torn brown paper with Ivan's picture attached.

The number of calls and letters abruptly went up after the CAB report hit the newspapers. Some openly accused Spong of committing suicide. One sadist phoned to say, "Now don't stop me, but they brought them bodies off the mountain in chunks and none of them had heads."

The crowning blow occurred when her five-year-old son, Mike, came home from school one day crying. "The other kids say Daddy's in hell," he sobbed, "because he killed people."

Jean and Mike would take long walks together, and when a plane flew over, he would invariably look up at his mother to ask, "Daddy sly [fly] right?"

And she would always responded, "Yes, he always flew right." She worried that Mike was in constant anguish about what other children said—that his father had been at fault. Three years after the crash, little Mike Spong developed an ulcer, rare for a child his age.

Jean Spong and her son stopped the onslaught by moving from Kansas City to Phoenix, where her husband's sister and cousin were living. Life there would prove to be more tranquil.

Fifty-one years after the event, Jeanette Phillips Ragan, superintendent of hostesses for the central region of TWA in 1955, described her still-vivid memory of the funeral of flight hostess Sharon Schoening. "She was a lovely girl and had many friends. As TWA's representative, I attended her funeral in Iowa. Her mother, of course, was quite distraught. Then I learned that a year later, her twin brother was killed in an automobile accident. I have thought so often of that family and that mother. How sad."

6
CAB Investigations

The Civil Aeronautics Board (CAB) began its investigation immediately after the crash, conducting official hearings in Albuquerque on March 24 and 25, 1955. They obtained considerable evidence concerning the weather conditions at the time of the crash from airport personnel; from an air force pilot who had observed the plane from his home to the north of town, watching it disappear into the clouds; and from two airline pilots who had landed or taken off from the airport about the same time. Unfortunately, the board neglected to interview TWA pilots who had discussed weather conditions with Captain Spong and First Officer Creason just prior to takeoff.

Electronics experts also reported their analysis of the radio control panel that had been recovered at the scene of the crash, stating that the radio frequencies selected on the panel were in agreement with the authorized flight plan.

A month later, CAB investigator Phil Goldstein asked representatives of the Air Line Pilots Association (ALPA) whether they would like to join him on another expedition to the accident scene after the snow had cleared the area. The ALPA representatives felt that their presence would accomplish little, but thanked him for his kind invitation. In early May, Goldstein and a CAB investigative team reached the summit of the pinnacle by ascending the TWA Canyon from the desert floor below. They succeeded in collecting reasonably intact, but badly damaged, navigational instruments from the downed aircraft.

On backtracking their way down to the base of the pinnacle, they were startled by the noise of a massive rock fall descending from the cliffs above. They eluded the avalanche by diving for cover behind an immense rock formation rising from the canyon floor, but Goldstein badly wrenched his back in the process. He was in great pain but knew from personal experience that evacuation by hand-carried litter down that canyon would be too perilous; he would have to escape the mountain on his own two feet, aided by his companions. The ensuing three-hour trip was sheer torture for him, but the party eventually arrived at the cars waiting on the East Mesa, from which he was rushed to a hospital. His injured back required a series of operations that put him out of action for months.

CAB Accident Report

The Civil Aeronautics Board's accident report did not appear to be controversial when it was published on October 12, 1955, eight months after the crash.

"The Board determines that the probable cause of this accident was a lack of conformity with prescribed en route procedures and the deviation from airways at an altitude too low to clear obstructions ahead."

This finding prompted the Albuquerque newspapers to explicitly attribute the crash to pilot error—a plausible explanation that seemed to match the circumstances that I had observed. The plane was probably off route because the pilot was attempting a shortcut across Sandia Crest on his way to Santa Fe. The newspapers, however, did not reveal the reasoning that had led the board to its conclusion. Had they done so, I would have strongly doubted the probity of its decisions.

The report, however, was not deemed acceptable by professional pilots; and the fascinating story of the ensuing investigations appeared as a chapter of a 1960 book, *The Probable Cause*, by Robert Serling, brother of television writer-producer Rod Serling. I had not paid attention to the book when it was published, perhaps dismissing it as wild conjecture by mistakenly associating it with his brother's TV program *The Twilight Zone*.

Much of the material that follows was gleaned from the files of TWA pilot Larry DeCelles, who supplied Robert Serling with a great deal of his information.

The Probable Cause

The first item that attracted my attention in the CAB accident report concerned atmospheric conditions. It seemed to be a relatively minor issue, but I had personal knowledge that cast doubt on what the board claimed.

"Wind velocity over the Sandia Mountain was indicated to be too light to produce an important 'mountain effect' such as severe turbulence, downdrafts, and erroneous altitude indications. Furthermore, such effects when present are manifest over the crest and lee slopes, whereas this accident occurred on the windward slope."

I was appalled by the board's need to base its judgment upon textbook fantasizing about "mountain effect" and "lee slopes." I had been on the windward slopes of the mountain that day and had experienced the intensity and capriciousness of the winds. Our later visits to the wreck site proved that the weather conditions there frequently did not mirror what was happening in town. Measurements made at the airport on the day of the crash certainly did not pertain to what was actually occurring on the high slopes of the Sandias.

The conjectured weather conditions were largely based upon the testimonies of ground personnel at the Albuquerque airport, rather than pilots in the air. As TWA pilot D. C. "Buck" Buchanan nicely phrased it, "We fly airplanes, not airports. No matter what a given station may be reporting in the way of weather, that weather may not exist twenty, ten, five, or even one mile from the observer point."

The second item concerned the crash itself. The report stated that the magnetic course from Albuquerque to the crash site (and to Santa Fe) was about 30 degrees and that the wreckage was strewn in a manner indicating a direction of flight of 320 degrees (essentially northwest) at impact, inferring that the aircraft had turned left about 70 degrees from its original heading. It was climbing just before the crash as if to avoid an obstruction.

The plane, instead, was heading westward (270 degrees) toward Albuquerque—a significant 50-degree difference—when it struck the pinnacle. I had personally observed the impact site, as had others, and their observations had accurately been reported in the newspapers. Yet the CAB officially declared otherwise.

The findings of the board had thus been founded, at least in part, upon conjectures rather than facts; but they had had no difficulty in explicitly blaming the pilots:

"The weather was such that the visibility along the airway was good for many miles ahead to the north. . . . *Even if all navigational aids and instruments had failed, all the captain had to do was look outside to determine that he was not following the airway*" (emphasis mine).

"Therefore, from all available evidence, and the lack of any evidence to the contrary, the *Board can conclude only that the direct course taken by the flight was intentional.*"

Larry DeCelles, along with most other TWA pilots, however, strongly suspected that Captain Spong had been lured into the Sandias by an erroneous fluxgate compass indication. He had been amazed and disgusted when the CAB report accused Spong and Creason of having "intentionally" deviated from their prescribed course.

Pilots from TWA and other airlines were also overwhelmingly shocked and dismayed by the absurdity of the CAB findings. They were willing to accept pilot error as the possible reason for the crash, but the CAB was implying that the pilots had purposely deviated from their approved flight plan in order to take a shortcut *over* an eleven-thousand-foot mountain by flying almost two thousand feet *below* its summit.

Those who had personally known the pilot, Ivan Spong, knew that he was not a happy-go-lucky fly guy recovering from a rough night on the town. His peers regarded him as a serious and highly competent professional who adamantly refused to deviate in the slightest degree from flying regulations. He had not earned that reputation by being stupid. A night on the town to him was an anthropology class at the University of New Mexico from Professor Hibben.

Testimony of Captain O. L. Hanson

This sentiment would later be substantially enforced by a letter from TWA Captain O. L. Hanson, who was aboard the TWA Flight 163 that had carried Captain Spong, First Officer Creason, and flight hostess Schoening to Albuquerque on February 18, 1955, the evening before the crash. Hanson was qualifying for the route from Kansas City to San

Francisco and had performed the normal copilot duties under Spong's direction from Kansas City to Albuquerque.

"Captain Spong was extremely conscientious in performing his duties in complete accord with TWA procedures and made no compromise with them. His skill and aptitude during the more difficult maneuvers was of an extremely high order. . . . Captain Spong was particularly helpful in pointing out the dangerous terrain in the Santa Fe to Albuquerque area [and] the importance of abiding by the en route procedures between Santa Fe and Albuquerque."

Instrument Landing Systems

A brief introduction to instrument landing system (ILS) terminology may prove helpful at this point.

The ILS allows a pilot to search for an airport and land safely in cloudy conditions and at night. It is based upon narrowly focused electronic beams (similar to radio waves) that mark the positions of airport runways. Localizer beams transmitted down the center lines of each runway are used to give the pilot a visual display of the plane's position relative to the ideal glide path to touchdown. The plane's position is shown relative to a vertical line indicating deviations left or right of the center line and a horizontal line indicating deviations above or below the desired glide path.

The pilot remains on the glide path by keeping the plane centered on both the vertical and horizontal lines. While the ILS does not provide the pilot with quantitative information concerning how far left or right he or she is, the plane's height above the terrain, or the distance from the runway, marker beacons directed upward from the ground demarcate the ends of the glide path. The outer marker indicates the position of the beginning of the path, roughly four miles from touchdown; and the inner marker signals that visual contact with the runway is imminent. When the plane flies over a marker beacon, it actuates an indicator on the pilot's instrument panel, and the beacon modulating tone is made audible to the pilot.

The localizer beams can also be used in taking off from an airport, but the meanings of the ILS displays will be reversed. As the visual cues were designed for landing, "right of glide path" for landing pilots on the "front course" must be interpreted as "left of glide path" for pilots taking off in the opposite direction on the "back course."

Fluxgate Compass Error Experiences

The Air Line Pilot's Association (ALPA) realized that they would have to discover new concrete evidence to challenge the board to reopen its investigations. That evidence would be developed by TWA pilot Larry DeCelles, who had recently succeeded in discovering both the nature of and the correction for some fluxgate compass errors aboard TWA aircraft.

DeCelles's own experiences with fluxgate compass errors provide us with valuable insight into what may have contributed to the crash of Flight 260.

He had been a copilot aboard a Martin 404 approaching Dayton, Ohio, from the east about 9:45 p.m. on January 6, 1954, flying the plane on instruments while the captain performed the copilot duties. They were at twenty-five hundred feet westbound on the west leg of the Columbus, Ohio, low-frequency range and were to intercept the Dayton ILS localizer course and turn southwest toward Dayton.

He had gone slightly past the Dayton localizer course before making his turn and consequently had to turn south to get back on track—at the same time letting down (descending) for his approach to landing. Shortly after completing the turn and rolling out of the south heading, he broke out under the overcast and could see the lights of two airports straight ahead where there should have been only one. The city of Dayton was to his right instead of to his left; and the lights of a mysterious third airport appeared still further to his right.

DeCelles was thoroughly bewildered, but his captain understood immediately what had happened. The latter reached down and activated the fluxgate compass gyro caging system, realigning the spin axis of the gyroscope to the direction in which the plane was then heading. The heading indicators immediately swung around and showed that they were flying southeast rather than south! The captain said he had seen it happen before.

A similar thing had occurred later in July, when the same pilot was picking his way—on and off instruments—through a squall line on a westbound flight between Washington, D.C., and Wheeling, West Virginia. It was pretty dark for a while, and he thought they might be in for a rough ride, but suddenly they came out into the clear. But it was too clear, and he felt instinctively that something was wrong.

Something seemed wrong, for the weather on the back side of a squall line is usually murky—the clouds being stratified, rather than cumuliform. Besides, it seemed strange that they could have passed quickly through what seemed to be an extensive storm area. Yet, still on instruments, everything else appeared to be perfectly normal, as the direction indicators showed him to be on course, heading westbound.

He continued flying with an uneasy feeling for several minutes before he happened to glance at the old-fashioned, obscurely located, and seldom-used float compass. It said they were headed eastbound, not westbound. Remembering his former experience, he caged the fluxgate gyros, and the heading indicators immediately swung around and indicated that they indeed were headed east.

Somehow he had developed a 180-degree error while working his way through the squall line and had unwittingly reversed course toward the east while his instruments indicated that he was maintaining a generally west heading at all times.

The Fluxgate Compass

The fluxgate compass was (and still is) used aboard aircraft instead of the common magnetic (wet) compass, for it remained stable during aircraft turns and was readily (and inexpensively) adapted to instrument panels. A simple electromagnetic device, it sensed the direction of the horizontal component of the earth's magnetic field and generated a small electrical voltage that was compatible with the commonly available electric meters already in use on the instrument panel. To maintain accuracy during the twists and turns of normal flight, the compass was kept as level as possible by mounting it on a gyroscope-and-gimbal system.

Ironically, the Achilles heel of the system was the very stabilizing gyroscope that was the key to its reliability. Steep turns could induce torques that surreptitiously caused rotor precession and tumbling (spilling), producing erroneous readouts until it eventually realigned itself—a process usually requiring several minutes of straight and level flight. The potential for disastrous consequences was high during that interim, unless the pilot had the good fortune to notice the problem and reset the gyros with the caging button.

DeCelles's experiences were unnerving, and he set out to learn more about the inner workings of the system to see whether he could devise some sort of warning system from the fact that airplanes were equipped with two independent fluxgate compasses. Both located in

Figure 31. TWA Capt. Larry DeCelles at the time he investigated the TWA Flight 260 accident in 1955. (Courtesy of Larry DeCelles.)

the left wingtip, they transmit heading data to the cockpit by means of an electronic circuit, displaying the data on a radio magnetic indicator (RMI). There are two RMIs, one for each pilot.

It seemed to him that some means could be found by which the data supplied by the two compasses could be mechanically or electrically compared so that a warning sound or flash would be generated whenever a significant discrepancy between the two was detected—it being highly unlikely that both would malfunction simultaneously, in the same direction, and to the same magnitude.

While studying the wiring diagrams for the plane, he was shocked to find that both RMIs were connected to the same transmitter: the pilot and copilot would always see identical heading indications. The second fluxgate was being used merely as a standby unit to which both RMIs could be switched in case of malfunction.

Obviously this was not a fail-safe arrangement. Consequently, on January 16, 1955, one month prior to the Albuquerque crash— DeCelles submitted a written memorandum to TWA calling attention to the hazard of the fluxgate hookup and suggesting that the captain's RMI should be hooked to one fluxgate compass and the first officer's to the other. The suggestion was in the "under consideration" stage when Ivan Spong flew into the mountainside, but it was implemented in all airplanes shortly thereafter. The company gave DeCelles an award for submitting the idea.

Captain J. L. DeCelles

Captain J. L. DeCelles was born on November 10, 1921. Known as Larry, he was the eldest of five boys. His childhood was an exciting though rootless one: he lived in Mexico during a revolution, changed schools thirteen times before he got out of grade school, and attended four high schools and two colleges. He enrolled in the Jesuit Rockhurt College in Kansas City, Missouri, in 1939. Experiencing an emergency appendectomy halfway through his sophomore year, he fell in love with his nurse, Betty Frechin. Circumstances then compelled him to interrupt his education to get a job.

Although aviation had been part of his life since his earliest years—his father, a commercial pilot since 1923, had his pilot's license signed by Orville Wright—Larry DeCelles began his aviation career by accident. At Rockhurst he had been a member of a radio speaker's seminar that broadcast a weekly skit dramatizing the history of some local industry. He had chosen TWA as his subject and, as a climax to the skit, interviewed TWA's vice president, Paul Richter. Shortly afterward, when he left school in June 1941, he called on Mr. Richter for a job. Richter hired him as a personnel clerk in Albuquerque, where TWA was training pilots to ferry bombers to England.

After Pearl Harbor was bombed in December 1941 and TWA lost its training contract, DeCelles went to work for Eastern Air Lines in St. Louis as an operations clerk. In June 1942 he left Eastern, enlisted in the Army Air Corps, and returned to Kansas City to await call-up, working in an ordnance plant in the interim and marrying Betty in October. The Army Air Corps assigned him to the 349th Troop Carrier Group that served stateside until sent to Europe just in time to see the end of the war.

After the war he went back to TWA and began copilot training, but nothing deterred him from his intense desire to do things for others. In 1953 he received the Christopher Award from the Christopher Society, an organization that encouraged people in all walks of life to bring Judeo-Christian principles to bear on the world around them. The Christopher Society's motto, "It is better to light one candle than curse the darkness," aptly matched his credo.

DeCelles was appointed central air safety chairman for TWA in March 1957, and his tenacious ability to search for the truth would play a major role in events that would transpire over the next three years. He had met Ivan Spong only once—briefly serving as his copilot on a leg of a longer flight—yet chose to dedicate himself to what some considered to be a futile effort to defend a dead colleague. His mission would absent him from his family for lengthy and stressful periods of time, but he remained focused on success.

The Air Line Pilots Association

Captain DeCelles's efforts to clear the Flight 260 pilots was featured in *The Probable Cause* by Robert Serling. The following narrative of his was derived from his letter to Serling of August 24, 1959.

A considerable portion of ALPA's activity was directed toward improving aviation safety. As pilots consider safety to be of primary concern, the home office maintained a fully staffed engineering and air safety department—then headed by Ted G. Linnert—that coordinated the activities of a host of local and regional pilot committees, thus allowing the influence of working airline pilots to be extended into every area where flight safety was concerned. ALPA local councils were found wherever airline pilots were based, and each one had an air safety committee, the chairman of which was a member of the ALPA Central Air Safety Committee for his airline. Except for the home office department, ALPA safety workers were unpaid volunteers whose activities were usually conducted on their own time between trips.

The philosophy of ALPA's president, Clarence N. Sayen, was that pilot error accidents existed, but no pilot ever erred deliberately or in the interest of self-destruction. Merely assessing blame to the pilots would do little to enhance aviation safety. If the maximum were to be learned from each accident, accident investigations should determine the probable origin of the problem—design error, fatigue limits, cockpit booby traps, inadequate training, et cetera.

Initial Concerns

When the CAB issued its report on the Sandia accident, TWA Central Air Safety Chairman Captain R. F. Adickes asked pilots to send him reports of any fluxgate compass malfunctions they had experienced. He forwarded them to the ALPA home office, where they were used to buttress the protest that the CAB had not given proper consideration to instrument malfunction as the probable cause of the accident. After Adickes's successor, Captain David Halperin, had collected substantial evidence, he requested a meeting with the CAB to discuss the case, but was denied by William K. Andrews, who was then in charge of accident investigation for the CAB. Andrews was reported to have been largely responsible for the "findings" expressed in the accident report. Andrews was to blunder badly again during the public investigation of the sensational Grand Canyon midair collision in 1956. Shortly thereafter, he "retired" from office and was succeeded by Oscar Bakke, whereupon a meeting was set for a CAB-ALPA discussion of the Sandia affair.

The CAB

In the meanwhile, Halperin had enlisted DeCelles as an assistant and was grooming him as a successor. DeCelles accompanied Linnert from the home office to Washington for the Sandia discussion. Captain Richard Flournoy of New York also attended for ALPA.

Bakke was tied up for most of the day, and they had to deal with his subordinates—finding them to be a good group, friendly, easy to talk to; but, except for the younger members, most of them appeared to still be living in the days of the Ford Tri-Motor or, at best, the DC-3. They were convinced that the weather had been virtually CAVU (ceiling and visibility unlimited), and all the fancy arguments about instrument malfunction were met by the objection: "But all the pilot had to do was look out the window to know the direction he was going."

ALPA pointed out that another airline pilot had taken off minutes after Spong and had testified that the mountains and the Rio Grande Valley were completely obscured by a snowstorm, but it fell on deaf ears. The weather was *good*—the report said so! When ALPA asked CAB whether they really believed—as their report had seemed to imply—that the TWA pilots had entered into some sort of a suicide pact, they replied, "No. No. We meant no such implication. We believe they were taking a shortcut."

"At nine thousand feet?" ALPA asked. "Yes," CAB incongruously replied. "We can't understand why they didn't climb higher."

The CAB people agreed to give consideration to the ALPA arguments and seemed willing to delete the "intentional" connotation from their report. The ALPA folks agreed to send CAB a written summation of their arguments. The conference ended on this note—ALPA hopeful, but not much encouraged. Halperin assigned DeCelles the task of preparing the written summation. He spent a good deal of time on it, and it was mailed to the CAB in mid-April 1957.

Albuquerque Localizer Errors

DeCelles replaced Halperin as TWA central air safety chairman when his term expired at the end of April 1957. One of his first official acts was to write a letter to TWA insisting on the need for a warning device to monitor discrepancies between the RMI heading indicators from the two fluxgate compasses. His efforts bore fruit, and such systems were installed on all new jet aircraft. As the approach used was not adaptable for obsolescent piston aircraft, the TWA engineering department cooperated with the ALPA air safety committee to develop one that was.

During the latter part of July 1957, a TWA pilot en route through the Albuquerque area chanced to overhear a Continental Air Lines pilot report to the Albuquerque control tower that the Albuquerque ILS localizer course—which Spong was supposed to be following when he flew into the Sandia Mountains—was displaced for the second straight day and was heading directly toward the Sandias. The TWA pilot immediately notified DeCelles, who alerted both the Civil Aeronautics Authority (CAA) and—through Ted Linnert—the CAB.

On August 16 the CAB replied to Linnert that the localizer course had been checked shortly after the accident and was found normal. The board concluded, therefore, that such a malfunction could have played no part in the Sandia accident.

Six days later DeCelles received a telephone message from the Kansas City office of the CAA, notifying him that preliminary investigations of the false course report concerning the Albuquerque localizer indicated that rain coming through a leaky roof on the transmitting shack might have caused the false indication. A new roof had already been installed. DeCelles immediately forwarded this news to Linnert for CAB attention, but was unfortunately too late. The board had already signed an amended report that was released on August 26, 1957.

CAB Amended Report

As anticipated, the amended report deleted the word *intentional*, but a lengthy paragraph had been inserted that said the same thing in a roundabout way. The implication was almost stronger than the original declaration. ALPA's arguments for an instrument malfunction were dismissed—almost contemptuously. They did not, said the board, even "warrant serious considerations." They were not a possible contributing factor.

In November 1957, Jean Spong sent a letter to the chairman of the TWA ALPA Central Air Safety Committee saying that she was surprised to learn from a Chicago-based pilot that Ivan's case had finally been reviewed and closed, with a thinly disguised finding that he had committed suicide and hence the murder of fifteen people.

"I find this so difficult to believe, even though the first reports said the crash was 'apparently intentional.' Ivan would never do such a horrible thing, to himself or to his passengers. . . . I was praying the very least that could be discovered was: cause unknown. Even though months have passed since the crash, what I heard today cut deeply and reopened old wounds and again has me wondering what really happened. Never will I believe that he committed suicide."

DeCelles's reply to Mrs. Spong stated that, while the CAB considered the case closed, ALPA did not. "You may be heartened that the vast majority of airline pilots—from both TWA and other airlines—have nothing but contempt for the CAB conclusion in this case. We will never forget it, and we will never rest until the record has been set straight."

On January 8, 1958, the local office of the CAA informed DeCelles that the leaky roof did *not* have any effect on the operation of the Albuquerque ILS. DeCelles immediately responded: "Will you please advise what *did* cause the localizer course to be displaced on these two occasions so as to lead to Sandia Ridge?"

Later in the month DeCelles received a reply to a request for TWA to assist ALPA in seeking a reopening of the case. TWA officials responded that they regarded the Sandia case closed. It would be fruitless to attempt to reopen the case after a second statement of findings had been issued. This was disheartening news, but TWA representatives were being realistic about the predictable functioning of a federal bureaucracy.

On April 8, 1958, nearly three months after his query, DeCelles received a reply from the CAA regarding the reported malfunctions of the Albuquerque ILS. "Reference is made to our previous correspondence on this subject, including your letter of January 16, 1958. We have been advised that the previously referred to false courses were not related to any malfunctioning, misadjustment, or inherent difficulties of the ILS and associated monitoring system."

As it was obvious that his question was being evaded, he placed a long distance call on April 14 to the Continental Air Lines captain who had originally reported the false courses on the Albuquerque ILS. What he told DeCelles made him realize that he had a club that could be used to get the attention of the CAB. They now had an authentic and verified report of a highly intermittent malfunction of the very radio facility that Spong was supposed to be following when he crashed—*and* the reported false course led to the very mountain range where the crash occurred. This was too hot to brush off.

Renewed Efforts

DeCelles was by now in possession of a substantial file of letters, telegrams, and teletype messages concerning the Sandia crash and would use it to reapproach the CAB. What he wanted was an opportunity to engage them in formal debate—preferably at a reopened public hearing—with respect to their dismissal of ALPA's arguments in favor of the instrument malfunction theory. The file contained numerous hair-raising pilot reports of malfunctions that supported the feasibility of ALPA's theory.

Fortunately, Ted Linnert was a very careful individual. He was open to requesting a new hearing on the developments, but he counseled preparedness. If DeCelles were willing, he would ask the CAB to forward to the CAB Kansas City office the transcript of the original hearing, including all subcommittee reports and all exhibits, so that a complete study of the record could be made in preparation for the proposed conference. DeCelles concurred, and Linnert made the request.

Meanwhile, DeCelles started plying the TWA engineering department with requests for data on the various possible causes and statistical rates of malfunction of fluxgate compass and navigational radio receiver components. And, on April 30, he again wrote the vice president of TWA requesting assistance.

The vice president's office replied on May 13 that they were making a study of the situation. When the study was completed, "we will be in a better position to discuss your request that TWA join with ALPA in seeking a reopening of the Albuquerque accident investigation."

Transcript of the Original CAB Report

On June 6 CAB wrote to ALPA to say that the CAB was making an exception to established procedures and that the board's duplicate copy of the Albuquerque accident transcript was being sent to the CAB Kansas City office, where it would remain and be available for ALPA representatives to review until July 15. Linnert forwarded this information to DeCelles along with an authorization for him to be reimbursed by the ALPA treasurer for the flights he would miss while studying the CAB material.

In June replies started coming in from TWA's engineering people supplying the technical data DeCelles was seeking. These letters would prove immensely important to the case they were building— B. M. "Bill" Meador, TWA's aircraft electrical engineering supervisor, deserving a great deal of credit for this contribution. This data was the beginning of a veritable flood of assistance that ALPA would now receive from TWA management.

The CAB transcript of the original hearing arrived at the Kansas City office of the CAB shortly before the end of June. A Mr. Stillwagen, investigator in charge of the Kansas City office, gave DeCelles a desk where he could begin his study, taking copious notes as he went along.

DeCelles's first concern was to dig out all the testimony conflicting with what he felt was an erroneous concept held by the CAB—that the prevailing weather at the time of the accident was such that "there is no understandable reason why the pilots would not know, by reference to the conspicuous terrain features, that they were not on the planned course."

To him, the CAB concept of the weather conditions seemed to constitute a mental block preventing the board from recognizing what seemed to him to be a simple and obvious fact: No rational pilot would intentionally try to fly a straight-line course from Albuquerque to Santa Fe at nine thousand feet, and no rational copilot would go along for the ride.

From this, three elementary deductions could be drawn: first, Spong and Creason did not realize they were off course; second, their failure to realize that they were off course was proof positive that their instruments were not indicating properly; and third, no "conspicuous terrain features" were visible to them.

Reading through the statements of the various witnesses who had testified at the original hearing, he found ample evidence to substantiate his deduction that the weather was such as to completely obscure the pilots' view of the "conspicuous terrain features" on which the board had hung its argument. It was all too evident that whoever wrote the original CAB report on the accident had made a careful selection from the witnesses' testimonies regarding weather conditions the morning of the accident and had disregarded all testimony conflicting with the opinion that the crew was trying "to go direct."

This evidence alone—and the simple deductions that could be drawn from it—seemed to DeCelles sufficient to convince the board that it should reopen its investigation of the case. Fortunately, however, he kept reading through the exhibits, unearthing exciting evidence that so strongly supported the position that, if necessary, ALPA would have no difficulty in attracting the interest of the federal bureaucracy.

When finished with his study, he felt that he could prove, beyond all reasonable doubt, that the crew of Flight 260 fully intended to follow its clearance—that they could not have "intentionally" deviated from it.

Moreover, he now had concrete evidence that the ship's compass was not indicating properly. There was a discrepancy of forty-seven degrees between the impact heading, determined from the distribution of wreckage, and the impact heading shown on the heading indicator that had been recovered. This discrepancy was of the proper size and direction to have led the pilots of Flight 260 to fly to the crash zone while believing themselves to be flying on the heading of the prescribed course.

The evidence was almost too good to be true.

He worried, however, that the impact heading determined by the wreckage distribution might not hold up for some reason; he did not know by what method it had been determined or within what tolerances it could be accepted. Or it might be argued that the heading indication found on the recovered RMI dial was not significant—the investigative subcommittee that had analyzed the recovered instrument had reported only that "upon disassembly of the instrument there were no marks to indicate the card [a circular disk attached to the compass needle and marked with compass directions] was moved on impact."

DeCelles felt he had ample deductive evidence that a compass error had led the flight into the mountains. He knew that the pilots could not knowingly have flown at such an altitude for such a period of time on a heading toward Sandia Ridge. He had no need for concrete evidence himself, but he was confronting a governmental agency that had prejudged the case and had twice issued a verdict against the pilot and copilot. He would need more than his personal opinion that no pilot would knowingly do such a thing; it would be far easier to accomplish his task if he could present unassailable evidence of an erroneous heading indication.

Searching for Concrete Evidence

Accordingly, during the first week of July, DeCelles sent out three letters. The first was to Phil Goldstein, who had been in charge of the accident investigation, asking him to qualify the means used for establishing the aircraft heading of 320 degrees and evaluate the accuracy of his finding.

The second letter was to B. M. Meador of the TWA engineering department, asking him for written verification that 273 or 274 degrees could confidently be interpreted as the RMI reading at the moment of impact because the dial was motor driven and, hence, not subject to rapid displacements.

The third letter was addressed to all TWA pilots, asking them whether they were in complete agreement with two opinions:

"No TWA pilot or copilot who has ever made even a single trip to Albuquerque during daylight hours would knowingly fly on instruments on a northeast heading from the Albuquerque airport at nine thousand feet for five minutes."

"It is a standard and necessary airline piloting practice to navigate primarily by reference to heading and course instruments regardless of whether the weather is IFR [instrument flight rules] or VFR [visual flight rules]. Naturally, the airline pilot observes prominent landmarks when they are visible from the cockpit; however, that part of his attention which is directed outside of the cockpit is necessarily devoted primarily to such important considerations as watching for other aircraft, studying the weather which lies ahead, etc."

The response was almost immediate. More than nine hundred pilots replied, unanimously in agreement with the two opinions DeCelles proffered.

While the replies came in, TWA Captain W. H. Johnson assisted DeCelles in preparing graphic exhibits to illustrate the evidence discovered in the CAB record. Johnson drew a profile representation of the mountain and a number of transparencies by which he could illustrate the testimony of the various witnesses concerning weather conditions. Another drawing illustrated the flight path that would have been flown with the erroneous heading indication found in the CAB record. Captain Johnson then took these to the TWA art department, where they were reproduced on material suitable for a view-graph projector.

In mid-July 1958, Ted Linnert forwarded DeCelles a copy of a letter from the deputy administrator of the CAA, disclaiming that the reported false courses of the Albuquerque ILS localizer had been caused by any malfunction of the transmitting equipment, but admitting that the possibility of "radio interference" could not be discounted. The two reports, said the letter, "may have resulted from interfering radio signals from an unknown source."

Also in mid-July, TWA, having decided to give ALPA all possible assistance, appointed David Halperin—DeCelles's predecessor as central air safety chairman—to coordinate the company's assistance program.

On July 21, TWA's Meador affirmed that it was quite possible, but not necessarily certain, that the 273 or 274 degree position reported represented the reading of the RMI card at the moment of impact of the aircraft.

Two days later, the CAB's Goldstein responded that a pocket compass had been used to determine the 320-degree magnetic heading referred to in the accident report. He was unable to determine whether the compass could have been affected by local magnetic disturbances.

Flight Tests

On July 28, a CAB representative replied to Linnert's request for a conference, stating that it would be impractical to hold a conference until his staff had had ample time to weigh both the ALPA seventeen-page critique and other material that was still in preparation.

On August 25, at DeCelles's request, TWA conducted an elaborate flight test with a Martin aircraft to simulate various types of fluxgate compass malfunctions, enabling them to duplicate exactly the type of compass error that would have caused the accident. A professional photographer filmed movies of the instrument panel throughout the simulation; these would later comprise one of their prime exhibits.

Later, on a scheduled flight through Albuquerque, DeCelles simulated the malfunction again. It was a clear day, and he took movies of the instrument panel as the airplane rolled out on a supposedly northerly heading. As he panned the camera up for a view out the window, he could see the middle of Sandia Ridge straight ahead.

Conference with the CAB

On August 14, ALPA President Clarence N. Sayen forwarded a letter to the CAB reiterating the request for a conference and attaching thirty-two indexed documents prepared by DeCelles and Johnson.

On October 10, Oscar Bakke, director of the CAB Bureau of Safety, personally presided over a meeting at the CAB office building in Washington, D.C. A group of about thirty persons were present, representing CAB, CAA, Bendix (manufacturer of the fluxgate compass), Collins Radio (manufacturer of the VOR receiver), TWA, and ALPA. (The VOR, or VHF omnidirectional radio range, is used by the ILS to determine the approximate position of the aircraft.) Bakke opened the meeting, remarking that, among other things, he had only recently taken over the Bureau of Safety and had not been connected with the original investigation.

He then turned the meeting over to Linnert, who turned it over to Captain DeCelles, who presented ALPA's case with the assistance of Captain Johnson, who ran the slide projector and the movies and otherwise sat at his elbow handing him the proper documents at the proper time. They had carefully rehearsed their presentation. The meeting took seven exhausting hours.

On October 14, Linnert wrote to James R. Durfee, chairman of CAB, to report to him about the October 10 meeting; he appreciated Mr. Bakke's scheduling the meeting and arranging for such complete technical representation from other parties.

On October 20, Bakke replied to Linnert's letter to Durfee, telling him that the matter had been assigned by the board to the Bureau of Safety for further study. They would:

1. Conduct flights, including photographic missions, during the next ten days to resurvey the accident site and obtain additional data on wreckage distribution, heading on impact, et cetera.
2. Visit Pioneer and Collins Instrument Companies to obtain further information concerning potential sources of error in the directional instruments involved in this accident.
3. Contact all of the parties in attendance at the October 10 meeting to obtain their opinions of the material ALPA had presented.

Once the data from these actions had been evaluated, the CAB would make a statement of plans for formally reopening the case for the introduction of new evidence. He concluded his letter by praising DeCelles: "Particular mention should be made of Mr. DeCelles. The manner in which the ALPA views were submitted was exemplary. It was apparent that considerable thought had been given to the careful selection and proper organization of the pertinent material."

Visits to the Crash Site

Toward the end of October, DeCelles received a long distance call from Phil Goldstein. The CAB was going to send people to reclimb the mountain in order to recheck the impact heading, using an astrocompass this time instead of a magnetic compass. Would DeCelles (representing ALPA) and Halperin (representing TWA) care to join him?

They flew out to Albuquerque and met Goldstein, and early the next morning all three set out for the foot of the mountain in a car from the government interagency pool. On the way they picked up a mountaineer-guide, mountain club team leader George Hankins, who was sixty years old by then, with long blond hair that reached over his shoulders. (His hair hadn't been noticeably long during the rescue and recovery efforts of 1955.) The beatnik era had yet to come, and George wasn't protesting anything other than recent increases in the cost of haircuts. Buffalo Bill Cody had worn his hair long, and so would he.

DeCelles thought highly of his guide, for he described him to Robert Serling (author of *Probable Cause*) as a man who "never sat down and could climb a cliff side like a billy goat. He was a fine gentleman—a machinist by trade, an inventor by hobby." (I knew when I first read this apt description of George that Captain Larry DeCelles was a man whose judgment I could trust. He had known George for only a few hours, while I had known him for eight years and couldn't have done better.)

The day was cold, the wind was brisk, and it was snowing on the mountain, the upper part of which was obscured by gray-white snow clouds that swirled and dipped with the eddying wind. The weather was supposed to clear, but if it didn't before they reached the foot of the wreck pinnacle, they would have to abandon the climb. They saw tumbleweeds blown by the wind as they traversed the mesa—looking lonely, somehow, rolling along, rootless and dead, past the gray boulders and the cactus plants. And then they entered the canyon and began the long climb up the trail, the clouds dropping lower and lower.

DeCelles looked at his watch, which showed a few minutes past seven—about the time that Flight 260 had flown up this same canyon nearly four years before. And then he heard the faint sound of an airplane. At first he thought it was someone running his engines up at the airport in the valley below, but then he realized it was coming closer. The sound grew louder and louder, reverberating from canyon wall to canyon wall. It grew to a crescendo and then began to fade. Finally it was gone, and he realized that it was an eastbound flight making the standard instrument departure—climbing in a spiral over the Weiler intersection to the minimum safe altitude, then proceeding through the clouds above the mountaintop and passing over their heads. The sound made him think of a bugle blowing taps.

Contrary to the forecast, the weather grew worse instead of better. When they reached the foot of the pinnacle, they found it obscured by clouds, and it was beginning to snow. They built a fire and rested. For the tenderfeet, it had been a tough climb. They weren't used to the exercise and particularly not at that altitude. DeCelles remembered asking Hankins if he wouldn't at least sit down; George's endurance embarrassed him.

When they were certain that the weather would not improve, they began the three-hour descent. Goldstein bore up well, but Halperin and DeCelles were completely bushed. They drove back to the Casa Grande Lodge, where Goldstein checked with the weathermen. The forecast had been drastically revised. It was going to be thick for a week or two. They would go home and wait for a better day.

On November 22, they tried again. There were just three of them this time—Goldstein, Hankins, and DeCelles—as Halperin had to attend to other business. Their route would be the one that we had pioneered on our first visit to the pinnacle from atop the mountain. This meant they would have to climb back up to the Crest at the end of the day, but Goldstein thought this would be easier than the long trek up and down the canyon.

The rock faces of the pinnacle were sheer cliffs, but the climb up the dirt slope leading to the notch was straightforward. As DeCelles described it, however, the ascent from the notch was not. Hankins's belaying him up ensured his physical safety but did not ease his fears. The handholds and footholds were scarce, and he could see all the way to the canyon floor, two thousand feet below, and imagine his body falling and bouncing down the mountainside.

When he reached the top and looked out to the west, he could see the Rio Grande Valley floor, nearly a mile below. It looked like a different planet—far different from looking down from an airplane.

But it didn't frighten him anymore, and he wandered all over the summit, marveling that he wasn't afraid. Goldstein cautioned him when he got too close to the precipice, where the sandy soil made the footing insecure.

I and others who have topped that summit have shared those experiences.

They discovered that little evidence remained at the crash site. Wreckage not deliberately pushed over the precipice at the close of the investigation had since slid or been blown over the cliff. Caught in the gnarled branches at the top of a tree was a long piece of twisted aluminum rattling in the wind.

They relied on the three-year-old recollections of Hankins and Goldstein to locate the spot where the bodies of the pilot and copilot were found lying side by side. Remnants of the windshield and other material verified that this was the point at which the cockpit had come to rest, fifty feet uphill from the spot on the cliff rim where the tail had rested.

Goldstein used the astrocompass to sight along the line from the cockpit site to the tail to determine its true bearing, then repeated the operation with a magnetic compass to determine its magnetic reading. While *true north* is the direction of the North Pole from any point on earth, *magnetic north* is the direction of the North Magnetic Pole, now lying near Ellesmere Island in northern Canada; it moves around because of changes in the earth's core. *Magnetic deviation* is the angle between magnetic north and true north—positive when magnetic north is east of true north. The magnetic deviation at Albuquerque in 1955 was 13 degrees; it is now 11 degrees. Another navigational term is *heading*, the direction that a plane is pointing, but not necessarily moving because of wind drift. Sometimes confused with *heading*, *bearing* is the direction of the destination.

The true and magnetic headings of the aircraft at impact were both 262 degrees.

As the magnetic deviation at Albuquerque was 13 degrees east, the measurements should have differed by the same amount. Identical readings meant that a local magnetic deviation of plus 13 degrees existed—the result of pieces of wreckage still remaining or, perhaps, an ore deposit. The aberrant deviation disappeared entirely when they moved to a position approximately one hundred feet southwest of the impact point.

Could this be a topsy-turvy tangle of the meaning of north? *True and magnetic north were supposedly distinct; yet Goldstein had found them identical twins at the impact point. If his explanations were wrong, could this new information be evidence of a deeper mystery?*

Correcting for the local deviation produced a likely magnetic impact heading of 249 degrees, essentially due west, and lag of 20 degrees from the RMI reading of 273 degrees—easily attributed to the great rapidity of the turn just before impact. *Magnetic impact heading* is the direction the plane was pointing at the time of impact. Lag occurs when an instrument cannot instantaneously respond to a sudden change. In a sharp turn, the RMI dial will take a while to adjust to the new direction.

In short, the fluxgate compass seemed to have been functioning correctly at the end.

They descended the pinnacle and started the long climb back up to the crest, where their Jeep was parked. It was a tedious climb, as they encountered a fair amount of snow and ice in patches. When they were still quite a distance from the top, Goldstein suddenly slipped on one of those patches, lunged to grab a tree root to stop his fall, and twisted his back in the process. The pain must have been severe, but perhaps what bothered Goldstein most was his recollection of the injury he had sustained several years before on this same mountainside when he was nearly caught by a gigantic rock slide.

He gritted his teeth and continued the climb, slowing down, his face turning pale. At first he would not let them help him, but as the climb became increasingly difficult he finally accepted aid from a rope—Hankins and DeCelles taking turns climbing ahead with one end and anchoring it while Goldstein climbed up it, hand over hand, slowly and painfully. The sun was going down, and they were afraid night would fall before they could get to the top; but at length they reached the crest.

As they were trudging through the deep drifts to where the Jeep was parked, DeCelles was afraid that Goldstein would go into shock, but he improved rapidly when they reached the vehicle and seemed in fine shape by the time they were back to the valley.

Goldstein and DeCelles had dinner together that evening at a restaurant on Highway 66, west of town. Looking through a huge picture window, they could see lights of the city in the valley below, and on the other side of the city barely make out the black outline of Sandia Mountain against the blue-black sky. It was a cloudless night, and the red lights marking the television towers on the ridge top were clearly visible. It looked very peaceful.

Less than "Concrete" Evidence

Flying back to Kansas City the following day, DeCelles mulled over the significance of what they had learned. They could be reasonably certain that the airplane had crashed while on a heading somewhere in the range from 240 to 260 degrees (magnetic) and that the fluxgate compass indicator—the RMI dial—was reading somewhere between 260 and 290 degrees. He could no longer argue that the RMI dial revealed an error that could have produced the fatal flight path. His concrete evidence had crumpled into dust.

His case was not lost, however, for stating that the fluxgate was functional at the moment of impact did not imply that it was functional throughout the flight. It would be impossible to prove absolutely that fluxgate error was the cause of the accident, but it appeared to be the only plausible theory that would explain the prolonged northeasterly heading toward the mountain.

If the initial compass error stemmed from tilting the stabilizing gyro during the first turn, the tilt could gradually have been corrected by the automatic gyro erection mechanism while the aircraft flew onward. And the erroneous heading indication might have conspired with wind drift—a fairly strong westerly wind was reported—to produce a track that initially led toward a point somewhat south of the crash site, but gradually curved to the north as the gyro tilt was corrected, the flux-gate reading correctly by the time the flight entered the canyon. The aircraft then could have proceeded northbound along the east wall of the canyon until the crew glimpsed the mountain and made a steep left turn, only to strike the peak on the way out.

Upon return to Kansas City, he prepared a report for Linnert discussing these issues and commending Goldstein for the cordial and capable manner in which he had handled the expedition. It had been a pleasure working with him.

Linnert forwarded a copy of DeCelles's report to CAB Bureau of Safety chief Oscar Bakke on December 17 with a cover letter expressing hope that he would soon hear from him regarding plans to reopen the hearing.

Meanwhile, DeCelles and Johnson realized that their case rested to a large degree upon their ability to demonstrate that gyro tilt could produce compass errors that would lead the plane to the crash zone and yet be nearly corrected within the five-minute period elapsing from the time when the flight took up its fatal heading until it met the mountain.

Visualizing the Evidence

They now drew heavily upon the spirit of cooperation they had developed with TWA management to develop graphic imagery for their demonstration. C. B. Brainerd, a member of Meador's aircraft–electrical engineering department, prepared a chart from data gleaned from a study of the compass errors that would be produced by various degrees and directions of the fluxgate gyro tilt.

DeCelles and Johnson perused the maintenance manual published by the manufacturer of the fluxgate compass system to determine the minimum and maximum rates at which a tilted gyro could be expected to erect. Coupling this information with the probable ground speed of Flight 260 enabled them to plot a series of curves representing the flight paths that would have resulted from various combinations of gyro tilt, gyro erection rate, and indicated heading. The results were highly gratifying, as the curves clearly showed that gyro tilt produced by a malfunction at any moment during the final third of the long turn made by Flight 260 after takeoff would cause compass errors of the required magnitude. Moreover, their data indicated that the compass error would be completely eliminated by the time of reaching the crash zone in many cases—and in the rest, nearly so.

Johnson used his drafting tools and colored ink to redraw their curves, then took them to the TWA graphic arts department to be reproduced as view-graph slides. By rearranging them so they could be pivoted to portray flight paths that would result from the pilot pursuing various headings, the team would be able to demonstrate that for each set of curves, there was a heading that would have led Flight 260 to the crash zone. These slides amounted to an animated cartoon in Technicolor.

Johnson also prepared a slide of a plan view of the Albuquerque area, including geographical, airway, and radio facility features; then another of the same area obscured by the snowstorm, which could be projected on the screen as an overlay to the original.

Other slides depicted a vertical cross-section of the flight path and a broadside view of the mountain, with overlays depicting mountain obscuration according to the testimony of various witnesses.

Johnson was thus concocting a vivid PowerPoint presentation by hand, long before modern computer imagery was ever conceived.

Other slides were more pedestrian, dealing with the fluxgate hookup before and after the accident, photographs of the pilots' instrument panels, as well as charts and tables depicting compass errors resulting from various combinations of fluxgate gyro tilt.

ALPA Critique

Meanwhile, DeCelles set about revising the CAB accident report as he thought it should read. The report was so full of errors that it was necessary to rewrite it almost completely.

He would use the CAB report as a model, addressing each section in turn, developing his thesis—that the pilots had intended to fly their prescribed route—from the words and phrases found in the CAB evidence.

His thesis began quietly in section 1 of the original report when he stated that a report paragraph should be revised to show that the TWA departure chart for Albuquerque did not depict the Weiler intersection and that the flight requested the tower to confirm that its location corresponded to that of the Alameda intersection on his departure chart when they were receiving takeoff clearance—a clear indication that they intended to fly the route stated in their flight plan.

His argument was further strengthened when the CAB attacked pilot reliability in section 2: "Flight 260 took off from runway 11 at 0705 on schedule. The time off (time when the plane left the ground) was not reported, contrary to company practice." DeCelles provided reasons why they may not have been able to do so, reasons supporting his central argument. As radio jargon will appear throughout what follows, I'll define a few important terms: VHF (very high frequency)—also employed for television broadcasting and FM radio—is used for short range (line-of-sight) terrestrial communications, because its propagation characteristics are ideal for ensuring that its signals won't interfere with those from remote locations. HF (high frequency), on the other hand, is used by pilots for communicating with distant airline operation centers, because its propagation characteristics do not restrict its use to local areas. VHF is ideal for communications between airports and nearby planes because it is less affected by local atmospheric noise (static) than HF.

TWA did, indeed, require reporting immediately after takeoff, but when the airport's Air Traffic Control (ATC) required a check on VHF frequency after departure—as they did for the Weiler intersection—it was customary to report the time on the airline's HF frequency instead. If unable to contact the company on HF—as was frequently the case—it was both company and general practice to wait until circumstances permitted, then change over briefly to the company VHF frequency; reverting to the VHF frequency used by ATC when the time-off report had been given. (There were two frequencies for ATC and a different two frequencies for TWA—comparable to each having both a phone line and a facsimile line.)

Equipment recovered from the wreckage would seem to indicate that an unsuccessful attempt to contact TWA on HF had been made and that the crew was in the process of setting up the radios to give the take-off time on VHF when the accident occurred.

Moreover, the quote from section 3, "It [the plane] passed over the eastern part of Albuquerque, near him, at an estimated altitude of three thousand feet (eighty-three hundred feet mean sea level) in a high-speed shallow climb," was incomplete. It should have been followed by, "The pilot was not climbing as though intending to cross the ridge at a safe altitude." The omitted sentence preceded the evidence that CAB selected from the testimony of the witness.

Excellent Flying Weather

The next section was originally intended to establish the CAB thesis that the day had been clear for flying, but it included a statement that provided DeCelles with an onslaught of contradictory evidence boosting his own ideas: "He [one witness] noticed that the upper portion of the Sandia Ridge was obscured by clouds." This statement was in direct conflict with other testimony by the same witness and with the testimony of several others whose qualifications were unimpeachable. It gave a seriously misleading impression of the extent to which the mountains might have been visible to the pilots of Flight 260.

The quoted statement was found in a slightly different form on page 24 of the official transcript of the CAB hearing: "The upper third of Sandia Ridge was obscured by clouds."

But, on page 30 of the transcript, the same witness testified that the altitude of the cloud base adjacent to the mountain was lower than seventy-five hundred feet—thus implying that 86 percent of the ridge had been obscured.

Other observers also corroborated this testimony.

"The clouds were right down to where the terrain starts leveling off."

"All you could see was just the little parts of the foothills."

"The Sandia Mountains were completely covered. The base of the mountains could be seen, the overcast did not extend to the rising ground of the approaches to the pass."

"The height of the base at the layer over the mountains was approximately eight thousand feet, and it lowered as you went south along the mountain. Around Tijeras Canyon it was nearly to the base, and that is approximately six thousand feet."

Observers in the air also corroborated the judgments from those on the ground.

A witness from Pioneer Air Lines Flight 62, departing just eleven minutes after Flight 260, testified that it was not possible to see up the Rio Grande Valley because they found a "solid wall" of cloud and "no forward visibility" just a few minutes north of Central Avenue. "The biggest peak was obscured from the top right down to the base." At an altitude of 10,000 feet, three to four minutes north of the airport, they had been skimming through the tops of a solid overcast extending over the entire Weiler intersection.

Yet, in spite of this testimony, the CAB report had claimed: "Before departure the pilots had been briefed on the weather, which was generally clear and would have permitted visual flight over nearly the entire route, with only short instrument flight probable."

The CAB claim thus conflicted with the Pioneer testimony, for had the Pioneer aircraft been flying a thousand feet lower at the altitude prescribed for Flight 260, it would have flown in clouds that would have required instruments for nearly the entire route.

More damning yet was the fact that the CAB report also misquoted both a tower operator and the Pioneer crew by stating: "Tower personnel watched this flight proceed out the back course of the ILS and still had it in sight when it reported over the Weiler intersection at nine thousand five hundred feet. Its crew testified that they encountered only approximately one minute of instrument flight near the intersection of the back course of the ILS localizer and the 240-degree radial of the Santa Fe omni range."

The tower operator had actually testified that he saw the Pioneer flight when it reported at ten thousand feet northbound over the south boundary of the airport and "one more time north of the field. It was a very short time after the report was made, and I don't think he could have been further than Central Avenue; and that is the last time that the aircraft was observed."

Furthermore, the Pioneer flight did not report over the Weiler intersection at ninety-five hundred feet. It was cleared to fly at ten thousand feet, and there was no reason (or testimony) to suggest that that altitude was not maintained.

The section 5 quote "The wreckage was sighted from the air just below the crest of Sandia Mountain" also drew DeCelles's attention. "Just below" was hardly congruent with the reported testimony, "Some 1,439 feet lower than the crest of the ridge. . . ." Nor was it indicative of the fact that they had then been flying *just above* their flight-plan altitude.

In summary, DeCelles found that the CAB accident report statements intended to support the CAB "clear day" thesis instead substantially bolstered the ALPA argument that the pilots had intended to fly the route prescribed by their flight plan.

Omitted Navigational Instruments Data

Section 8 listed recovered aircraft components that had been used in determining the cause of the crash, with the statement that "other navigational instruments were either not recovered or were so extensively damaged that they could not be tested nor their settings learned."

DeCelles found not only that the statement was false, but the supposedly unrecovered or too-damaged navigational instruments had proven to be of crucial importance to his subsequent investigations. This false statement was all the more remarkable in view of the fact that it had been added to the original version of the CAB report in response to the ALPA suggestion that malfunction of navigational instruments might have caused or contributed to the accident. The omitted data included settings for the tachometer indicator, a propeller blade, radio equipment, and the RMI dial.

All Possible Evidence

Section 10 included the statement "The Board, in an attempt to determine a reason for the pilot's actions in pursuing the course flown, explored all possible evidence and circumstances." This drew fire from DeCelles, as the board had in fact not "explored all possible evidence and circumstances."

Had they done so, they would not have failed to comprehend the significance of such arresting facts as these:

1. The crew questioned and requestioned the location and definition of the Weiler intersection.
2. The aircraft's receivers were found set to the proper frequencies for complying with the flight clearance.
3. The omni bearing selector had been set to check the Weiler intersection.
4. The aircraft was in cruise power, at the cruising altitude specified in the clearance.
5. This cruising altitude was some three thousand feet below the absolute minimum safe altitude for crossing the ridge.
6. The Sandia Mountains, as viewed from flight altitude, were completely obscured.
7. The Rio Grande Valley to the north of Albuquerque, as viewed from flight altitude, was completely obscured.
8. There had been numerous instances of fluxgate compass malfunction. (A graphic file of such malfunction reports had been submitted by ALPA to the board prior to its writing of the amended report.)
9. Some types of fluxgate compass malfunction were extremely difficult to detect. (At that time several carriers—including TWA—were actively pursuing development of a device to warn pilots of such failures.)
10. The primary heading references for both the captain and the first officer (their respective RMIs) were wired to the same fluxgate compass.
11. The RMI dial that was recovered from the wreckage was stopped on a heading that was significantly different from the heading on which the aircraft struck the mountain.
12. The magnitude and direction of the error of this RMI were equal to that which would have been required to lead the flight into the crash area.
13. There had been numerous instances of malfunction of VOR navigation receiver components. (A file of such malfunctions was submitted by ALPA to the board prior to its writing of the "amended" report.)

14. Several types of VOR navigation receiver malfunctions were of such a nature as to have readily contributed to this accident.
15. An incident of simultaneous dual failure of fluxgate and VOR receiver equipment had occurred on at least one occasion and had been made known to the board.

Unfounded Conjectures

Section 11 was even worse because it set forth conjectures that the board admitted were not substantiated by evidence at all.

The first was the possibility that the pilots had chosen a beeline from the Albuquerque airport to Santa Fe.

"Consideration was given to a possible misunderstanding in the ATC clearance. It is interesting to note that the 026-degree radial off the Santa Fe omni range, which is 206 degrees from that range, is very nearly in line with the Albuquerque airport and the crash site. This is considered to be a highly remote source of navigational error, particularly considering the excellent weather existing along the authorized route."

The second conjecture was founded upon the (false) premise that the first officer was relatively unfamiliar with the route and had therefore flown the beeline path because he tuned into the Santa Fe omni instead of the Albuquerque omni. Which was contradicted by the board's admission that the aircraft navigational frequencies had been set to the frequencies specified by the flight plan. All of which led to the board's astonishing conclusion that the flight had not followed the flight plan at all.

"As previously stated, the First Officer was relatively unfamiliar with the Albuquerque area. In identifying the location of the Weiler Intersection the 026-degree radial of the Albuquerque Omni was mentioned. Had this course been flown with the receiver tuned to the Santa Fe Omni instead of the Albuquerque Omni, the aircraft could conceivably have arrived close to the point of impact. It is impossible to know what changes may have been made in the radio frequencies just prior to the accident. This thought is offered with the full realization that it is entirely unprovable and completely conjectural. The aircraft's receivers were found set to the proper frequencies for using the Albuquerque Localizer and Omni Range in accordance with the flight clearance. However, the flight did not follow this plan."

DeCelles's response was that he agreed with the board's admission that the theory offered in these two paragraphs was "entirely unprovable and completely conjectural." The fact was that the theory was ridiculous and fantastic and had no place in a serious attempt to understand this accident.

In order for the CAB theory to be viable, it would require that First Officer Creason—a commercial pilot with nearly four thousand flying hours and more than three years' service as an airline copilot, flying a route that he had flown at least three times within the previous six weeks—would:

1. Tune in the Santa Fe omni instead of the Albuquerque omni.
2. Attempt to fly the en route course by means of the intersecting radial rather than the en route radial.
3. Fly a steady northeast heading for four or five minutes out of Albuquerque at nine thousand feet.
4. Fly into an overcast on that heading.

Furthermore, the theory would require that Captain Spong—an air transport pilot of excellent and conservative reputation, with more than twelve thousand hours and nearly thirteen years' experience on the airline, flying a route that he had flown eleven times during the preceding three-week period—would sit idly by and let this fantastic error occur in an area of extremely hazardous terrain.

Shortcut to Santa Fe

Section 12 should have explained why the pilots could not possibly have intended to fly the direct route to Santa Fe. Instead it delineated why the board presumed the pilots had flown the route knowingly.

"It is difficult to conceive of the crew attempting to cross a 10,682-foot ridge at 9,000 feet, especially when the aircraft was capable of climbing to an altitude which would more than clear the ridge. The Martin 404, grossing 40,027 pounds, should, at maximum continuous power, climb at 1,500 feet per minute up to 9,000 feet and slightly less than that thereafter. This rate of climb would have brought the aircraft several thousand feet above the ridge starting from Albuquerque, only thirteen miles away. Even with much less power the ridge could have been easily topped. There appears to be no plausible explanation of why the airplane was not climbed, presuming the pilots flew the direct route knowingly."

DeCelles's response was accordingly blunt.

In view of the dramatic immensity of Sandia Ridge and the fact that its elevation was well known to all TWA pilots qualified on the route, it was not only "difficult" to conceive of the crew attempting to cross a 10,682-foot ridge while in cruise power at 9,000 feet, it was *impossible*. He therefore concurred with the final sentence, "There appears to be no plausible explanation of why the airplane was not climbed, presuming the pilots flew the direct route knowingly."

It was regrettable that the board had not taken the next logical stop to conclude that the pilots did *not* fly the direct route knowingly.

Flight 260's deviation from flight-plan course was either intentional or it was unintentional. If it was intentional, either the pilots conspired to commit simultaneous suicide and mass murder, or they were mutually ignorant of the facts that the Sandia Mountains block the direct route and the minimum safe altitude for crossing these mountains was four thousand feet above the altitude at which they were cruising. As the board had previously protested that it has never intended to suggest—and did not believe—the pilots were attempting suicide, it certainly could not be seriously suggesting that the pilots were unaware of the location and height of the Sandia Mountain range.

Therefore, it could only be concluded that the deviation from course was not intentional.

But, if the course deviation was not intentional, some explanation must be offered for the facts that the flight pursued an extremely hazardous heading for an extended length of time and had entered an overcast on that heading, and the crew did not detect their departure from the intended course.

It was also obvious that, if the course deviation was not intentional, the prolonged heading that produced that course deviation was also not intentional. Logically this could only mean that Flight 260 experienced a malfunction of the compass system.

Probable Cause

DeCelles then laid out the reasoning behind his contention that the probable cause for the crash was the malfunction of the fluxgate compass, not pilot error.

Failure to detect departure from the prescribed course could probably be attributed to:

1. Possible malfunction of the airborne ILS localizer receiver.
2. Possible malfunction of the Albuquerque ILS transmitting system.
3. Possible confusion by the crew with respect to proper sensing of the course deviation indicator during a back-course ILS departure.

Details of these discussions can be found in chapter 16, "ALPA Critique of the CAB Amended Report."

CAB Hearing

Ted Linnert phoned DeCelles to tell him that the CAB would reopen the accident hearing on January 15–16, 1959, in Kansas City. It would be a full-dress affair in the Phillips Hotel with a court reporter and all the trimmings.

Harold Crowley, who had presided at the original hearing in Albuquerque, presided here—flanked by the CAB's able expert on aircraft system engineering, Tom Collins, and by equally able Phil Goldstein, investigator in charge of CAB, Santa Monica, California. The room was crowded with a battery of representatives from the manufacturer of the fluxgate compass, the Eclipse-Pioneer division of Bendix, and from the manufacturer of the radio navigation equipment, Collins Radio.

Two representatives of TWA management were present to testify in support of the ALPA position: Captain Dave Halperin, now head of the safety program, and Bill Meador, of its engineering department. Their participation was especially meaningful for DeCelles, as few airlines would have backed the pilots' union in an accident long forgotten by both the press and the public.

Also in the room were DeCelles's wife, his mother, his secretary, Bill Johnson's wife, and a sizeable number of TWA pilots, many of them in uniform.

DeCelles's presentation took a day and a half. He called to the witness stand Phil Goldstein, who testified about the new determination of impact heading on their mountain climb. He also called up two TWA pilots. Captain Al Gettings, a friend of the deceased copilot, produced Creason's logbook, proving—contrary to the board's report—that Creason had been through the Albuquerque area a great many times and was thoroughly familiar with the route. And Captain R. K. Ownby, copilot on the Constellation flight that passed through Albuquerque on the morning of the accident, had discussed the weather situation with Spong and Creason while they were preparing to board their flight.

DeCelles's personal life had been absorbed for four years by the combination of this case and by his other activities as central air safety chairman. He estimated that the accident investigation had comprised nearly a third of his activity as air safety chairman.

His golf clubs were rusty, and he had neglected both his family and his property. It was over now, and he began playing a little golf and getting reacquainted with his wife and kids.

His wife was proud of what he had done. It has been hardest on her because she shouldered more than a fair share of family responsibility during his lengthy investigations. She was glad that he was done, but she had never suggested his quitting on the Sandia case; she realized it could have been her husband instead of Ivan Spong flying that plane, and besides, she knew that he was too stubborn (or blockheaded) to quit when he thought there was a chance to win.

Had he ever met Spong? Yes, once, in early 1948. Spong had just returned from the TWA's international division, and DeCelles was about to go there. They had a trip together—to New York, he believed. Spong was a large, quiet, friendly man—kindly, conservative, competent—not at all the daring or foolhardy type.

He had never met Mrs. Spong.

CAB Supplemental Aircraft Accident Report

The CAB issued its report on June 15, 1960, more than five years after the crash in 1955. It absolved the pilots from blame for the accident, but its findings were inconclusive.

"In view of the foregoing discussions, the Board believes that the former report did not accurately reflect all the circumstances of this accident. It is believed that insufficient evidence exists to substantiate the reason for the deviation from the prescribed flight path. The probable cause therefore will be changed accordingly.

"Probable Cause: The Board determines that the probable cause of this accident was a deviation from the prescribed flight path for reasons unknown."

Although the Civil Aeronautics Board had previously had no

difficulty in blaming the pilots for this accident, it now came to the conclusion that the cause of the accident was not precisely known. A malfunction of the fluxgate compass system could not be blamed for the accident because there was no certainty that there had been such a malfunction.

In all probability, "probable" to the board meant absolute certainty.

The gyro tumbling problems of the fluxgate compass that Captain DeCelles revealed in his investigations have never been cured. Pilots are now trained how to avoid them.

In later years DeCelles continued in airline safety work as a member, then chairman, of the ALPA's All Weather Flying Committee.

He also developed an omnidirectional glide path, for which he received a patent. This device used the signal of a transmitter located at the airport to provide a pilot with instantaneous and continuous data for establishing a glide path to any runway he or she chose to use.

He was awarded the Laura Taber Barbour Air Safety Award in 1988 and the International Federation of Airline Pilots Associations' Scroll of Merit.

7
The Fiftieth Anniversary Trek

Hiatus

I continued my rock climbing ventures after the crash by summiting New Mexico's Shiprock a few months later. (Shiprock is now off limits, as it has been acknowledged as sacred to the local Navajos.) I then married in 1956 and began learning the responsibilities of parenthood; our three children were born in Albuquerque. When my air force tour ended, I remained in the same job at Kirtland as a civil servant, then transferred to Sandia Corporation (now known as Sandia National Laboratories) as a staff member in the mathematics research department, performing computer systems software development. In 1962 I returned to Stanford for a master's degree in computer science, working part time for Control Data Corporation as a systems programmer. Then I worked with Woodrow W. Bledsoe at Panoramic Research, as a mathematician, using the computer to recognize human faces, and with Iben Browning at the Thomas Bede Foundation, as a member of the technical staff in designing methods for the automatic layout of printed circuit boards.

Woody Bledsoe had been my department manager at Sandia Labs and would later become chairman of the mathematics department at the University of Texas, Austin, where he served on my dissertation committee. One of the founders of artificial intelligence, he made early contributions in pattern recognition and automated reasoning. Continuing to make significant contributions to artificial intelligence and academia throughout his long career, he also served as bishop for the Mormon Church. He died in 1995 of Lou Gehrig's disease.

Iben Browning was one of the most intelligent people I have ever known; he told me all about continental drift, the extinction of dinosaurs, tektites from the moon, and climatology long before they became accepted by the experts of that era. The *New York Times* credited him with accurately predicting high-stress periods of seismic activity that coincided with the volcanic eruption of Mount St. Helens in 1980, the Mexico City quake of 1985, and the Loma Prieta, California, quake of 1989. He gained unfortunate notoriety for erroneously predicting a major quake along the New Madrid fault in 1990. He died in Albuquerque a year later.

After moving to Austin, I received the first PhD diploma ever awarded in computer sciences by the University of Texas, then became a computer science academician at Penn State and Virginia Tech, before moving to Atlanta, Georgia, to become a computer information systems professor. My research specialty was computer graphics, developing techniques and applications for scanning digitizers. Computer graphics started out as a cure looking for a disease; it is now the mainstay of the interactive computers in use today.

Having been a nerd all of my life, I took up running at the age of fifty-four and learned the joys of being a competitive jock—earning eight national age-group titles in U.S. Track & Field Masters competitions after age sixty. I switched to racewalking competition in 1975, just after the modern phase of this crash saga began.

Return

The saga started up again in March 2004 on a vacation to New Mexico, when my wife and I took a ride up Sandia Crest on the Sandia Peak Tramway. The world's longest aerial tramway, it rises about four thousand feet in just under three miles to an altitude of ten thousand four hundred feet. The tram had been constructed after we left Albuquerque in 1962.

I asked the tram operator whether he knew anything about a TWA plane crash that had occurred in the 1950s. He replied that the tram passed above the site, but the wreckage would not be visible. He had in-depth knowledge of the crash, but I was surprised that some of his facts were wrong. He knew the date of its occurrence and the number of passengers and crew aboard; but he also averred that the plane was flying northeast when it struck the mountain. I contradicted him. The plane was headed west toward Albuquerque when it hit the pinnacle— I knew, because I had participated in the search-and-rescue efforts.

I did not recognize the wreck pinnacle when he pointed it out to me—hardly surprising, as I had never viewed it from above; but I wondered about the absence of wreckage. The rubble heap of twisted metal that I well remembered was missing from the pinnacle that he showed me. Wind could not have blown it off, nor could vegetation have covered it. I must have been looking at the wrong place.

We stayed in Albuquerque that night, and I took an early morning run up the La Luz Trail the next day. Parts of the trail were new to me, but old sections sparked my memory of the search for the missing plane soon after it had crashed. I proceeded at a rapid pace and was pleased that my heart rate remained reasonably low in spite of the altitude. Icy sections of the trail impeded my progress, however, and I turned back at an altitude of eighty-eight hundred feet.

Back in Atlanta, I signed up for the La Luz Trail Run to be held on August 1. Ascending forty-four hundred feet in nine miles to Sandia Crest from the East Mesa, it has been described by *Trail Runner* magazine as "one of the 12 most grueling trail races in North America." As I had first hiked the trail in 1954, I would call it my Fiftieth Anniversary Race.

I decided to renew contacts with old friends and phoned Zelma Beisinger, a former climbing buddy who had also worked with me at Sandia Labs. She later e-mailed me to say that she would be glad to see me and that everyone she had talked to seemed surprised that I had turned up.

It was pleasant seeing Zelma again and recalling our friends and climbing experiences. Bill Stamm, a ninety-two-year-old founding member of the New Mexico Mountain Club, had asked her to give me a brochure for the club's fiftieth anniversary banquet. It listed me both among the early members and the dearly departed—thus explaining why some folks were surprised that I was still around. When Bill later apologized for the mistake, I thanked him for the opportunity to claim kinship with Mark Twain.

I ran the La Luz Trail Run the next day, placing second in the seventy to seventy-four age division but behind Dave Hammack in the seventy-five to seventy-nine age division. He didn't seem to know that he's too old for that kind of thing. Dave was a rock-climbing legend in the Sierras and the Sandias.

Zelma emailed me in mid-January 2005 that someone named Hugh Prather was researching the TWA accident and would contact me soon. He did so, and that is how I became involved in the recent episodes of the Flight 260 saga. Hugh had contacted Bill Stamm to ask whether he knew of any mountain club members who had participated in the search-and-rescue efforts; and Bill, now knowing that I was still among the living, remembered that Zelma would know how to reach me. In short, I became involved because of a sequence of whimsical steps.

My wife had the whim to visit Albuquerque again; I had the whim to sign up for the La Luz Trail Run and then to phone Zelma Beisinger. who remembered that I was not supposed to be alive and had the whim to tell Bill Stamm about it; Hugh had the whim to call Bill, who remembered that I was a still-living member of the TWA rescue efforts and that Zelma might also know how to contact me.

Hugh Prather

Hugh Prather was a twelve-year-old boy in Espanola when he became fascinated by an article in the February 20, 1955, Sunday edition of the *Albuquerque Journal*. The headline, "Air Liner Search Continues," had inspired his search for the truth about the accident for over fifty years. He has collected voluminous material from original sources in preparation for a book describing his findings.

Although he had had no technical rock-climbing experience, I was to discover that he had little fear of heights and rock scrambles. He is a retired superintendent of schools, an organizational consultant, and an avid hiker who frequently conducts trips to wilderness areas throughout the Southwest and as far away as Mexico.

My phone conversations with Hugh were highly productive. He was a good interviewer, but I was still surprised at how easily I recalled details of events that had occurred a half century earlier. He told me that he was going to place a memorial plaque at the base of the pinnacle on February 19, 2005, the fiftieth anniversary of the crash; and I decided to prepare and send him a manuscript describing my experiences at the time of the accident.

We then agreed that a fiftieth anniversary reenactment of the recovery expedition might be a good idea, and I e-mailed Susan Corban, president of the New Mexico Mountain Club, to determine whether she could get me topographic maps of the Sandias along with technical rock-climbing support for a try in early April 2005. Maps magically appeared via the Internet, but Dave Hammack, the climbing legend who had bested me in the trail run and who had direct knowledge of the conditions, responded that early April would not be a good idea—Albuquerque was experiencing record snow falls, and we would encounter packed ice.

We waited until early May, when the snow levels had abated, and then settled on Wednesday, May 25. Susan lined up Jim Linn from the mountain club, who was concerned about the severity of the proposed trip. We would be having to bushwhack for quite a ways at high elevations through heavy vegetation and perhaps face snow on the northern slopes. He was also worried that an elderly flatlander like me might find the going especially difficult. Nevertheless, the climbing organization would be happy to support the expedition. He volunteered his services for the technical climbing work, and I put him in contact with Hugh Prather so they could coordinate their efforts.

Lots of mountain club people were interested in the project, but Wednesday was not a good day for working folks. I was despairing that we might not have enough technical support when an out-of-the-blue e-mail arrived on May 10 from my old climbing buddy, Reed Cundiff, who asked whether he could join us. I accepted on the spot, and our climbing party was now complete, with two weeks to spare.

The Trek

May 25, 2005. At 7:00 a.m. I entered Shoney's Restaurant on Menaul Avenue in Albuquerque and looked for familiar faces. Seeing none, I turned to the manager, who kindly pointed me to a table where a group of people were seated; they introduced themselves to me.

Jim Linn, a retired chemist from Sandia National Laboratories, had over thirty years of climbing experience and was a past president of the New Mexico Mountain Club. Having worked at the labs myself, I was especially pleased that he had joined us.

He was accompanied by Frances Robertson, a well-established haven't-been-there, haven't-done-that, must-do-that-today kind of person. She was also a past president of the mountain club and retired teacher from the Albuquerque Academy with an in-depth knowledge of New Mexico botany and its lore.

She had also been an alto soloist with the New Mexico Symphony Orchestra and the Orchestra of Santa Fe, as well as with productions of Handel's *Messiah* all over the state. And she sang leading operatic roles with the Southwest and the Four Corners Opera Companies—Carmen in Bizet's *Carmen*, Suzuki in Puccini's *Madame Butterfly*, Regina in Blitzstein's *Regina*, and lighter roles from Gilbert and Sullivan productions—Buttercup, Iolanthe, Ruth, Katisha—as well as Anna in the *King and I*, et cetera, et cetera, et cetera, and so forth.

Hugh Prather arrived later. I recognized him from his newspaper picture, but did not fare as well with Reed Cundiff, who appeared moments afterward. I must have been expecting the fifteen-year-old boy with whom I had enjoyed numerous rock-climbing adventures in the Sandias. He hadn't acted like teenagers usually do and was a delightful companion for all who ventured with him into the wilderness. He developed into a super climber, gaining renown for his first ascents with Dave Hammack in the Sandias and later, on his own, in the Organ Mountains near Las Cruces. When I first contacted Reed in March, he accused me of being a major figure in his growing up and in his rock climbing. I pleaded innocent—he would have done very well on his own.

After a stint as an army ranger in Vietnam, he went back to graduate school and is now a physicist at the White Sands Missile Range. He served for two and a half months in Iraq as a government scientist determining how labs and research/development centers could help troops in the field.

In an earlier e-mail, I had asked Reed why the wreckage that I had remembered atop the pinnacle now lay at the bottom of the canyon. He explained that, while the tramway was being constructed, TWA officials and others had contracted to have the wreckage taken out by helicopter or dumped and buried at the base of the pinnacle; visible wreckage would have been bad publicity for the airline industry. In his response to my e-mail, Reed had volunteered to join our expedition.

We were an improbable lot for this venture. With ages ranging from sixty-two to seventy-three, a betting man might wager good odds that we had gathered for a leisurely stroll through the neighborhood.

After treating us to breakfast, Hugh led us to the Sandia Peak Tramway, where we grabbed the first ride up. Although it was my third trip on the tram, I still had trouble identifying the crash pinnacle from the air. Hugh surprised me by showing me that it was actually visible from the tram visitor center atop Sandia Crest—virtually indistinguishable from the towering cliffs that rose behind it.

We left the tram visitor center and headed about a mile northwest along the Spur Trail in the direction of the La Luz Trail when Frances unexpectedly announced that we were at the place where we would head down the TWA Canyon.

I instantly contradicted her—a remark that surprised us both. I had never been on the Spur Trail before, I was not familiar with the terrain, and I was not aware that I was even in the TWA Canyon. Yet, assuredly, I knew that the trail could not be where she said it was—I didn't know where it was, but I did know where it wasn't. I later realized that I may have been influenced by the fact that we were immediately below limestone cliffs and the trail down the canyon did not negotiate limestone cliffs.

We continued another mile along the Spur Trail to the Y where it meets the La Luz Trail so that I could photograph the vertical north face of the Thumb. The trip over was pleasant, and Hugh was able to show us a distant view of the top of the wreck pinnacle—it didn't look at all familiar. We then reversed our path and headed back. When the TWA Canyon came into view, I immediately recognized the place where the trail down the canyon had to be, passing beneath an insignificant tree rising from the slope below the Spur Trail. I was viewing that tree from a position where I had never been before, but I somehow knew that the old trail had passed beneath it.

When I examined the tree from the Spur Trail, there was no evidence of a trail headed downhill beneath it, but I was certain that it had been there before. We began our descent from the spot that Frances had initially pointed out—a short, steep slope of rubble anchored by steel mesh that was part of the Spur Trail construction. The trail abruptly traversed left at the bottom of the slope to a point directly beneath the tree, then suddenly turned right, down the canyon, where I thought it ought to go. My initial judgment had been correct.

The canyon did not seem at all familiar to me on this trip. It was now encased in vegetation where none had stood half a century before. I had not visited the pinnacle since 1955 and had been in the upper regions of this canyon four times at most. Yet, from here until we quit the Dragon's Tooth, there were times at which I knew precisely where I was and where other things had to be. When I was off track, I had a feeling that things were not quite right, but I could make them so by slightly altering the direction of my travel.

Down the Canyon to the Pinnacle

My initial steps down the steep slope were tentative at best. I was afraid that my running-injured knee might give way or that I would trip on vegetation and really mess my body up. I was a cliff hugger—leaning inward to avoid falling outward, with the predictable consequence that I slipped and slid all over the slope. Gradually, I gained confidence by traveling more vertically, even leaning slightly outward, away from the slope, preserving my balance by pointing my boots in the direction of travel. My stature, sense of balance, and fluidity of motion gradually returned to me as I ventured downward.

I also began to gain a sense of the inclined surface, learning to judge how to negotiate loose rock so that it would not rattle the heads of friends below, knowing when to take giant steps downward and when not to, and, above all, gaining the art of twisting my body gracefully through malevolent vegetation that was remarkably adept at gouging treasured things. I succeeded in defending the beloved La Luz Trail Run T-shirt that I was wearing, but my bare arms were bloodied from their first encounter with oak brush. I gained some intangible skill at that point and remained unscathed from then on.

The terrain was far more treacherous now than it had been fifty years before. The scant vegetation of that era had been pressed flat by snow, and we could see far down the canyon to discern the best path forward. The canyon floor was now oppressed by greenery. Bushes of every description—some with hidden thorns—choked the valley and hid our feet from view. We stumbled and tripped on invisible objects, and our destination was rarely in sight.

Our best views were upward, where we were awarded with the sights of the magnificent cliffs rising vertically above us. Jim Linn pointed out improbable climbing routes to me that were rated class 5.9 and higher. Hardware is used in class 5 climbs to protect climbers from falling; in class 6 climbs it provides direct assistance to the climbing process.

Hardware in my day was comprised mainly of pitons and carabiners. The pitons were hammered into cracks in the rock by the leader and were retrieved by the last climber on the rope so that they could be reused. They came in a variety of shapes and sizes with names—wedges, spoons, wafers, blades, verticals, horizontals—indicating their appearance or the character of the cracks for which they were intended. Pitons that can damage the rock have now largely been replaced by chocks that are inserted into cracks without hammering.

We came to a clearing further down—a beautiful place with a rare clear view of the top of the pinnacle. Surprised to see rock dust at my feet, I elevated my gaze to discover that the top of a towering fir tree had been cleanly sliced from its trunk, revealing an immense cliff looming above it. I looked for recently fallen rock and found instead a small sprig of greenery that emitted the pungent smell of freshly crushed spruce. Here was ample evidence that rock avalanches were frequent, each stone humming through the air in its free fall from the heights above.

Shortly afterward, Hugh announced that we were at the base of the pinnacle, and we turned right to begin our climb upward to its notch. Frances discovered the vestige of a trail and scampered up the right edge of a talus pile. I followed her for a short time, then headed straight up the center, calling to her to bear left, but she continued on her route and rapidly disappeared from sight. I ascended rapidly as the footing was good and was pleased that my heart-rate monitor indicated my pulse was far below my anaerobic threshold; I seemed well acclimated to the altitude. The talus pile, however, soon became enveloped by scrub oak wielding formidable spines and blocking the pinnacle from view. Cliffs ahead, however, were visible, and I realized that I must traverse left to reach the saddle. Calling out to Frances to do the same, I got no reply.

I heard the crunch of metal beneath my feet, which were hidden by deep brush. Reaching down, I picked up a small piece of wing fabric and knew I was near my destination. I had encountered wreckage blown free of the pinnacle by the force of the explosion fifty years earlier. A few moments later blue sky appeared dead ahead, and I broke free of brush shortly after that. I had finally arrived, right on target at my destination, not more than ten feet above the saddle. The top of the pinnacle rose from its notch before me.

I yelled for my companions to join me, and Hugh arrived about five minutes later. I pointed out the climbing route to him, then called again for the others. Reed soon appeared, and then Jim and Frances together some fifteen minutes later.

I was thankful when Jim belayed me up the pinnacle, for my legs were unaccustomed to the steep rocks.

I did not recognize the crash site, for it was now devoid of metal, and the scraped-cleaned rocks and sandy slopes seemed strange to me. I did, however, locate the spot where I had seen Mrs. Schoonmaker lying. The slope on which she had landed was above the debris and was little changed by the ravages of time.

The top of the pinnacle was a lovely, serene place with marvelous views of the surrounding terrain, but to my eyes the wreck site was devoid of intrinsic beauty, an ominously foreboding place—a reaction probably occasioned by memories of the events of half a century ago.

Jim and Hugh attempted to pose me to recreate my 1955 *Denver Post* photo, but to no avail. The pinnacle was strangely different now, and I could not picture how things had been. We then retreated from the summit, with Jim belaying Frances and me to the notch.

We retraced our way from the saddle back down the steep dirt slopes to the canyon floor, then headed southward toward the wreckage at the base of the pinnacle. When we discovered the first signs of debris, I began complaining to Hugh that something appeared to be wrong— the wreckage should not be where we were finding it.

He later explained that we had not been at the base of the pinnacle, but were instead at the eastern face of an immense fin of rock that separated us from the defile where the tail section, left wing, and its left engine had plunged. The wreckage in the defile had been carried to its current position while the tram was being constructed. My memory had not failed me; the wreckage had been moved.

Atop the pinnacle, I had felt great compassion for the victims, but this non–in situ trash dump held no meaning for me. The war ground—and cemetery—at the crash site had been desecrated and could never be restored.

We trekked downward toward the East Mesa from the pinnacle. The going was easier now on a well-defined trail through lush vegetation sprinkled with tiny flowers that Frances joyfully pointed out to us. A small creek flowing along the canyon floor provided us with waterfalls. This green and narrow wilderness might well have been along an Appalachian trail, but flowering cacti would soon appear on the desert mesa below.

We arrived at the Sandia Peak tram terminal near dusk, weary but delighted by our travails. Jim Linn praised our 1955 recovery efforts. The rugged terrain over which we had done our work was the most challenging that he had ever experienced.

Frances Robertson thanked me profusely for including her on the trip. Her last words to me were, "I had a blast!" I couldn't have phrased it better.

8
Treasures from the Past

I returned from Albuquerque elated by my adventures and by the pleasures of bushwhacking over immensely spectacular and challenging terrain, but disgusted that I had failed to capture anything meaningful on film—the pictures I'd taken had turned out badly. Hugh later supplied me with wonderful shots of the pinnacle from the tram, but I had no record of what we had experienced on foot.

October 25

The ensuing lengthy silence lasted until October, when I received two e-mails concerning Flight 260. The first was from Hugh Prather, who reported some exciting news: Albuquerque Sunport officials had just alerted him that the Ambassadors Lounge was being remodeled for conference room space, and it would include a memorial plaque honoring TWA Flight 260. His marathon efforts with Sunport officials, TWA representatives, and the Clipped Wings group—retired TWA flight attendants, who had been known as "flight hostesses" in 1955—had finally paid off.

This was indeed welcome news, and I promptly responded, then proceeded to read the second message, from a Ginny Campbell in Leawood, Kansas.

10:00 a.m. She introduced herself as the daughter of Bill Campbell and the granddaughter of Dorothy and Alfred Schoonmaker. Several family members had joined her earlier that month to trek up to the crash site with Hugh Prather. He had supplied her with a copy of my narrative of the crash and our recovery efforts.

She thanked me for such a detailed report; it was wonderful getting a clearer idea of the complexity of the recovery and the determination of the people who had brought her loved ones back to their families. It was comforting to know that her grandparents were found together at the pinnacle. They were joined at the hip and very devoted to each other. It had been great trekking to the site to get more of an understanding of those somber events. She was glad that there were people who were not immediate family and yet who cared for those lost aboard Flight 260.

This was astounding news indeed! I recognized the Schoonmaker name immediately and was amazed that a granddaughter of that couple had actually contacted me at seemingly the same instant that Hugh had sent me his message. (I noticed later that her message had actually been sent about an hour and a half after his—the e-mails described below are listed in the order that I read them.) The name Bill Campbell, at the moment, did not ring any bells; I did not remember a Campbell being a victim of the crash.

I was appalled, however, that Hugh would think it appropriate to share the details of my narrative with a close relative of crash victims. Surely, he must have known that such knowledge could only reawaken pangs of grief that had dissipated with time.

And yet, a victims' granddaughter had purposefully contacted me to thank me for what I had written.

11:48 a.m. I responded to her immediately that I had never known her grandparents, but my memory of them at the scene of the wreck had been indelibly etched into my mind. They had been the only bright spot in what was otherwise an appallingly grim reality. After a lapse of over fifty years, I was amazed that I still recognized the spot where they lay at the crash scene.

11:53 a.m. I then e-mailed Hugh to learn more about Ginny's visit to the crash site. A half hour later Ginny Campbell responded to my message, asking whether I remembered if her father had been up on the pinnacle. When her mother had received his effects, the ring and gold cuff link from his right arm were missing. She knew why now, but was hoping that she might miraculously find the items when she went there a few weeks ago. It would be nice to know where he was found.

I was confused by Ginny's question concerning her father. Albuquerque newspaper accounts of the crash had not reported that three members of the same family had perished in the accident, and as I had no recollection of a passenger named Bill Campbell, I unwittingly associated the ring and cuff link (which were probably on his body, but no one had mentioned them to me) with her grandfather rather than her dad.

Accordingly, I sent her an incongruous reply that I didn't remember any family member accompanying us to the wreck scene at any time. We went up with fellow climbers or crash investigators. Her father might have visited the scene with someone else—perhaps George Hankins—after I left Albuquerque in 1962. We were reluctant to tell family members how their loved ones ended up. Indeed, I worried about including the description of her grandparents in the write-up I had sent to Hugh. Thanks to her, I was glad that I did.

I was interested in learning about her grandparents and why they were on the flight. I had met Worth Nicholl, who was a fellow passenger, but knew nothing about the others.

Had Hugh taken her to the top of the pinnacle?

12:24 a.m. Ginny's graceful reply cleared things up considerably. I was beginning to learn that e-mails concerning Flight 260 should be read with care. They would reveal the events of a remarkable tale.

She had had a lifelong mission to visit the crash site, and Hugh had guided her and other family members there; they had left a small memorial atop the pinnacle. It had been great going up there and understanding things more clearly. She hoped to return in the near future to leave more things at the memorial and spend more time on the pinnacle. The views had been spectacular!

She explained who her father was and the circumstances concerning the trip to Santa Fe. While up on the pinnacle, she had had a wild hope of finding her dad's other gold cuff link and college class ring, which were never recovered. She had been led to believe that "rescuers" had trouble locating him—thinking perhaps he had been the victim thrown to Echo Canyon. If that were the case, the gold cuff link and ring would never appear. Knowing where her grandparents were found had set her wondering about her dad. She was only twenty-one months old when he and her grandparents were killed.

I was excited by Ginny's emails and was amazed to be in contact with a person who was intimately connected with the events of half a century before. I was especially elated to be thanked for what I (and others) had done for her family. I spent a restless night recalling the events of those days in 1955.

October 26

I woke up the next morning convinced that I might have seen Ginny's father at the scene of the crash. I had memories of individual sights that I had to put into a sensible sequence that might correlate with what she had told me.

9:33 a.m. While composing my thoughts, I opened a message from Hugh, who was responding to my question concerning Ginny. He told me that he had guided the son of the copilot, Gary Creason, to the top of the pinnacle in early September; then Ginny and her family on October 8. It had become a little easier each time he climbed to the summit as he learned exactly where to make transitions and where the handholds were.

He included Ginny's photo (Figure 36) of a piece of wreckage that none of us had observed when we were there in May—probably the most poignant remainder of the accident. It was a piece of the aircraft that was wedged into a crevice between two boulders with such force and intensity that it was inextricable. It must have been at the precise impact spot where Flight 260 and the cliff came together. The tail section must have ridden up onto that area as the fuselage disintegrated. He was sure that was exactly where the tail section was hanging.

Larry DeCelles had sent him his whole archive on Flight 260; and Gary Creason and his sister Jana had loaned him their father's flight manual for a Martin 404.

Unexpected news was beginning to be the norm! The son of the copilot had actually visited the pinnacle, and I now had visual evidence of the wreck scene itself—unmarred by the cleanup that had occurred when the tram was constructed—and the photographer was my e-mail correspondent from Kansas.

12:33 p.m. I had much to wonder at, but greedily e-mailed Hugh to ask how far the wedged metal was from the eastern cliff. Was it near the place where my picture was taken in 1955, or was it lower down where the hostess had been?

Treasure from the Past

2:59 p.m. I had lunch and in midafternoon was about to e-mail Ginny about my conjectures concerning her father when I discovered two messages from Bill Pearson in San Diego, whose existence was unknown to me. His mother, Anne Schoonmaker Pearson—daughter of the Schoonmakers—lived near Charleston, South Carolina. Ginny was his cousin, and they had hiked to the crash site with Hugh.

While atop the pinnacle he had found a small hinged case with "Beltone Mono-Pac" inscribed on the side; he thought it might have been something the passengers or pilots plugged into for communication. He hadn't known that his grandfather wore a hearing aid device, but when he had sent the item to his mother earlier in the week, she had relayed the accompanying story, which she also shared with Hugh Prather.

This burst of information made no sense to me at all, but I read on, learning that my description of the rescue efforts—especially about his grandparents being adjacent to each other outside the plane—represented new information for their family and his mother, who, at seventy-five years of age, took great comfort in it. He couldn't thank me enough for the time and effort I had taken to recap my experiences after the crash.

As I seemed to have a fairly clear recollection of his grandparents—and where they came to rest—he wondered whether I would mind receiving a call from his mother regarding my memories. He was confident that his parents would love to meet and speak with me if I were ever in the Charleston area.

Though my brain was spinning at this point, I proceeded to read the accompanying e-mail that his mother had just sent to Hugh Prather.

2:14 p.m. Anne Pearson thanked Hugh for guiding her son and her relatives to the crash site, then related a fantastic story about what her son had found there.

While her son was atop the pinnacle, he looked around for souvenirs for his mother and picked up a stone that she had asked for, as well as fragments of a broken cup and a small piece of shiny metal. He mailed them to her a few weeks later.

When they arrived, she initially thought that the metal was a piece of an ashtray, but then realized that it was part of a hearing aid.

Her father was deaf in one ear from World War I and had worn a Beltone unit for years, carrying it in his jacket breast pocket. Her mom would cut a small hole in his jacket beneath his left lapel, so that the wire from the hearing aid would run from his jacket pocket, through the hole under his lapel, under his arm, around his back, and out of his jacket below his right ear.

She had contacted Beltone the previous day—October 25—and they had just advised her that Mono-Pac was popular in the 1950s and that it was a small silver-cased instrument. Unfortunately, their customer sales records did not go back that far.

The second message from Bill Pearson included a 1945 photograph of the Schoonmaker family and a 1953 photo of his parents' wedding in 1953.

4:01 p.m. Overwhelmed by this experience, I decided to collect my senses by responding to Ginny's earlier message. I apologized to her for not realizing that her father had been on the plane.

It was possible that I had seen her dad. I remembered a body (in reasonably good shape) that lay a short distance to the right (north) and perhaps slightly uphill from her grandparents. His was the first that I saw atop the pinnacle. (There was another badly charred one that was downhill and closer to the north face of the pinnacle.) George Hankins had taken descriptive notes of the victims for Dr. Szerlip, and they were probably given to the New Mexico State Police. If they still existed, the notes might corroborate my memory—they might be available to her as next of kin.

Her father was probably sitting near her grandparents on the plane, and his body may well have ended up near theirs. The fact that she had received his personal effects indicated that he was found reasonably intact.

I asked Ginny to let me know when she intended to revisit the site. I would like to revisit it myself in order to correlate some of Hugh's great aerial (from the tram) photos with these recollections.

Evidence supporting this message to Ginny would arrive some three months later, on January 19, 2006, when Sherman Marsh e-mailed me photos taken during our first visit to the wreck site. "I knew these would turn up sooner or later (the curse-blessing of a family that *never* throws anything away!)."

One of the photos showed Gene Szerlip bending over the charred body that I had remembered, with George Hankins standing by taking notes; but in my memory, George had been taking notes from the opposite direction, and he and Dr. Szerlip had been looking at another victim lying south of there.

The state police did not have George Hankins's notes, but in July 2006 his grandson Michael Thornton would supply me with entries from his grandfather's diary—including the notes that I had mentioned—verifying the relative positions of the bodies that I had given to Ginny.

The notes indicated, however, that I had erred in believing that the body lying next to Mrs. Schoonmaker was her husband's; it was that of the Reverend Earl F. Davis instead. I had fallen into the same trap as others in this narrative by making an unwarranted assumption about what seemed obvious.

4:31 p.m. My thoughts were somewhat collected by now, and I responded to Bill Pearson in San Diego, thanking him for his incredible e-mail. I asked him where he had found the hearing aid case, as I was interested in learning whether it was near the place where his grandmother had lain. I would appreciate getting images, videos, or whatever else he had of the crash scene that he had mentioned.

5:02 p.m. The response from Ginny thirty minutes later gave credence to some of my conjectures about her father. She had just received the news about the Beltone and had talked to her aunt in South Carolina.

Her mother had received only a tie tack and the jewelry that her dad wore on his left hand. Her brother had worn their dad's wedding ring on their trek to the site on October 8. They assumed his right arm was never retrieved. She had looked for his fraternity class ring and gold cuff link that day on a million-to-one chance that she would find it.

Her aunt had told her that her dad and grandfather would have been sitting together, since her father had flown out from New Jersey just to talk with Grandpa about their meeting in Santa Fe. Her grandmother would have been across the aisle.

She hoped to trek to the pinnacle again the next year, when the weather would be more predictable. They planned on coming out when the Sunport had the memorial dedication.

5:09 p.m. Seven minutes later, Bill Pearson responded that his mother would, indeed, be phoning me and would like for me to visit her in South Carolina at her home on Seabrook Island.

He had found the hearing aid case on the pinnacle, west of the impact point, where parts of the plane remain embedded in the rock, facing east. It was in a dirt and gravel area partway up the slope from the immediate impact point.

Lone Butterfly

Nearby, he had seen a lone butterfly sitting on a rock sunning itself and was surprised that it could be at such a high altitude. It was the only butterfly he was to see that day, and it apparently was near the place where his grandparents had come to rest.

The more he learned about the accident site—where his grandparents had been found and where he had found the hearing aid case— the more confident he became that he had stood where they lay. I would know better than anyone whether this was so.

A copy of the photo disk was on the way, and he would soon mail me the video disk. In the meantime, he gave me access to an Internet site where he had posted photos.

The video disk recorded the lone butterfly that Bill Pearson had seen a few moments before he unwittingly discovered the hearing aid case belonging to his grandfather. The soundtrack recorded his statement at the time: he wondered whether the butterfly might be an omen.

A neighbor's photo of twenty-one-month-old Ginny Campbell, taken a few days after the crash, shows her wearing a dress adorned with two butterfly appliqués.

Thoroughly confused by this time, I was having serious difficulty in grasping the complexities of what had just transpired. I had yet to comprehend why this family wanted to deluge me with such attention and felt puzzled trying to sort out the identities of the various individuals involved.

I pulled up the pictures that Bill had posted on the Internet and rapidly became enthralled by a multitude of marvelous images of scenes that I remembered from our trek, but had failed to capture with my own camera.

I was in the midst of this exhilarating experience when Anne

Pearson called from Charleston to echo what her son had said and retell me the story about the hearing aid case.

5:52 p.m. I e-mailed Ginny, telling her that I had just had a wonderful conversation with Anne Pearson and that her cousin had just given me access to more than one hundred photos of the wreck scene, which were doing wonders for filling out my knowledge of the topography of the pinnacle. The Beltone story was incredible!

7:52 p.m. Ginny responded two hours later that her brother—Bill Campbell Jr.—had also videotaped the trek and was planning to combine his video with that of their cousin, Bill Pearson. She and her brother had a combined total of over two hundred fifty digital pictures. Would I care to have any of the above?

Thus, by the end of the day, a stranger from San Diego had (1) introduced himself to me, (2) thanked me for having written a narrative about the crash that he knew was a comfort to his mother, (3) alluded to his having found his grandfather's hearing aid case atop the pinnacle, (4) sent me a copy of an e-mail from his mother to Hugh Prather describing how she identified it, (5) attached 1945 and 1953 photographs of his family, and (6) said that his mother would soon call me from Charleston—his mother validating his statements by saying that she would like me to visit her in the near future.

And I was overwhelmed by becoming the proud possessor of over a hundred marvelous photos of their trek—with two hundred fifty more to follow, along with ninety minutes of superb video.

October 27

I received an e-mail from Hugh Prather describing the location of the wedged metal. It was probably near where the tail section was hanging off the cliff. If you looked at the metal, made a 180-degree turn, and took one large step, you'd quickly descend seven hundred feet. The spot was right where the cliff began its straight-down descent.

He was pleased that I was having a dialogue with Ginny. He thought that the experience of going up there had been quite cathartic for her, her brother, and their cousin, and they had become wonderful friends of his in the process.

That evening, he e-mailed Anne Pearson important information concerning the hearing aid case.

When he was up on the pinnacle over Labor Day weekend, early in September, with Gary Creason, the son of the copilot, they had discovered that small shiny item and left it up there. Hugh could not be sure that there were no other passengers who wore hearing aids, but Anne Schoonmaker Pearson's father was one of the older men on the flight, so it seemed highly probable to Hugh that the Beltone piece had belonged to him.

October 28

Anne Pearson e-mailed Gary Creason to tell him about the October trek to the pinnacle and the discovery of the Beltone case.

She had never before had contact with him or his family and hoped that he would not mind her writing him. She just wanted to let him in on the Beltone find, especially since he had also handled the object. It was now back with her family, and she thanked him. Had anyone else found it, it would have been just a plain ole artifact, but to her it was a small piece of Dad back after fifty years.

November 13

Gary Creason e-mailed Anne Pearson, apologizing for not responding earlier, but he was recovering from surgery that he had undergone in late October.

Her story was truly remarkable. Indeed, he clearly remembered picking up the small, silver-colored metal case with "Beltone" engraved on it. As he recalled, Hugh Prather had noted at the time that Beltone was a hearing aid company, and he recognized the name as well.

Why had he replaced the case on the ground after examining it? It was a personal artifact, as opposed to a piece of the airplane. And he knew that it didn't belong to his own father.

As he would have liked to see the impact site remain essentially undisturbed, replacing the Beltone case on the ground simply seemed like the right thing to do. He hadn't been consciously analytical about it at the time, but that was his basic mindset.

He was delighted to learn that the case had found its way to her. He could only try to imagine what it would feel like if he were to recover one of his own father's personal possessions from the crash site after fifty years had passed.

In short, Gary Creason—the son of the first officer—had discovered the hearing aid case at the wreck site and had returned it to the place where he had found it so that Bill Pearson—the grandson of its owner, Alfred Schoonmaker—could unwittingly find it a few weeks later and return it to Alfred's daughter, Anne Schoonmaker Pearson.

I am inclined to believe that these events were meant to happen.

January 2006

I had a delightful visit with Anne and her husband, Bud Pearson, at their lovely home at Seabrook Island, South Carolina. Ginny Campbell, Bill Pearson, and Barbara Schoonmaker—Anne's sister, the eldest daughter of Alfred and Dorothy Schoonmaker—were also there, along with Bill's wife, Alyssa, and their infant daughter, Ava.

It was a moving experience getting to know them and telling them what I knew about the crash.

Ancient Lore

NAMING THE PINNACLES

I became concerned that I lacked distinctive names for the two imposing spires that towered above the wreck site and the massive pinnacle to its west. I had labeled the spires Upper Spire and Lower Spire for want of something better, but hadn't thought of a name for the massive pinnacle.

Jim Linn kindly supplied me with the fact that climbers knew the upper spire as Alioth—exotic sounding, but unfamiliar to me. I looked it up and to my surprise learned that I had long known it, though not by any name—Alioth being the brightest star in the handle of the Big Dipper. Might the names of the remaining stars in that handle perhaps serve my purpose?

Next to Alioth was Mizar (pronounced *my czar*), meaning "cloak" in ancient Arabic, and derived from *azara*, "to surround." It seemed a perfect match for the lower spire, whose southeastern edge has the outline of a cloak like garment. Mizar is a (visually) double star whose barely visible twin, Alcor, was often used as a test of visual acuity.

The name of the next star, Alkaide, at the western end of the handle, also seemed appropriate. It was the origin of the Spanish word *alcaide*, meaning "the commander or governor of a fortress"—and the massive pinnacle to the west could aptly be termed a fortress.

I then extended my investigation to Ursa Major, the constellation that encompasses the Big Dipper, and discovered an early legend:

> In ancient Mesopotamia the constellation of the Great Bear was seen as a funeral procession, around a bier or coffin, represented by the stars outlining the bowl of the dipper. The coffin was followed by three mourners: Alioth, Mizar, and Alkaid—the daughters of Al Na'ash, who was murdered by Al Jadi, the polestar (Polaris). They nightly surround him in their thirst for vengeance—Mizar holding in her arms her newborn infant, Alcor.

I chose the legend name Alkaid because Alkaide sounded too much like that of the terrorist organization Al Qaeda. I've recently discovered that rock climbers call the massive pinnacle Hail Peak, but I like my name better.

But what about the terrestrial counterpart of the child Alcor? I hadn't known about him when I began my search for names, but as he was a key element in the ancient tale, where was he to be found?

And then I realized that little Alcor was there also exactly where he should be, close by the skirts of his mother, Mizar, his spire being the most consequential of all: the final resting place of TWA Flight 260.

The terrestrial Alkaid, Mizar, and Alioth thus stand in silent tribute to the victims of that tragedy, while the mute celestial daughters of Al Na'ash continue their endless march toward Polaris.

Butterflies

I also chanced across the knowledge that in ancient Greek, *psyche* was the word for both "butterfly" and "soul," with my 1953 *Webster's New International Dictionary* informing me that "Psyche in Greek antiquity was a lovely maiden, the personification of the soul, usually represented with the wings of a butterfly, emblematic of immortality."

I had heretofore tended to regard ancient myths as fanciful and impractical. They may instead reveal ancient wisdoms about ourselves.

9
Family Trek

In the middle of September 2005, Anne and Bud Pearson had passed through Albuquerque while returning home from visiting their new grandchild in San Diego and decided to take the tramway up to Sandia Crest. She was interested in seeing the Sandias because her parents, Alfred and Dorothy Schoonmaker, and her brother-in-law, Bill Campbell, had perished aboard Flight 260. Amazed that the tram gondola passed over the wreckage strip, she identified herself to tramway personnel, who obligingly halted the gondola above the wreck pinnacle on the trip down.

They also put her in contact with Hugh Prather, who arranged a trip to the pinnacle on October 8. Included in that party were Ginny and Bill Campbell Jr., children of Bill Campbell and grandchildren of the Schoonmakers; Cheryl Campbell, Bill's wife; Bill Pearson and his sister, Lynn Myers, children of Anne and Bud Pearson, and grandchildren of the Schoonmakers; and retired airline pilot Jake Jacobson, a friend of Ginny's.

October 8, 2005

They arrived at the tram terminal at dawn, the tram cables disappearing into the clouds above them. Their ride up would be spectacular for them, and they took a multitude of photos and camcorder footage recording their journey.

Their tramway ride began in the foothills above Albuquerque's East Mesa and proceeded northeast to the top of Sandia Mountain. The mesa (meaning "table" in Spanish) appeared to be flat but was actually a tilted plane rising from the Rio Grande to the base of the mountain—its slope contrasted against the foothills in the background, with Albuquerque suburbs near the base of the tram visible in the foreground. Early morning fog hugged pockets on the desert floor and the Rio Grande in the far distance.

The lower regions of the Sandias were boulder-strewn desert slopes that eventually merged with vertical and overhanging cliffs of

Figure 32. Upper regions of Echo Canyon, where granite cliffs merge with the lighter limestone layers above. The Kiwanis Cabin appears as a light dot atop the limestone sloping to its right. Below it, the silhouetted Alioth and Mizar spires tower like tombstones above the crash pinnacle rising a short distance above its notch and saddle. (Photo by Ginny Campbell.)

Wreck Pinnacle

Figure 33. The crash pinnacle from the southeast. When the tail was cut free of its control cables, it fell from the tail ledge to the shrub shaped like a Christmas tree, then into the narrow cleft. The left wing fell to the base of the south face of the buttress upon impact with the cliff. Alkaid rises to the left of the pinnacle and Mizar, beyond it, to its right. (Photo by Hugh Prather.)

granite, their size difficult to judge in the clear desert air. The cliffs higher up—far more massive—revealed an arced fin of granite sliced off from its parent ridge, the gap between filled with sand and rubble descended from the cliffs above.

Then Echo Canyon came into view, with the Kiwanis Cabin appearing as a tiny white dot atop sloping limestone layers disappearing to its right. Alioth and Mizar were silhouetted against the dark blue sky, hiding TWA Canyon behind them.

Their first good view of Alcor was from the southeast, its western face bathed in shadow and its southern in bright sunlight, but barely distinguishable from the vertical cliffs of Mizar rising behind it. The "Christmas tree," where the tail had initially lodged when cut free from the pinnacle, was clearly visible against the narrow shadowed floor of TWA Canyon. The wreckage of the plane atop the pinnacle would have been easy to see from this angle, but as the granite spires behind it were no longer silhouetted against the sky, they blended in with the backdrop of other granite and were difficult to discern.

Because of the massiveness of the rock, the scale of what they were observing was difficult to ascertain. The tram car passed the pinnacle about level with the crash site but hundreds of feet south of it, directly over the Flight 260 plaque that Hugh had placed at its southern base.

As the tram moved onward, the full eastern face of Alcor came into view, revealing a shining piece of wreckage still remaining near the point of impact. The pinnacle face began blending with the massive cliffs of Alkaid behind it and would soon become indistinguishable from it as they traveled upward and eastward to Sandia Crest.

At the tram terminal atop the Sandias, the tram cables descended into the void. The pinnacle was obviously in view, yet its featureless expanses of granite were demarcated only by the vertical shadow of its north face. The streets of Albuquerque trending westward far beyond it toward the Rio Grande Valley, marked by a narrow band of fog.

Hugh pointed out the airport to them and explained the path that the plane had traveled to its doom. Then they exited the terminal and headed westward on the Spur Trail, with infrequent views of the Kiwanis Cabin before them and spectacular glimpses of the wreck pinnacle silhouetted by the morning fog. A tall tree in shadow stood in the V-shaped defile between the Mizar and Alioth spires, and they could see a small cairn lying atop a sunlit chimney-shaped rock, placed there by climbers who had ascended it.

They paused for photos at the head of TWA Canyon while Hugh cautioned them about the treacherous, incessantly downhill path they would follow to the pinnacle in a chasm now choked with vegetation.

The upper regions were a great mass of shrubbery enveloping the travelers, hiding them from their companions and blocking their progress forward, their feet disappearing into greenery that threatened to trip them at every step. Soon the foliage was replaced by aspen, still in fall plumage, and then by towering spruce. This was alpine territory, and desert cactus did not abide here; but mountain locust and scrub oak had sharp spines that could also wreak their damage.

They found the cliffs rising up on the western side of the canyon awe inspiring, and views of what lay ahead increasingly became available. The presence of cliffs behind them—hidden from sight by the oppressive greenery—became apparent when the forested regions permitted magnificent views back up the canyon, the northern sky a memorable blue in the clear mountain air.

Glimpses of the cliffs far down the canyon gave them a measure of how far they had descended, but the presence of the cliffs was not

Figure 34. View from TWA Canyon of the crash pinnacle, Mizar, and Alioth. The ledge on which the tail section rested and the "Christmas tree" below it are visible here. Wreckage and four bodies were thrown over the vertical north face to the slope directly below it. A tall tree in shadow stands in the V-shaped defile between the Mizar and Alioth spires. Further to the right, a small cairn lies atop a sunlit chimney-shaped rock, placed there by climbers. (Photo by Ginny Campbell.)

nearly as intimidating as the immense overhangs that towered above their heads, matching the grandeur of the looming cliffs emerging beside them.

Alcor came into view to the south from a small clearing, the top of a tree in the foreground sheared off by a rock avalanche that had free fallen from a cliff rising above them. Smaller branches on a tree to their left had suffered similar fates, the tall fir seen in profile at the base of the crash pinnacle bearing evidence that it too had suffered the ravages of falling rock.

The glade where they were standing appeared peaceful but was in fact a death-dealing battlefield, visited far too frequently by stony missiles from above.

Shooting with a telephoto lens, Ginny Campbell took a picture of the crash site from this clearing that was surprisingly similar to one

Figure 35. October 8, 2005, photo from the same clearing as in Figure 25, the former taken a half century earlier. The foliage on the canyon floor is far more abundant now, but trees on the skyline are little changed. Falling rock splintered the tree in the foreground. (Photo by Ginny Campbell.)

taken in 1955. The foliage on the canyon floor was far more abundant now, but the trees on the skyline where the tail had been hanging over the cliff were little changed. Dead trees silhouetted on the skyline fifty years ago still stood tall today.

A short distance later the Mizar spire ended abruptly, to be replaced by a talus pile heading upward toward the cliffs of Alkaid rising to the west. The massive talus boulders were perhaps the remnants of the rock wall that originally joined Alcor with Mizar to its north.

If memory serves me right, that talus pile was not there in 1955. The dirt slopes to the notch, which our rescue team had ascended when we first ventured to the crash site, had in the last half century migrated downhill to expose the shattered tumble of rocks they now confronted.

Hugh Prather, Bill Campbell, Ginny Campbell, and Bill Pearson began their ascent to the notch, while the others remained at the base of the pinnacle. The climbers were rewarded with a magnificent view northeast of the limestone cliffs atop Sandia Crest, framed in part by the vertical wall of Mizar rising on the left. To the east, they could see a tram car silently traversing overhead toward its terminal. It seemed impossible that they could have begun their journey there.

The saddle provided them with a spectacular panorama of rocky heights: the nearby summits of Mizar and Alioth towering to the north, a distant view of Echo Canyon to the northwest through the adjoining notch, the massive cliffs of Alkaid to the west, and, to the south, a diminutive Alcor rising a challenging forty feet, shining tram cables descending to the right behind it.

The climb to the top of the pinnacle was short, tricky, and nerve-racking, with menacing views of the desert floor and the Albuquerque suburbs lying thousands of feet beneath them. Hugh Prather led the way while the others anxiously waited their turns.

They climbed unroped—it still scares me to think about it.

The summit of Alcor provided its own set of panoramas. Views directly south revealed desert vegetation on western slopes of the Sandias that suffer the afternoon sun and shadowed northern slopes clothed with dark evergreens. Downtown Albuquerque appeared in the distance

Figure 36. Wreckage jammed beneath a giant block of granite above the south face of the buttress provides evidence that this may be where the plane first struck the pinnacle. (Photo by Ginny Campbell.)

to the left of the immense vertical cliffs of Alkaid, a few hundred feet to the west. The tram cables descended to the East Mesa below, and plane wreckage still hung from a tree that had been stripped bare at the time of the crash but was now luxuriously green.

The party explored the terrain, looking for evidence of the crash, but finding little besides pulverized shreds of metal, broken crockery, a piece of cockpit window glass, and an aluminum fragment of the right propeller. They were amazed to discover that it weighed a ton. Aluminum is a surprisingly heavy metal, but its strength permits it to be molded into extremely thin sections that are ideal for reducing the weight of aircraft components.

Bill Pearson called his mom on a cell phone and, while the others explored lower down, camcorded a butterfly, commented about omens, and collected souvenirs to send her—the piece of shiny metal belonging to his grandfather among them—then shoved the collection into his rucksack, where the items were forgotten until he remembered to mail them to her a week or so later.

As they say, the rest is history.

The three cousins created a shrine in memory of their loved ones beneath a cairn atop the summit ridge above the wreck site, leaving behind porcelain flowers that Ginny had carried in her pack. But for the size of its rocks, the cairn had the appearance of being man-made. Perhaps it was jumbled together with the aid of the helicopters used to lift the wreckage from the pinnacle. It's nice to conjecture that the cairn marks the spot where we buried victim remains on the day we found the plane's fluxgate compass. Then they exited the pinnacle to retrace their steps to the canyon floor, where they rejoined the others.

The party traversed the eastern base of the pinnacle amid great boulders and lush vegetation, walking past recognizable pieces of wreckage—propellers, a wheel with remarkably intact tire, a major section of numbered wing—to begin winding their way down the canyon to the mesa.

Their initial path, a dry creek bed punctuated by fallen tree trunks, eventually became a full-fledged trail alongside a gurgling brook. This forested wonderland, reminiscent of the Appalachias, was soon followed by an abrupt exit from the verdant canyon into a desert country ruled by prickly pear, cholla, and yucca.

Looking back, they saw a view of a blue tramcar passing the face of Alcor, the horizontal bands of limestone near the top of Sandia Crest in the remote distance. The sky was gray now and dusk was falling as they hiked across the mesa toward the tram terminal where they had begun their journey at dawn. They ended their trek in total darkness.

The next morning, the upper regions of the Sandias were enshrouded by clouds, much as they had been on February 19, fifty years before.

10
TWA Memorial Dedication

Plans for the Flight 260 memorial dedication to be held at the Sandia Vista Room of the Albuquerque Sunport began forming in early summer 2006. Who would be attending the ceremony? Ginny began sending e-mails to people she knew were interested in attending, receiving responses that perhaps ten to twelve people would be there. She then started making a list of potential attendees and suggested that a short biographical sketch of each might be of value.

Biographical sketches began to trickle in, and I was selected to be in charge of the final product. Ginny would receive the information, forward it to me for editing, and at day's end I would send the results back to her for broadcasting to all concerned, using Hugh Prather's "all concerned parties" e-mailing list.

The results were immediate and astonishing. She received return e-mails from daughters of Captain Larry DeCelles and First Officer Creason. As they all lived nearby, Ginny proposed that they have lunch together. Passenger, crew, and investigator family members who had unknowingly been living near each other for decades at last met one another. The luncheon was an outstanding success.

An avalanche of new attendees and biographies then descended upon us—wives wanted to join husbands, husbands wanted to join wives, and there were cousins, nieces, nephews, children, and devoted friends. They were purposeful, interesting people who had led fascinating and fruitful lives. They would travel to Albuquerque from California, Arizona, Colorado, Kansas, Texas, Georgia, New Jersey, and Massachusetts.

Ginny also began to get e-mails concerning the crash itself. A cousin of the pilot e-mailed her that his sister in Austin, Texas, had recently met a man who had been a policeman in Albuquerque. I asked Ginny to find out more—Bill Lucas might be that person. A few weeks later she received the word that indeed he was. She phoned him immediately, as did I the next day.

Bill Lucas told me initially that he did not recall me at all, but when I mentioned the mountain club and that he had given Sherman Marsh and me a lift in his car on the day of the crash, he responded immediately: "I remember you! You were the coldest, sorriest-looking kids with runny noses that I've ever seen."

Not quite the heroic image that I had in mind, but he had recollected us for half a century—and I told him that I still had a runny nose. Bill then supplied me with details of his experiences during those days, helping resolve the confusing accounts that had been reported in the newspapers.

Planning for a supper after the memorial dedication on September 22, Ginny called an Albuquerque motel to see whether she could reserve a table in their restaurant; then called later to arrange for another table as the attendee list began to swell. The motel eventually reserved their entire dining facilities for our use and made arrangements to hire additional staff.

Ginny called the *Kansas City Star* to alert them that the memorial dedication would take place. The editors responded that they did not believe their readers would have much interest in a memorial dedication being held in Albuquerque. She replied by deluging the paper with the ever-growing list of biographical sketches, many of them from individuals who were still connected with the Kansas City area. The *Star* editors relented and agreed to send their own reporter to Albuquerque to witness the dedication and visit the scene of the crash.

The *Albuquerque Journal* joined the fray a week before the ceremony, with columnist Harry Moskos interviewing Ginny by phone and writing a front-page article about the crash and the coming dedication. (Neither Ginny nor I knew at the time of the dedication that Moskos had been involved with the crash, as an eighteen-year-old getting crash photos onto the

Figure 37. TWA Captain Larry DeCelles (middle) meets Jana Childers and her brother Gary Creason, children of First Officer J. J. Creason.

Albuquerque Tribune telephoto machine in 1955.) The result was an avalanche of e-mails to the *Journal*, dutifully forwarded to Ginny by Harry—one from Arkansas from a surviving relative of a passenger, and another from Colorado written by Sheriff's Captain Rodgers, who, with Bill Lucas, had weathered the long frigid night upon the mountain. We have been in e-mail and phone contact ever since.

A federal judge e-mailed us about how the crash had affected him as a schoolboy growing up in Albuquerque. He wanted to join us in the trek to the base of the pinnacle the day following the dedication.

Retired Deputy State Police Chief Steve Lagomarsino also contacted us. As a patrolman sidekick to Bill Lucas, he had searched for the missing aircraft in his squad car and still had vivid memories of the mountain enshrouded by clouds that day. He would bring eleven professional-grade photographs of the search-and-rescue activities to the dedication ceremony; many of them grace these pages.

The Flight 260 article received the second highest number of e-mail responses from *Journal* readers that week—not bad for an event that had occurred a half century before.

A special supper on the eve before the memorial dedication was the occasion of the first meeting between Captain Larry DeCelles and the children of First Officer J. J. Creason. Gary Greason and his sister, Jana Childers, thanked the man who had absolved their father from blame for the crash. The event was witnessed by *Kansas City Star* reporter Steve Rock; TWA Pilot Chris Clark, a longtime friend of Larry's and former associate of Captain Ivan Spong; Hugh Prather, the

Figure 38. Victim family member Ginny Campbell, a model of the airliner atop the TWA flight memorial plaque, and keynote speaker Hugh Prather at the TWA Flight 260 memorial dedication at the Albuquerque Sunport in 2006. (Courtesy of Ginny Campbell.)

man responsible for getting everybody together; a large contingent of DeCelles family members and friends; and a host of interested folks from Albuquerque.

TWA Flight 260 Memorial Dedication

The next day's memorial dedication ceremony included a remarkably diverse assembly of people—veteran pilots who had flown Lockheed Constellations and Boeing 747s; retired TWA airline hostess Kathleen Kadas, who had attended Flight 260 on its flight to Albuquerque from San Francisco the day before the crash; twenty-six family members (eight from the crew, seven from the passengers, eleven from Larry DeCelles); and three rescuers (accompanied by their spouses), who renewed friendships after a lengthy hiatus.

We had accumulated a list of some sixty attendees, along with forty-seven biographical sketches, but multitudes of others would also register at the ceremony, accompanied by camera people from the local TV stations.

Hugh acted as keynote speaker, introducing Captain Larry DeCelles; Chris Clark, TWA captain and board member of the Airline History Museum in Kansas City; Gary Creason, son of the first officer; former TWA flight hostess Kathleen Kadas; and then Ginny Campbell, who called upon Ken Spong, second cousin of Captain Ivan Spong; Janet Crownover, Ivan's niece; Barbara Schoonmaker, Ginny's aunt and the oldest of the Schoonmaker children; and, finally, me.

Hugh Prather used slides to outline the details of the crash, the bungled CAB report, and Larry DeCelles's splendid role in setting things right. He introduced Phil DeCelles, who spoke briefly for his dad.

Chris Clark spoke extensively about the remarkable professionalism and dedication of Captain Spong, including an anecdote of his own experiences with him as a fledgling pilot. He also praised Larry DeCelles for exonerating the pilots of blame for the accident and for his long-lasting contributions to airline safety.

Clark's characterizations of Ivan Spong's character were accentuated by Ken Spong and Janet Crownover, who related wonderful stories about him. A giant of a man—at six foot four and two hundred fifty pounds—he was also huge in his dedication to his profession and the safety of passengers and crew and in his devotion and service to his family. It was inconceivable that a man who would never have knowingly deviated in the slightest from established flight procedures could actually have been accused of purposely doing so—all the more devastating to his family and those who knew him best.

Gary Creason, proud son of the First Officer J. J. Creason, presented a gripping account of his vivid memories of his father, who died when he was only four—a man who had been universally loved, admired, and respected by all who knew him.

His father had been a constant companion to Gary when he was home from flying, and it had taken the boy years to understand that he would never return; he had thought of him daily ever since. His father's entry into the cockpit that fateful day had been the prelude to a tragedy but, nonetheless, was a remarkable achievement: J. J. Creason had grown up in Great Depression poverty, with only a ninth-grade education, in a house that did not get indoor plumbing until 1960, five years after his demise. Gary's loss had been a personal struggle, and he thanked those present for remembering his father.

First Officer Creason would have been proud of Gary too—a Boston biopharmaceutical intellectual property attorney with a PhD in plant physiology from Cornell and a law degree from Fordham.

"My heart is always on the mountain" were the opening words of Kathleen Kadas. Having lost her own husband to an aircraft accident, she knew the suffering that the surviving families had endured. Being a flight hostess had been the greatest job on earth to her, and she was intensely proud of having served.

Then the oldest of the Schoonmaker offspring, eighty-five-years young Barbara, lightened the somberness by thanking everyone for attending the memorial dedication. She had never expected anything like this—it was like having a big extended family.

I was exceedingly grateful for Barbara's smooth transition away from distress and for Ken Spong's compliments and expressed gratitude for the efforts of the recovery crew. They made my job easier in sketching the bizarre details of our search-and-recovery efforts. I stated that I was especially proud of the profoundly dedicated efforts of the untrained volunteers who had made our work successful. I had been continuously astonished by the caliber of the individuals associated with this crash, especially those in the audience before me.

The impressive quality of the people connected with this saga has been substantiated time and time again since then.

Ginny Campbell terminated the presentations with a very moving description of the travails of her own family and the miraculous discovery of her grandfather's hearing aid case.

She then revealed seventeen crosses that she had commissioned, each engraved with a name of a crash victim—thirteen passengers, three crew members, and the airliner itself. She would carry them to the top of the wreck pinnacle the next day, and we would place them in the memorial there.

11
Return to Alcor

The next morning, still on Atlanta time, I woke up early, dressed, and ventured outside to be welcomed by a clear, starry sky—a wonderful sight, as the possibility of snow had been talked about the night before. Turning to the east, I could see the silhouetted outline of the Sandias, but were the upper slopes enshrouded by low-lying clouds—and hence snow—as they had been in 1955? Icy going at the wreck pinnacle was a fearsome challenge then, and I had little stomach for it now. As the motel blocked my view of the Crest, I anxiously walked up a small rise to get an unobstructed vista and was rewarded by being able to see the lights on the TV towers at the summit. The slopes seemed clear, and I hoped that any lingering rime would have burned off by the time we reached them in a few hours.

The trip up the tram was spectacular, as usual, and required two gondola loads as our party numbered about thirty-five, including thirteen who would venture to the summit of Alcor. The air was cold, but dead calm at the top of the tramway—a slight dusting of snow on shadowed sections of the Spur Trail making it treacherous but providing us with a well-defined track of a mountain lion that had passed by a short while before.

Mountain club rescue team member Dick Heim hailed me about this time to say goodbye. I was sorry that he would not be able to venture with us further, but a slippery mountain was no place to be with his reluctant knee. And a few moments later we discovered that the initial steep plunge down TWA Canyon from the trail was especially hazardous. The frozen, crusted surface lay atop a slippery layer of mud and had a penchant for migrating downhill—especially nasty for me, as I was slow in getting a sense of balance on the uneven terrain.

The vegetation was far more luxurious than the year before; record rainfalls had created a green haven in the canyon. Our way was partially blocked by a recent landslip that had left large boulders atop still-green bushes and small trees—not a spectacular avalanche, but it would have been a terrifying movement if someone nearby had witnessed it, a substantial section of rock and earth oozing and grumbling a few feet down the mountain.

I began to fret whether my names for the pinnacles might prove improvident. Having just conceived them a few weeks before, they were recorded in my first draft of this book, which now resided in the TWA memorial room. This trek would verify or vilify my judgment.

When we began glimpsing views of the immense cliffs of what I thought was Alioth on our right I asked Jim Linn to point it out for me and was suitably appalled when he indicated down the canyon to what should have been the skirts of Mizar instead. I had apparently interchanged the order of Alioth and Mizar when I named the pinnacles to match the stars in the Big Dipper. I had been meticulous in checking the map, but had somehow botched the job. The little Alcor pinnacle must be standing close to Alioth instead of near his mother, Mizar—at deviance with both astronomy and the ancient legend.

Reality obviously did not match my poetic symbolism. The grandeur of the scenery remained intact, but its mystical aura had been impaired. I began facing the quandary of a serious rewrite of my tale as we ventured downward. What type of scenario would make things right, or would I find it necessary to omit all references to ancient lore?

Then, just as suddenly, things were righted once more: joy had no bounds when the skirts of the actual Mizar came into view down the canyon. As ascending climbers are often maliciously teased by the false summits towering above them, I in descending had been tricked by a devious pinnacle below me.

We stopped at the talus pile that separates Mizar from Alcor, waited for the rest of our party to join us, and had lunch. Thirteen of us would ascend to the saddle, where we met the rescue party that had weathered the long night fifty-one years before. The rest would continue down the canyon with Hugh to the desert regions of the East Mesa.

I announced to the party that I intended to bushwhack my way to the north face of the Alcor buttress and ascend to the saddle along its base to explore the area where four crash victims had been hurled from the pinnacle. Everyone was welcome to come with me, but it would be far easier to go directly up to the saddle.

Gary Creason, Ken Spong, and Steve Rock volunteered to join me, while the rest accompanied Jim Linn up the right edge of the talus pile. I began traversing horizontally, hoping to find the narrow cleft in the north face into which the aircraft tail section had fallen after we cut it free of the summit. We were only a few hundred feet from our destination, but our view and passage were impeded by a dense thicket of brush—seemingly benevolent greenery in that it was devoid of thorns, stickers, and sharp edges that could wound, but in truth, relentlessly possessive vegetation that encompassed us, embraced us, ensnared us—a supple, resilient greenery that entangled our limbs and seriously impeded our progress; and we lacked machetes that could have cleared the way.

Grim determination gained us a little distance, and I eventually encountered the trunk of a fallen tree lying on top of the brush. As it was pointed up the slope in roughly the desired direction, I clambered on top to use it as a bridge over the tangled mass of foliage and was rewarded by an unencumbered view of a section of the north face. As the cleft was not visible, I assumed that it must be downhill from us to the left and would require the traversal of still more brush—not an inviting prospect—so I opted for beeline paths to the north face that would avoid as much vegetation as possible. These were conveniently supplied by narrow tracks that coursed uphill through the thicket, evidently cleared by rocks plummeting from the cliffs above during rainstorms, and highly beneficial to us now that we were favored by the absence of both liquid and stony precipitations.

The uphill climb was arduous but reasonably free of impediments.

I hoped that when we encountered the north face we would find relatively easy going along its base in the narrow gap between the granite and the brush—and so we did.

Metal

I immediately turned right when I met the rock and after a few steps glimpsed something shiny under a bush slightly downhill from me. I yelled, "Metal!" and proceeded to investigate while the others joined me. It was obviously a piece of wreckage with the surface scored by its slide down the rough granite wall. I knew that this isolated piece of metal must have come from the crash itself. As no other wreckage was evident, it had not been tossed off the summit by cleanup crews.

But what was it?

Gary Creason immediately supplied the answer: it was part of the wing. Obviously wrong, I energetically told him, for the bulk of the debris from wing and fuselage had been found on top of the pinnacle, and we were at the base of the north face, where four bodies but virtually no wreckage had descended. Surely, this could not be a piece of the wing.

Figure 39. Gary Creason (left) and Ken Spong in dense foliage view the wingtip found at the base of the north face of the buttress in 2006. (Photo by Steve Rock, Kansas City Star.)

Figure 40. Close-up of the wingtip shown in Figure 39. The straight edge at the top right appears to be aerodynamically sculpted, and a vented slot is visible on the top edge. (Photo by Steve Rock, Kansas City Star.)

But he was adamant, showing us that both sides of part of the object were aerodynamically sculpted. Indeed, it even looked somewhat like a miniature wing. But what could it be, and why was it here? It was too small to be the tip of the wing itself. It must have been part of something else, perhaps the tail. When the fuselage was stopped abruptly by the pinnacle, the piece might have snapped off and continued onward in its original direction of travel—and thus over the north cliff. As the plane had been in a steep left bank, the tip of the right horizontal stabilizer would have been high in the air, away from the impacting fuselage, and would have been subjected to the maximum degree of torque.

I opened my pack, pulled out pictures of the wreckage taken in 1955, and examined the photos of the horizontal stabilizer (Figures 21 and 23). No luck—except for a dent, the right stabilizer was intact; and the left stabilizer must have been below the tail assembly.

Could it have been a piece of the tail's vertical stabilizer? Yes! A photo that I pulled from my backpack clearly showed that a piece of its leading edge was missing—Gary had been right after all, and we had succeeded in identifying the vertical stabilizer as the source of the piece of metal!

My excitement knew no bounds. Fate seemed to have sent me purposefully and directly to the metal. I had discovered it immediately after reaching the base of the north cliff—our intended destination—in spite of the fact that the dense brush precluded my having any knowledge of where we would end up. Indeed, our location or even approximate altitude on the pinnacle remained a mystery, as the brush still screened us from views of the nearby slopes. Gary Creason, the son of the copilot, had been there to identify the metal with Ken Spong, a cousin of the pilot, as witness; and Steve Rock, an objective newspaper reporter, could corroborate the discovery.

Photos of me taken at the time revealed a tense and immensely focused expression on my face. My intense reaction must have seemed far out of proportion to what had actually occurred. It had, after all, been just a solitary piece of crafted metal among countless fragments of wreckage that had descended from the sky.

Yet subsequent events would later justify my exaltation.

We left the metal where it lay and traversed the base of the cliff in the direction of the saddle—a reasonably easy journey, as the uphill grade was relatively slight—and we stayed free of the brush by pressing so close to the adjacent rock that we gained no sense of the towering granite immediately above our heads.

Rounding a corner to our left, we were plunged into a shaded alpine wonderland with immense fir trees blocking our view of the sky. The sun-worshiping brush had suddenly vanished, and we now trod on a thick carpet of rich dirt. The hillside rising steeply before us, we would climb to the saddle in a terrain never graced by the rays of the sun.

We greeted the others at the saddle and were belayed to the summit of the pinnacle by Jim Linn, who was running a superb show. I was truly thankful for the security of his rope, as I was exhausted, my supply of adrenaline having been expended by the steep climb and the excitement of discovering the metal.

Up at the top, I did my best to find the spot where we had buried the body parts a month after the crash, but I failed to find topographical features that I remembered. Perhaps they had been obliterated by the cleanup crews scouring the summit of wreckage. Perhaps the memorial cairn that was erected fifty years later was near the spot.

The wreck site had a tranquil quality to it this day, serene and quiet in the absence of wind except for the soft voices of our party exploring its slopes; the forbidding feel that I had experienced the year before had vanished. I maneuvered from place to place, searching for the scenes that the cameramen of 1955 had captured, delighting when I discovered the spot where the rescuer had eaten his breakfast from a can, finding the remnants of an old can nearby, and wondering whether it was the original.

I also found the place where the right engine had come to rest (Figure 30), the steep cliffs of Mizar in the background; I noted that a long horizontal crack in that face was no longer present. Sometime in the last half century the apparently solid features of Mizar had been altered when an immense section had broken free, obdurate granite crumbling into scattered talus while long-dead trees atop the pinnacle stood tall.

I asked Gary Creason to identify the spot where he had discovered Alfred Schoonmaker's hearing aid case. After a lengthy search, he pointed to its approximate location on the upper slopes; and I told Ginny that her grandmother had been found a few yards to the left, and that the first victim that I had seen that day had been lying a few feet uphill—it might easily have been her grandfather.

Figure 41. Ginny Campbell and crosses at the memorial cairn atop the pinnacle, the streets of Albuquerque far below. (Photo by Bill Campbell.)

Figure 42. The author, Collin Campbell, Ken Spong, Jim Linn, Gwen Murphy, Gary Creason, and Bill Campbell bow their heads as Ginny Campbell places the cross for the plane into the shrine under the cairn atop the crash pinnacle. (Photographer unknown.)

Bill Pearson's feeling that he had been standing at the spot where his grandfather had perished appeared vindicated. His omen of the sole butterfly landing on a rock seemed real indeed.

A few minutes later we placed seventeen crosses at the memorial cairn for the victims and the plane that had perished fifty-one years before. Ginny intoned the names as we placed each cross in the shrine beneath the cairn, her brother Bill videotaping the ceremony. I was honored to place the cross for flight hostess Sharon Schoening, whom I remembered all too vividly. Ginny had handed me the cross for passenger Lois Dean at the memorial dedication ceremony at the Sunport the day before—Dean had shared my love for educating others. It was a moving, sad, yet joyful experience with a magnificent view of Albuquerque as a backdrop amid a crescendo of nature's perfect silence.

We then departed from the summit of the pinnacle.

The trip down the spire was uneventful except for foolishness on my part. Frances Robertson was attempting to show me hand and footholds for descending the final section when I decided to demonstrate my climbing expertise by descending face forward, leaning outward from the rock, and walking straight down the ridge from the summit with the tension of the belay rope holding me firm. It was a technique that I had used countless times before.

Only I had forgotten one minor detail—the tension of the belay rope was supposed to come directly from behind. The last and most precipitous part of the descent was down a steep buttress that veered sharply right from the ridge, causing the taut belay rope behind me to begin pulling me sideways, off balance. I plunged over the cliff to my right.

The belay rope easily checked my free fall, and I gracefully swayed like a pendulum away from the cliff. The gentle swing back, however, was interrupted by my chest and knees meeting the rock, spinning me around so that my subsequent swings were parallel to the rock face. The jarring impact was replaced by repetitious scraping of my bare arm on the rock wall. The fall had been uneventful, but my body's greeting the rock had sparked my attention.

I yelled to Jim Linn that I was in midair, and he paid out rope to get me down to terra firma.

Being more embarrassed than hurt by the experience, I asked Steve Rock not to mention it in his newspaper story. He replied that, as he had not personally witnessed the event, in his eyes it had never happened. Steve had been a delightful companion on that trip; quiet and unobtrusive, he was one of us, and we valued his presence.

The initial impact with the rock had bruised my chest and knees and put a small, bullet-hole-like puncture in my favorite shirt, but there was no evidence of further injury. The back side of my left arm was extensively scraped but not bleeding badly. I declined Bill Campbell's kind offer to patch me up—though later I wished that I had accepted it, for I must have been a sorry sight to inflict on my companions. As my bruised chest began to bother me later that evening, I asked doctors Bill and Cheryl Campbell to have a look. Discovering extensive abrasions on my chest and both knees but nothing else, they applied Band-Aids and Neosporin to everything in sight and admonished me to get a tetanus shot when I returned to Atlanta. The lingering soreness of that inoculation disappeared a few weeks later along with my chest pains.

Our trip down the mountain was made especially enjoyable by Frances holding forth on the folklore of the local botany and relating her recent experiences in the Peruvian wilderness. Her floral knowledge was especially interesting to seventeen-year-old Collin Campbell, son of Bill and Cheryl—a welcome companion and highly impressive young man. The bounteous contributions of both Jim Linn and Frances Robertson to this expedition were beyond measure.

We were later treated to a magnificent sunset that silhouetted Mount Taylor eighty miles away in vivid red—an ancient volcano, rising six hundred feet higher than the Sandias, but diminished in size by distance. Hollywood producer Mike Todd, then married to actress Elizabeth Taylor, had perished in a plane crash near its base in March 1958. The area is now part of a national monument appropriately named El Malpais ("the badland" in Spanish). We could also see Cabezon Peak, a volcanic neck rising two thousand feet above the Rio Puerco Valley; a popular rock climb destination, it is part of the Mount Taylor volcanic field.

We arrived at the base of the tramway just as the sun was setting, its soft latent glow still bathing the upper cliffs of the Sandias in watermelon red.

The next day, Steve Rock's article "Crusade to Clear Pilots' Names Brings Healing" appeared on page one of the Sunday edition of the *Kansas City Star*, along with a photo of Larry DeCelles with Gary Creason and his sister, Jana Childers.

Included was a quote from Gary Creason:

> From the time I was four years old, I've had visions of the plane hitting this mountain. But that mountain was just an abstraction to me. To actually stand on the site where the plane hit the mountain, to see small fragments of the windshield and coffee cups lying on the ground, that's powerful stuff.

12
Solving the Riddle

Aftermath

After returning home to Atlanta from Albuquerque, I phoned New Mexico Tech University for information about crash victim Robert Balk, who had been carrying a five thousand dollar geological map aboard the plane. The operator suggested that I call campus historian Robert Evelyth, who astonished me by saying that he was highly familiar with the story of Dr. Balk. He had been a personal friend of Balk's widow, and his own wife had recently returned from Albuquerque, where she had attended a certain TWA Flight 260 memorial dedication! Small world!

Bob Evelyth did not believe the map had been recovered, but said he would check his files. A few days later he mailed me beautifully written tributes to the Balks that served me well in my biographical sketches. I am also indebted to him for setting me straight about lots of the geological tidbits that permeate these pages.

Wedged Metal

I then began investigating the location of the wedged metal at the impact point (Figure 36). I had always thought that it was near the eastern cliff where I had recovered the body of the hostess, but e-mails from Ginny seemed to indicate that it must be elsewhere.

Examining a photo of Ginny's stepsister, Gwen Murphy, near the metal, I was surprised to notice that her face was bathed in sunlight, while her right leg was in shadow. Had she been above the eastern cliff, the camera would have been pointed west, and her face would have been in shadow. It was late afternoon, and the camera must have been pointing north instead of west.

Something was seriously wrong, for my eastern cliff had suddenly morphed to a southern one—a topsy-turvy tangle of east and south.

Hugh Prather had not known where the body of the hostess had lain and had assumed that it must have been near the wedged metal at what he correctly judged to be the impact point above the south cliff.

I knew where the hostess and tail section had rested above the eastern cliff, but had not associated the piece of shining metal in the photographs of the pinnacle with the impact point.

More importantly, I had incorrectly assumed that the plane had been traveling westward when it struck the pinnacle, for that belief was consistent with the position of the hostess and the tail wreckage.

It now seemed evident that somehow the plane had been traveling northward instead of westward.

The "WORL" Photo

I also examined a photograph (Figure 28) that appeared in an *Albuquerque Tribune* clipping that Sheriff's Captain A. S. "Governor" Rodgers had sent Ginny. The photo depicted a piece of fuselage at the base of a large rock, inscribed with the lettering "WORL," a fragment of the Trans World Airlines logo. I now began to understand why Phil Goldstein's apparently conflicting statements about the aircraft heading were both correct, and why the bodies of some of the victims were found ahead of the plane and above the wreckage.

But to prove my point, I needed to identify the mysterious piece of wreckage that I had just discovered beneath the north cliff of the pinnacle.

I had experienced a feeling of incredible elation when I first found it. Yet when I returned home, I began to have doubts that I had located anything significant: pictures of Martin 404s revealed that the piece did not appear to be part of the tail assembly at all. The most likely candidate—the rudder—was far too large and did not remotely resemble it. Indeed, its small size seemed to mitigate the case for ailerons or flaps as possible candidates.

Larry DeCelles's Birthday

Nevertheless, I remained hopeful, and Larry DeCelles would provide me with an opportunity to investigate matters firsthand by celebrating his eighty-fifth birthday on November 10 in Kansas City. Family members of the Flight 260 victims would attend, as would former TWA Captain Chris Clark, board member of the Airline History Museum, who arranged for us to have a tour of a Martin 404 at the museum. If Chris could not identify the metal from my photos, perhaps he would know aircraft mechanics at the museum who might, as they would be intimately familiar with the plane. Until recent years it had been a frequent flyer to air shows around the country.

Ginny borrowed the pictures (Figures 39 and 40) from me at Larry's birthday luncheon banquet and showed them to Chris, reporting back a few minutes later that he could not identify the piece of wreckage. I found this strangely positive news because it implied that the metal was not something that would normally concern a pilot, something that he would check in preflight inspections of the aircraft. But what was it?

The Airline History Museum

The Airline History Museum provided our group guided tours of a Lockheed Super-G Constellation, a Martin 404, and a Douglas DC-3 housed inside a large hangar. My wife and I visited the Constellation first. I well remembered the incessant drone of its engines in my travels east from Albuquerque to Chicago—in those days, flights to East Coast sites had always refueled in Chicago. First-class passengers had been seated at the rear of the aircraft, as far away from the roar of the engines as possible.

The Constellation was fascinating, but I was impatient for the tour of the Martin 404 that was to follow. Descending the steps from the Constellation, I saw the Martin 404 across the hangar and proceeded purposely toward it. I looked intently at the leading edge of the left wing for anything that remotely resembled the wreckage in my photos—but found nothing. I passed under the wing and peered intensely at the tail section as I marched under it—nothing there either. I then turned to direct my gaze along the trailing edge of the left wing at the ailerons and flaps. Walking slowly under it toward its tip, hoping that I would see something, my search again proved fruitless.

I was under the end of the wing when I looked directly up above my head and was astonished to view a twin of the metal that I had found upon the mountainside—the wingtip itself. I went ballistic with excitement and pointed it out to everyone who would listen. Ken Spong and Larry DeCelles's son-in-law, Joe Horvat, were kind enough to take photographs of the wingtip. They both agreed that the wingtip was the incongruous piece of wreckage.

Doubts

Yet, when I returned to Albuquerque, I soon began having serious doubts again. Something was decidedly amiss. The orientation of the piece of wreckage on the wing made no sense to me now, for the prominent aerodynamically sculpted surface (Figure 40) was nowhere in evidence. The photos that Ken and Joe e-mailed me did not help matters at all when I compared them to the ones that Steve Rock and Ken had taken on the mountain. They revealed a slotted vent along one edge that correlated with Ken's museum photo, but the aerodynamically sculpted surface had somehow vanished.

I had not made sense of the piece of wreckage at the crash scene either, for I couldn't understand why a slotted vent should be immediately adjacent to what was apparently a trailing edge of a wing. But in the new photos, the slotted vent structure was clearly an integral part of the wingtip, while the trailing edge had mysteriously been absorbed into the wing itself. Though no longer a protruding object, its straight outline was still evident.

Joe's photo, however, revealed a shadowy line between the wingtip and the aileron that was lying in a neutral position, and I—at last—had the solution to the problem. Had the aileron been extended up or down, the pointed end would clearly have been evident. The pointed, sculpted end was part of the wingtip itself, not the aileron. Similarly pointed wingtips are used on modern Piper Pups.

Slots

But why would any competent aerodynamic engineer have chosen to disrupt the aerodynamic quality of wings by inserting slots into their tips? I considered the possibility that the slots might have something to do with the reduction of wing turbulence, but my research revealed nothing. Then I phoned the Airline History Museum for answers. I was put through to the president, who said that he was not aware of the slotted wingtip, but would put me on hold while he walked out onto the hangar floor to investigate things himself.

After rolling a maintenance platform under the wing and climbing up it, he came back and reported that the slot was there indeed. He didn't know its purpose, but would put me on hold again while he asked someone who did. Two minutes later he informed me that the slot was part of a "hot wing" anti-icing system. Hot air from the engine exhaust was funneled along the leading edges of the wings and then vented out at the wingtips to prevent icing from ever happening. (Deicing systems remove ice after it has formed.) He also explained that air turbulence was not considered to be a problem when Martin 404s were designed.

A ten-minute phone call to the Airline History Museum had thus resolved the mystery of the slotted wing.

Wingtip

Gary Creason had immediately recognized the piece of metal as a wingtip. But why would this lone piece be at the foot of the north cliff when the rest of the wing was found elsewhere? That didn't make sense. But as it turned out, I had been at fault in using common sense to talk him out of his perception.

And how could an experienced pilot like Chris Clark fail to recognize a picture of a wingtip?

That's an easy one. Wingtips are not items that pilots tend to worry about. They don't have moving parts, are not known for malfunctioning or falling off during bumpy landings, and are out of sight at the far end of the wing.

Ah, but why did this wingtip break off and sail over the north cliff when Flight 260 struck the mountain?

That's an easy one too, and I had actually voiced an explanation for it when Gary first tried to convince us that the metal came from a wing. The right wingtip sheared off when the plane met the rock, for it extended up in the air furthest from the point of impact, thus experiencing the greatest amount of torque. The rest of the right wing apparently remained attached to the fuselage, but the tip soared off in the original direction of travel.

Gwen's photo had later made me see the light—literally. But strangely enough, even the knowledge that the plane had impacted on the south face hadn't permeated all of my skull. I still had the notion that the tail section had somehow arrived up at the top from the east instead of the south.

Final Conclusions

But then things began to make sense.

I came to the realization that Phil Goldstein had initially been correct when, sighting along the line from the tail location to the nose location, he measured the approximate magnetic heading of impact as 320 degrees, roughly northwest. (The wreckage distribution was 320 degrees.)

And, surprisingly, he was also correct later when he determined that the plane's fuselage was pointing at an angle of 273 degrees, or roughly west.

These apparently conflicting statements were resolved when I realized that the pilot had spun the plane on its axis while making his climbing turn to escape the mountain. The plane was heading west, but its original momentum kept it moving northwest—much like an ice-skater who spins around but still skids backward.

Impact

When the plane struck the mountain, it was pointed west in a severe— perhaps sixty degree—bank to the left and climbing upward at roughly a forty-five degree angle, parallel to the sloping summit of the pinnacle buttress ahead, while sideslipping northwest in its original direction of travel.

When its left wing struck the south face of the buttress, the left wing and left engine were sheared off by the force of the impact and fell to the base of the south precipice. The undercarriage of the fuselage struck the upper edge of the large rock appearing in the "WORL" photo, while the weakened fuselage above the missing wing disintegrated and peeled off from the undercarriage to come to rest atop the rock, leaving the "WORL" section behind to slide back down to its base—the only major piece of wreckage found there.

The plane thus pancaked onto the top of the buttress while sideslipping northwest instead of moving west, the direction that it was pointed.

The bodies of the pilot and copilot remained near where they initially struck the pinnacle because their seatbelts tethered them to the rigid spine of the aircraft, which stayed reasonably intact. Unbelted passengers, however, continued moving upward to the northwest—thus uphill parallel to the sloping face of the pinnacle and to the right of their original positions inside the aircraft. Those seated on the right would travel further than those on the left, as the right seats were banked higher than ones on the left.

Those near the front of the aircraft—perhaps Mrs. Schoonmaker and Rev. Davis—thus landed uphill and to the right of the pilots. The right engine landed above all of the passengers because it was above and in front of them when it began its free flight.

As the fuselage apparently pancaked onto the sloping top of the pinnacle, the hostess remained near where she initially landed. The massive tail could not wound her because it was not headed her way.

The tail section was still southeast of the rock when the wing struck the south face of the buttress. It was rotated backward over the eastern cliff by the weight of the vertical stabilizer and kept from falling by rudder control cables that were still attached to the rigid spine of the aircraft.

Explosion

An enormous fire must have engulfed the wreck site, but there is no evidence that there was an explosion. Had there been one, wreckage would have been blown in all directions—thus over the southern base of the large rock where only the "WORL" section of the fuselage was found. There is no indication that the left wing caught fire at all.

But what about the twisted strings of metal that remain hanging high in the once-shredded tree to this day?

That's a mystery too. Perhaps it has a solution.

13
Compassion

I remained confused about why victim families could possibly have been grateful for my writing about the crash until clarification began making its entrance in the form of an e-mail from Barb Skudlarick to Ginny shortly after the memorial dedication. Barb had been highly moved by visiting the Flight 260 display at the Albuquerque Sunport.

Barb was a director of the National Air Disaster Alliance/ Foundation (NADA/F), the largest grassroots air safety organization in the United States, representing disaster survivors, those who had lost loved ones, aviation professionals, the traveling public, and others impacted by air disasters worldwide. The purpose of this nonprofit corporation was to "raise the standard of safety, security, survivability, and support through constructive communications with all levels of government, public and private agencies, manufacturers, and industry associations."

Quite a mouthful, but its mission was typified by Barb's actions: she spent three weeks in Washington, D.C., immediately after

September 11, 2001, assisting victims whose loved ones were killed in the attack on the Pentagon.

Barb Skudlarick put Ginny in contact with Carolyn Coarsey, the cofounder and vice president of the Family Assistance Foundation (FAF), vice president of Aviem International, and president of Higher Resources, Inc. Carolyn invited Ginny to share her experiences at the Fifth Annual FAF Conference in Atlanta, one of its purposes being to bring together survivors, aviation and marine industry personnel, mental health specialists, and spiritual care professionals to discuss and improve upon the initial response to major disasters. The overall goal was to mitigate the emotional devastations of such tragedies as major airline crashes, the 9/11 attacks, the subsequent London bombings, and the Indonesia tsunami of 2004.

The mission of FAF is to help organizations around the world—airlines, cruise lines, rail companies, and industrial firms—successfully meet the needs of those affected by large-scale disasters, including customers, employees, victim families, rescuers, and the public at large. Aviem International provides FAF members with logistical support, disaster planning, and response, including emergency call center services, on-site disaster management, and family assistance. Higher Resources, Inc., produces training media, videos, and other materials that are used in conjunction with FAF and Aviem efforts. Carolyn Coarsey founded it when she was a graduate student at the University of New Mexico.

I am indebted to Carolyn for the bulk of the material that follows. Much of it was excerpted from her *Handbook for Human Services Response* and from her PhD dissertation, "Psychological Aftermath of Air Disaster: What Can Be Learned for Training," which was sponsored in part by the Civil Aero-Medical Research Division of the Federal Aeronautics Administration and published by the University of New Mexico.

Carolyn V. Coarsey

Carolyn Coarsey began her professional life in 1972 as a flight attendant with Eastern Airlines in Miami. She encountered her first air disaster soon thereafter, when Eastern Flight 401 crashed in the Florida Everglades and killed 101 people, including two of her fellow flight attendants. Shortly afterward she became a base training instructor, retraining flight attendants to keep their certifications current with

Federal Aviation Administration (FAA) regulations. Several students in her class had just survived that crash.

She was told to hide pictures and pretend that the accident had never happened when flight attendants came to class. Like that of other airlines, Eastern management's philosophy was, as she put it, to "shut them up as soon as possible so that we can forget about it and get on with running an airline."

Unaware of the harmful effects of emotional trauma caused by accidents, management simply wanted the crash to go away, as it was bad for business. As psychological studies had shown that natural disasters had no lasting emotional traumatic impact on survivors, it was logical to assume that airline disasters would also have no lasting impact on their survivors.

Nevertheless, Carolyn felt that "ignoring the enormity of what they had experienced was to dishonor them and their very survival." She did what she was told, however, for she knew that no one meant harm.

Although airline accidents had come to be relatively infrequent by then, airline officials still worried that the public might be discouraged from air travel if accidents were publicized. Accordingly, employees were never to discuss airline crashes with the public—especially since errant words might result in lawsuits from victim family members.

Carolyn was distressed by how little was known about helping employees who had survived the crash. She could only imagine how bad it must have been for the families of the victims.

Unfortunately, she was destined to find out.

In 1977 she was again promoted to work in the airport operation offices—among other things, writing procedures for the 112 airports that the airline served and updating the Passenger Assistance Reference Guide with new policies.

As Eastern Airlines had experienced three major crashes in her five years there, Carolyn was especially interested in learning about the procedures that airport agents were supposed to follow at the time of an accident. To her amazement, she discovered that such procedures did not exist. Her boss explained that airline crashes were such a rarity that airport agents just called Miami, and "we would handle it from there." As there were just four people in her office, she wondered who "we" were.

In 1985 she learned firsthand how little airline and airport employees knew about dealing with the public in the aftermath of a crash. She was meeting her fiancé, Jeff Warner, a former airline employee who was traveling as a passenger aboard Delta Flight 191. He and 136 others were killed when the plane encountered a wind shear, crashed, and struck a car in its final approach to the Dallas/Fort Worth International Airport.

While the rescue and recovery personnel were doing their best to save lives and recover bodies, employees in the airport were behaving as if it were a normal day. Her fiancé's flight was not on the screen, and when she approached the agent at the gate where the flight was supposedly deplaning, he reacted as if he had no idea what flight she was asking about.

She eventually learned that something was amiss when she heard an announcement that passengers who were traveling to Los Angeles on Delta Flight 191 should approach the ticket counter to be rescheduled for a later flight. Her fears were confirmed when she saw the press arriving.

She again approached the ticket agent, who then told her that the flight had crashed. People might go to the hospital to look for survivors; she could get a ride there by going to a room down the hall. She had no desire to enter that room filled with distraught strangers and was pondering other options when another agent came up to her. When Carolyn explained to her about Jeff, the agent abruptly turned away and quickly walked through a door marked "Employees Only."

Carolyn immediately understood what was happening and even had empathy for the Delta employees. She knew that there were caring individuals among them who wanted to help, but simply did not know what to do and were afraid of the consequences if they made a wrong decision.

Indifference in times of tragedy was a better policy than expressing heartfelt sympathy—or so the airline personnel believed.

The next day a counseling psychologist and close friend called to console her and, with the best of intentions, lectured her on grief, telling her that she was in shock and implying that she perhaps would have more pain in the future than she was already experiencing—a fearsome prospect, indeed. Thus began the first of a series of well-intended yet distressful comments and gestures from kindly people who wanted to help, but didn't know how.

Carolyn set about delving into the subject of grief so that she could help others in similar circumstances and train colleagues to do the same. Surely there must be some easily understood, practical concepts that would be useful in educating frontline disaster response helpers to support survivors in their first hours of grief.

She enrolled at the University of New Mexico and began studies toward a PhD, discovering that academia was reticent about supplying her needs. Death, grief, and mourning were presented as purely cognitive, intellectual processes. Her classes were devoid of discussions that would tell her how to approach a grief-stricken person without inflicting additional emotional wounds; and she was disappointed when faculty voiced professional opinions that did not mesh with her own experiences. A highly regarded psychologist flatly stated that mourning lasted about six months. He obviously did not understand that grief didn't work that way. Others ventured comments indicating that they did not understand that she was addressing important real-world problems. "Why don't you ask the airline people what they are doing, and do that?" "Why don't they just remove the frontline employees and replace them with counselors who know what to do?"

But then she discovered a counseling psychologist, Dr. Joan Guntzelman, PhD, who also taught at the medical school. She used a more empathetic approach to grief, thereby validating Carolyn's belief that there was something besides the typical methods being taught in the classrooms. A softer, less clinical approach might do far better.

Beginning to see the vast differences between clinical counseling and the immediate human service support required at the time of disasters, Carolyn started to formulate her own ideas about how to train helpers. And she came to the realization that grief experiences were unique to the individual.

Grief had no timetable and no predictable pattern of events.

She began interviewing crash survivors to determine how the behavior of airline and airport employees following a disaster had impacted their lives. What had worked? What had failed? Was there some pattern of experiences that could be exploited to improve matters?

Travails of an "Uninjured" Survivor

Carolyn's interview with a forty-one-year-old international marketing executive revealed how badly things could go wrong. (To preserve his anonymity, Carolyn did not reveal either his identity or the circumstances of the accident.) His flight had crashed during landing at a large airport in the early evening, causing fatalities and numerous injuries. Airport authorities had concentrated their limited resources on caring for the injured and in the interest of efficiency had instructed uninjured passengers—including the wet and disheveled marketing executive—to walk a short distance to the airport terminal building immediately after the accident. He had survived a crash, apparently unscathed, and had accompanied other passengers to the terminal immediately after the accident, waiting fifteen to twenty minutes for airline employees to arrive and provide coffee and blankets. The mayor of the city and news crews also appeared, then medical personnel who offered telephones.

He was taken to a hospital, where he was admitted but somehow overlooked. After waiting several hours in wet clothes and no shoes or socks, he identified himself as a crash survivor. The hospital employees duly apologized for having forgotten him and gave him a brief physical examination. An airline employee then told him to take a cab to a hotel where he could shower and make arrangements to fly home. As his clothes remained too wet to wear, airline employees provided him with a sweatshirt and size 38 slacks, even though his waist size was 34.

Clean but still bereft of footwear, he returned to the airline terminal. There he was provided a free breakfast, which he could not eat, as he was in a state of shock.

Airline representatives then phoned and told him to take a shuttle bus to the airline office at the airport. Unable to find the office, barefoot, and holding his pants up, he stumbled into an airline pilots' check-in lounge, where he was immediately assisted by both employees and pilots. They determined he was a survivor of their company's accident the previous night, supplied him with shoes and pants that fit, and insisted that he relax on a sofa until time for his flight.

No one escorted him to his flight, however, and a security guard stopped him and asked for identification—which he didn't have, because he had lost his wallet. Somehow he cleared security, but then he boarded the wrong flight. He got off and successfully managed to board the correct one on his next try, finally returning home without further ado.

The following evening, he collapsed. A physician living nearby recognized the symptoms as stress and recommended immediate medical care.

Under psychiatric care, taking sleeping pills and medication for his emotional state as well as medication to help him subdue his newly acquired fear of flying, he continued his job as a marketing executive. His wife accompanied him on trips for a year in the hope that her presence would help him return to normality, but to no avail. He was forced to resign his position and start his own business where flying would be at a minimum.

Despite having been a well-paid executive throughout his career, he had to tell his son that he could not attend the college of his choice, as his income had gone down by fifty percent. His medical bills, including psychiatric treatment, were covered for one year only, but after that he was still bothered by nightmares, flashbacks, and depression. After settling with the airline's insurance company, he stopped the psychiatric care, as he could no longer afford it.

He could no longer obtain affordable medical insurance because he had seen a psychiatrist following the crash.

This passenger had voluntarily relinquished control of his personal safety to the airline when he first stepped aboard the plane—a simple act that he had done many times before and a mandatory one in order for him to earn a good living in international marketing. This time, however, things had gone woefully wrong. The plane had crashed, and part of his trust in his stable, predictable world had crumbled with it. His memory of the chaotic sights, sounds, smells, and terrors that accompanied his escape had been distressingly vivid while he walked to the airline terminal with the other passengers, but he trusted that his intense emotional state would wane once he entered its orderly world. His sense of equilibrium would be restored in that safe haven.

Only the orderly world of that safe haven turned out to be a malevolent mirage—a bewildering assembly of incongruous events that assailed him at every turn.

It wasn't that the airport, airline, and hospital employees were indifferent or unkind. They saw things from a different perspective.

Airliner crashes were not routine events, and few airport and airline employees had ever experienced the turmoil that accompanied them. Safety was of immediate concern for the airport personnel: the prevention of subsequent accidents and collateral damage. Rescue and firefighting crews were at the scene saving lives, containing and putting out fires, preventing others from starting, directing incoming and outgoing flights away from the wreckage, keeping the public out of harm's way, and expeditiously getting medical care to the seriously injured.

Survivors with lesser injuries might be wet or cold or untidy, but they were alive and could be attended to with far less urgency. Their arrival at the terminal—their condition and number—had neither been predicted nor planned for. They were purposely isolated from the public (as well as from their kin) to preserve some measure of decorum. But they were not isolated from the mayor or the press, as doing so might disrupt good public relations. Though unexpected, in the case of the marketing executive who survived the crash, the visit of those notables had been appropriately handled by experienced public relations personnel.

Treating survivors of major disasters was not routine for hospitals either, and an avalanche of patients in the middle of the night would have severely tested the best of well-planned organizations and necessitated triage considerations so that patients would be prioritized on the basis of the severity of their wounds.

The airport employees may well have regarded the marketing executive as having survived the crash with flying colors. His clothes were wet, and he was disheveled, but he probably didn't appear worse off than his fellow survivors. He may not have complained about his condition, perhaps providing contrition for others who did. The blankets and coffee were late arriving, but that was a matter of organizational priorities. The airport personnel used triagelike considerations to dole out their limited services to those who most needed them.

He was low man on the totem pole to the hospital employees, because he obviously didn't need the medical treatment that others did. Newly arriving automobile accident victims may well have bumped him down the list. Delaying his examination was not a life-threatening decision either, nor was the matter of inadequate clothing.

And the airline employees had treated him with courtesy, as they would any passenger. He was a seasoned traveler and could easily fend for himself if they provided the necessary instructions.

The environment of the pilots' check-in lounge was different, however, as pilots had a special awareness of air crashes—perhaps knowing crew members of the flight the marketing executive had been aboard. They furnished him with appropriate clothing and cautioned him to rest on a couch. Yet they failed to recognize that he might require personal assistance in boarding his continuing flight.

The marketing executive's perspective was utterly different, however. He had boarded the plane thoroughly confident in both his own abilities and those of the airlines that had served him well over the years. Though thankful that he was physically intact, part of his confidence had been shattered by the crash—a brief, terrifying experience that would be one of the most important events of his life. Every action of his body and mind then had been focused on survival—getting himself out of harm's way.

Matters would be far easier once he was in the safety of the terminal building; and he had no qualms about entrusting the airport with his own care. They had earned his trust in the past, and they could be trusted now.

But then they failed him when he needed them the most. There were inexplicable foul-ups, and the airport personnel, at best, treated him as they would any other passenger. But he wasn't just another passenger. He may not have looked it, but he was dazed and befuddled; and his attention was still focused on the tragedy that he had just endured. He might not have needed coddling, but he couldn't be expected to solve all of the simple problems that might arise in the tasks that they set before him.

And each failure stripped from him some measure of self-confidence, as well as his confidence in the airline system.

What survivors needed immediately after a traumatic experience were often simple things: food, transportation, lodging, toiletries, and help dealing with officialdom, locating missing baggage, seeing that the kids were picked up at school, and getting the cat fed at home. Their well-ordered worlds had to some degree been shattered by the disaster, and they would gain back control of their lives by different mechanisms. Overcoming bewilderment, panic, fear, anxiety, and loss of confidence would be of high priority now and would be greatly affected by the competence of those who first responded to their needs.

And, incredible as it may seem, these first-response helpers would also prove to be of immense value to both the airline and the airline industry by being the first line of defense against unwanted lawsuits and public enmity. Survivors and surviving family members tended to forgive airline errors if they believed the organization was truly caring. To err was human, and organizations were composed of humans.

Any act of apparent callousness or neglect, however, could easily turn that benevolence into unreasoning, lingering hate and result in lawsuits that benefited neither party.

Carolyn interviewed a surprising number of successful litigants who felt degraded by their legal experiences. They hated the legal process, and materially benefiting from the death of their loved ones gave them little solace.

Those who hate are doomed to domination by that which they detest. Those who forgive may live lives unfettered by the past.

Survivors complained that lawyers were everywhere, even in hospital waiting rooms, memorial services, and funerals, telling them that they would protect their interests against the airline, asking them to sign documents before it was too late, offering to help with funeral arrangements even when they had scant knowledge of the process. Their presence was usually undesirable and greatly exacerbated the emotional trauma that survivors were suffering.

Carolyn also learned that survivors wanted some measure of control of the supposedly benevolent acts of officialdom. Some wanted to visit the crash scene; some did not. Some wished to view the remains of what was left of their loved ones—though officials believed doing so would be too traumatic. A sister wanted a tattered piece of garment worn by her mother; her brother wanted no memento at all.

There was no pattern to these desires except that they were integral components of the emotional healing process. Survivors wanted facts, but not necessarily all of the facts about what had happened to their loved ones. When they asked specific questions they expected truthful, specific answers—but never false hopes or suppositions. Even if the facts were grim, they wanted to hear them. They were prepared to accept the truth if it were known. Giving them less—or more—was not acceptable.

If death of a loved one was not instantaneous, they still wanted a straight answer. Surprisingly, a grieving mother who asked about whether her child had suffered received some measure of solace by hearing the awful truth; less might easily have lead to future embitterment and disillusionment if she had later learned otherwise.

Coming to terms with a tragedy or loss was never a guarantee, but the truth did set some free.

Testimonies of those interviewed by Carolyn also revealed that airline companies would do well by immediately involving themselves directly with both crash survivors and family members to express concern and sorrow that the accident had occurred.

When the president of an airline personally called to say, "I'm here to let you know what happened and to see your family through this," families felt connected to the company and could see that it had not been the firm's intention to harm them. There would be legal settlements and insurance payments with any disaster, but when representatives from the company approached families with acknowledgment and support, they typically did not look for a fight in court. Family members still had to work through emotional pain and loss, but they didn't have the additional burden of anger and resentment towards the airline.

Carolyn also learned that the duties of initial-response disaster care teams were best handled by uncredentialed volunteers who chose to be there because of compassion, as opposed to professionals licensed to practice. Grief-stricken family members were especially receptive to the presence of caring strangers who had themselves lost loved ones in similar tragedies. Their consoling words were often not even needed; their mere presence was sufficient.

In Carolyn's words, "We don't have to farm out the job of dealing with the public to people with MDs and PhDs. When customers and the employees see the humanity of the company—as opposed to viewing it as a perpetrator—that makes all the difference."

The problem with professional grief counselors was that they too often felt the need to speak, when empathetic silence would do far better.

Indeed, in many instances a disaster care volunteer could ease the emotional wounds of a grief-stricken family member by merely listening to what the other wanted to say—the volunteer listening attentively, yet quietly, while the other spoke at length.

Empathy and sympathy are best conjoined to promote emotional healing.

Carolyn believes that grief is not a psychosis. It is a natural human response to tragedy and is best treated by the quiet sympathy of caring people who respond naturally from the heart, not by professional counselors who are trained to speak carefully scripted phrases.

Closure is a business term, well suited for the finality of contracts and business agreements, but ill suited to matters of grief. Grief does not come to termination in any predictable fashion. It may stop suddenly for seemingly inconsequential reasons; it may fade with time; it may continue unabated; or it may never happen in the first place, a phenomenon far too often attributed to callousness on the part of supposedly uncaring kin, when in fact they may have cared greatly for their loved ones, but were able to accept the reality and finality of death.

Carolyn does not believe that grief will out. "Grief becomes our teacher and—if properly integrated—can be the call to consciousness that guides our lives forever. It is the adjustment to grief—not its finality—that we are looking for. Forgetting is not only impossible, but unhealthy."

In 1991 Carolyn participated on a task force with the American Hospital Association, writing guidelines for handling mass transportation disaster. She was awarded her PhD in 1992; her dissertation was one of the first epidemiological studies of air disaster survivors.

The National Air Disaster Alliance/Foundation

In October of that year, the International Air Disaster Group Conference met for the first time in Washington, D.C., leading to the charter meeting of the National Air Disaster Alliance/Foundation (NADA/F) on June 8, 1995, in Pittsburgh, Pennsylvania. Family members from USAir Flight 427, which had crashed in Pittsburgh on September 8, 1994, were most active in this, and had influence with Pennsylvania Congressman Bud Shuster, chair of the House Transportation Committee, who proved helpful in passing the legislation that would follow the next year. Soon thereafter, on June 20, NADA/F founding members met with National Traffic Safety Board Chairman Jim Hall and Department of Transportation Secretary Frederico Peña to present fourteen issues and recommendations on family needs following disasters. (NTSB was the successor to the CAB.) On August 2 aircraft disaster families met with Chairman Hall, Secretary Peña, ten major airlines, the Air Transportation Association, Amtrak, and the International Claims and Litigation Management Group (ICALM) and presented issues and recommendations concerning family needs following disasters. Their stated mission was "to raise the standard of safety, security, and survivability for aviation passengers and to support survivors and victims' families."

Issues raised by airline disaster family members at a hearing held on June 19, 1996, by the Congressional Subcommittee on Aviation included horror stories of the inappropriate behavior of lawyers approaching families of victims immediately after the crash of ValueJet

Flight 592 in the Florida Everglades earlier that year, in May. Lawyers in Florida were characterized as overzealous attorneys who relentlessly pursued grieving relatives of crash victims. After employees from one law firm handed out business cards in the hotel lobby where family members were staying—as well as before and after a memorial service at the Everglades crash site—some relatives requested an injunction against them.

They also spoke about insensitively impersonal messages left on answering machines after accidents. "This is Pan Am calling. Your daughter Diane was on Pan Am Flight 103. The plane went down over Scotland. There were no survivors. If you have any questions, you may call us."

And there were stories of the careless treatment of victim remains and belongings. After an accident near Pittsburgh, some families claimed that thirty-eight caskets of unidentified human remains were buried without their knowledge the day before a special service was held where only two caskets containing unidentified human remains were shown. An airline spokesman said at the time that the airline did not tell relatives about the thirty-eight caskets unless they asked because it thought the knowledge would be too distressing. Some families considered the airline's attempt to protect them both unnecessary and deceitful.

Six months after the accident, relatives of those who died aboard U.S. Airways Flight 427 near Pittsburgh found some of the personal belongings of their loved ones in a trash bin outside the hangar where the wreckage of the plane was stored. They discovered rings, watches, jewelry, personal planners, address books, wallets, and other things that were important to the families. These belongings were in poor condition, as they had been lying in the mud in a dumpster for half a year.

Seemingly benign negligence had also caused considerable distress. A family had called a hotline number when they heard about a crash, but did not get any information until the next morning, when they learned that their son was indeed a passenger. The responder offered to report back every fifteen minutes with additional information, but never called back again.

The Aviation Disaster Family Assistance Act of 1996 became law on October 9, 1996. The act established a task force of representatives of the NTSB, the Department of Transportation, the Federal Emergency Management Agency, the American Red Cross, air carriers, and families who had been involved in aircraft accidents. Its duties were to examine the legal and social issues related to aviation accidents in order to create guidelines and make recommendations to assist air carriers and other agencies in responding to aircraft accidents.

Carolyn was not involved in these activities, as she was doing a study funded by the FAA and NTSB that looked at crash investigator stress. Many of the survivors in her research were, however, and their participation is what drove the law home.

The Aviation Disaster Family Assistance Act

This law codified what many airlines already wanted to do and prevented local laws from interfering with their efforts. They had willingly cooperated with the congressional efforts to draft a law that would address the needs of passenger families, establishing common practices for the airline industry. Foreign governments would soon follow and adopt legislation based upon the act, thereby making it applicable around the world.

The task force had proffered guidelines for the initial notification of family members by air carriers in the immediate aftermath of air disasters, requiring that family members be briefed about the accident, its causes, and any other findings of the investigation, as well as individually informed of and allowed to attend any public hearings and meetings of the NTSB about the accident. The law applied to families of all those aboard the plane—both passengers and crew—as well as to families of victims on the ground.

The news media were to alert the public when an airliner had crashed and inform them of a toll-free phone number they could call to ascertain whether a family member might have been aboard; each air carrier was required to establish a toll-free call center for that purpose. The call center would be provided with a list of the names of individuals (including crew members) aboard the plane, but the news media and general public would not.

Callers who inquired about specific individuals who were on the list were to be connected to another call center responsible for establishing communications with victim family members and friends. (As the passenger and crew member manifest might initially be in error or incomplete, liberal allowances were made for misspelled or mispronounced names. The airline would not be liable for damages arising out of the preparation or provision of that list.) A database for each family would be established, and family members were assigned to specific care-team members accessible round the clock via toll-free numbers.

Air carriers were also required to assist family members with travel to accident sites and memorial services, providing such physical care as lodging and meals.

Major air carriers had already adopted plans to ensure that family member travel should not be delayed by full flights or requirements to fly on a particular airline; other carriers would voluntarily assist with travel. As *family member* was not rigidly defined, close friends or companions need not meet legal definitions of *next of kin*. Air carriers were advised to be liberal in their interpretation of the term. The U.S. State Department would provide special facilities for family members who did not have passports or visas so they could obtain them quickly.

The act also stipulated that "nothing may be construed as limiting the actions that an air carrier may take, or obligations that an air carrier may have, in providing assistance to the families of passengers involved in an aircraft accident."

An NTSB employee would be designated as the director of family support services for each accident—the point of contact within the government for the families and a liaison between the airline and the families. An organization (currently the Red Cross) would coordinate victims' families' concerns. As with natural disasters, the Red Cross could quickly mobilize and have an immediate response team to deal with victims' families.

The privacy of victim families was also protected. Other than the media releases by the airline on the progress of family notification and the release of passenger names, all media inquiries and releases concerning family support operations would be referred to the NTSB family support public affairs officer, with the NTSB advising and assisting local medical examiners on any media affairs in their areas of responsibility. There were no restrictions, however, on victims or family members meeting with the media if they so desired.

Victim families were also protected from voracious lawyers. The act prohibited attorneys from unsolicited contact with families for forty-five days after the accident.

The act addressed the issue of the return of personal effects to the family members by the airline. Family members were to be consulted about the disposition of all human remains and personal effects. And each family would be consulted concerning the construction of any monument and its inscription.

Furthermore, air carriers were required to provide adequate training for their employees and agents to meet the needs of survivors and family members following accidents. The Task Force recommended that airline training programs use survivors and family members to share their personal experiences either in person or on videotape during the training process.

Congress also addressed the need for volunteers when it later amended portions of the Family Assistance Act, adding language prohibiting state or political subdivisions from preventing employees or volunteers from providing mental health and counseling services within a thirty-day period after an accident. The designated director of family support services might extend that period an additional thirty days if deemed necessary for meeting family needs.

Congress also adopted the European Union Council regulation in 1997 that required their member airlines to compensate air disaster family members within fifteen days after the identity of the deceased was established. Advance payments were to be made to meet immediate economic needs—proportional to the hardship suffered—but the minimum payment would not be less than twenty thousand dollars.

The success of this act has been phenomenal. Major airlines around the world have adopted these policies, as have cruise ship companies and smaller airlines, though they were not required by statute to do so. All major airline disasters are now subject to the regulations, and their victims have benefited accordingly.

Airports, competing airlines, governmental bodies, and metropolitan districts now work in concert using tenets of gracious human kindness in attempts to salve the emotional wounds left by mass disasters.

Unfortunately, however, all provisions of the act did not pertain to the 9/11 terrorist attacks, for the 9/11 deaths were deemed to be the result of military actions, not of airline disasters. The family members of its victims were not treated well initially, and they instigated a multitude of lawsuits, as well as suffering bitterness and grief. The 1996 act also influenced the passage of the Foreign Air Carrier Family Support Act of 1997 and the Rail Passenger Disaster Family Assistance Act of 2001.

Air Safety

Nor do the acts address air safety issues, as only the Federal Aeronautics Administration—not Congress—has authorization to enact air safety regulations. The FAA subjects each recommendation sent to it by the NTSB to a cost-benefit analysis, attempting to estimate the number of disasters that would be prevented by the regulation, the number of lives saved thereby, and such associated costs as the plane and litigated payouts.

Subjecting lifesaving regulations to cost-benefit analyses may seem crassly materialistic, but the purpose is to avoid prohibitively expensive air travel. We can never hope to devise regulations that will eradicate the possibility of air disasters, but commercial air travel is remarkably safe and inexpensive. Even in 1955, far more pilots were killed in automobile accidents than in plane crashes.

As Carolyn has explained to me, however, mere laws are never enough: "As the Dalai Lama teaches, law can never create compassion." Nor can it create the knowledge of what to do—and what not to do—to avoid further wounding emotionally traumatized victims.

Caring and knowledgeable humans can, indeed, work their magic to conquer the lingering grief of human tragedy.

14
Rescuers

Frank C. Hibben

Frank C. Hibben, professor of anthropology at the University of New Mexico, was the leader of the first TWA Flight 260 recovery expedition. He was also a noted archeologist, author, outdoor adventurer, big-game hunter, and philanthropist.

Earning an archeology degree from Princeton in 1933, he journeyed to New Mexico on an expedition to collect small mammals and birds for the Cleveland Museum of Natural History. Fascinated by the Native American cliff dwellings, he decided to attend graduate school at UNM and make New Mexico his home. He earned his master's degree in zoology in 1936 with a thesis on mountain lions. He then left UNM to study for a PhD in archeology at Harvard. He astonished everyone by completing the task in only one year. Later he explained, "I had to do it in one year. If I didn't come back to UNM in a year, I lost my job."

Shortly after returning to New Mexico, he excavated Sandia Cave, where he unearthed fragments of a Pleistocene mammoth along with a few ancient flint spearheads that he estimated dated back to 9000 to 8000 BCE. As a result he coined the concept of Sandia Man, which proved controversial because many professional archeologists doubted the validity of his research.

During World War II, Hibben served as a naval officer and aide to Admiral Foy (conceivably A. J. Foy, skipper of the battle-ship *Oklahoma*, sunk at Pearl Harbor) of the Joint Chiefs of Staff in Washington, D.C., and was awarded the Legion of Merit for his efforts. His duties were to memorize battle plans and repeat them verbatim to commanding officers in the various war theaters. His plane was shot down by a German submarine, and he carried shrapnel in his body until his death.

Following the war, he did field studies of Chaco Canyon in New Mexico, and beginning in 1946 he made a number of trips to Africa for archeological field research, including work with Louis and Mary Leakey in their discoveries of the earliest human remains. He later made secret U.S. State Department missions at the behest of his friend, President Richard Nixon, who offered to name him undersec-retary for African affairs.

Hibben devoted much of his time to creating a museum of anthropology at UNM. And he persuaded a friend, Gil Maxwell—discoverer of the San Juan oil field in northwestern New Mexico—to donate 50,000 shares of Occidental Petroleum stock, along with a collection of Navajo rugs, to the university. This was the beginning of the university's Maxwell Museum of Anthropology, where Hibben served as director from 1961 to 1971.

Figure 43. Rescuer Frank Hibben with chimpanzee art and hunting trophies. (By permission of the Maxwell Museum of Anthropology.)

He also established himself as a world-renowned big-game hunter, setting numerous world records and receiving the Weath-erby Hunting and Conservation Award in 1964. As chairman of the Albuquerque Zoological

Board, director of the Albuquerque Zoo, and chairman of the New Mexico State Game and Fish Commission, he was instrumental in introducing numerous exotic species into the wilds of New Mexico.

In 1996 he donated his own residence to be used as the future site of the Hibben Center for Archeological Research, and in October 2004 U.S. Senator Pete Domenici sponsored and passed a bill providing federal funds to complete the center. Hibben had earlier donated four million dollars of his own funds.

His books included *The Lost Americans* (1946), *Treasure in the Dust* (1951), *Prehistoric Man in Europe* (1958), *Digging Up America* (1960), *Hunting in Africa* (1962), *Kiva Art of the Anasazi* (1975), and a series of limited editions, of which the most recent was *Under the African Sun* (1999). His articles appeared in the *Saturday Evening Post, Reader's Digest, Field and Stream, Outdoor Life*, the *Denver Post, Empire*, and many sporting magazines and professional periodicals.

Artists

On a lighter note, I remember that he also entered several paintings into a modern art competition held at the New Mexico State Fair in the early 1960s. The contest officials objected, however, when they learned that the artists were chimpanzees. Hibben responded that entry rules did not specify the artists had to be human. The officials agreed, but pointed out that the rules did require the artists be over the age of twenty-one.

Being chairman of the Albuquerque Zoological Board gave him clout with his artists but not with the art committee.

I am pleased to report that the chimpanzee masterpiece shown in Figure 43 is now mounted of the wall of the director's office of the Maxwell Museum of Anthropology.

Dr. Hibben died in 2002 at the age of ninety-two.

George D. Hankins

George Hankins, the leader of our mountain club rescue team, was an ageless, dynamic, serene, and quiet man who had his own beliefs about how things ought to be and lived his life accordingly. His physical endurance seemed boundless, and I remember climbing trips to Colorado in which the rest of us eagerly hit the sack at the end of the long day, only to learn the next morning that George had spent most of the night sitting awake by the campfire, thinking things out.

George was born and raised in Delaware County near Muncie, Indiana, and had been earning a good living as a machinist in 1945, near the end of World War II, when he and his family abruptly decided to move to Albuquerque. They had never been there before, but hoped that the dry climate might help his wife, Villa, with her acute and recurring sinusitis.

In Indiana George had been having problems with the CIO labor union that he had belonged to for seven years. He had gone to a union meeting in which the speaker told the members for whom to vote and roused them to vote for a strike. The union blackballed him from future jobs when George refused to comply with the strike order.

He learned that the Warner Gear Company (later Borg Warner) was not a closed shop and that he could work any shift that he could get in. Although he went to each of three shifts a day for three months, union guards barred his entry, and he got into work only once. When he came out, they threw his toolbox into the river with the threat that he would be next. His picture was on the front page of the local newspaper, captioned "One-Man Strike Against the Union."

When his wife, Villa, became frightened by the turmoil and admonished him that one man could not change the world, George replied, "Jesus did." When she countered, "I hope you don't think you are another Jesus," he rejoined, "No, but I'm an adult, free American, and no one has the right to tell me how to vote."

His opposition to the union could have cost him his life, and he could no longer earn his living as a machinist.

Villa Mae Hankins

Villa Mae Hankins graduated from Ball State Teachers College in June 1945 with a major in English and minors in chemistry and library science—the latter mandatory, as English teachers were also in charge of libraries. As all of the local jobs were held by tenured teachers, she applied to the Arizona school system, but discovered that they would hire only single women; so she settled on New Mexico and Albuquerque because she might also work toward a master's degree at the university there. (The New Mexico school system would not have hired her had she been divorced.)

Train Trip to Albuquerque

They sold their house, taking a personal note for the last five hundred dollars—which they never received—then sold the cows and everything else that they could. George, who stayed in Muncie to settle up the sale, took Villa and their three daughters to the train station for their trip to Albuquerque.

The train trip was the first one for the girls. They had packed their bedclothes, curtains, a new set of dishes, and surplus clothing into a large wooden box and shipped it by freight. Each of the girls had her clothes in a small suitcase, and each carried her wrap. Villa, forgetting hers, had to use a doll's blanket.

They ate breakfast in the dining car because Villa wanted the girls to have that experience; the oatmeal, toast and jelly, and milk were the cheapest items on the menu at 85 cents each. The train was old, and the coaches smelled of urine. It was full of soldiers who helped keep the girls entertained; and they were glad for handouts from the country food basket that Villa had packed. The girls had coloring books, crayons, and a doll, and one of the girls, Ethel, had brought her violin, as Villa wanted her to keep up with her music studies.

They had to change trains at Kansas City at midnight, but the girls behaved well, except for vying for attention. As they got into New Mexico and began seeing small adobe houses from the windows, the middle daughter, Jo, kept saying, "I don't want to live in a mud house. I want to go back to our nice big brick house. When I get enough, I'm going to buy it back."

Albuquerque

They had left Muncie at 4:00 p.m. Saturday and arrived in Albuquerque at 1:00 p.m. two days later, on Labor Day, to discover that they could find no place to stay. The war had just ended, and all the soldiers from both the Sandia and Kirtland bases had brought in their wives and sweethearts. Villa couldn't find a room—not at the YWCA, the YMCA, nor any of the hotels.

She didn't know anyone, but her minister in Muncie had given her the address of a small church on North Second Street. The minister, a Mr. Mills, answered her call from the train station, explained that he was busy helping build the bell tower on the church, and handed the phone to his wife.

Villa said that she was "a Christian in distress" with three young girls and had come to work in Albuquerque but couldn't even find a place to spend the night. Mrs. Mills promptly replied, "Stay where you are, and I'll come for you."

She took them back to the church, where they were living in one side. The church had been a saloon and dance hall a few years before. When Mr. and Mrs. Mills asked, "What can we do for you?" Villa answered that they needed a bath, rest, and food, in that order; these were graciously supplied. Villa phoned a hospital and got a job, which she was told she could start the next day or whenever she wanted.

The Millses took them by car to search for a room and found one at a second-rate hotel with a double bed that had just been vacated. They took it, and Villa and her three girls all slept crosswise on the bed. The next day, the manager said he had a room with two beds for ten dollars a day. They stayed ten days.

Villa went to work as a nurse at Presbyterian Hospital, leaving the girls in the hotel. (She was a licensed nurse, and nurses were in more demand than teachers at that time.) When Villa got off work, she took the children to a grocery to get some food, which they ate in a nearby park; then they walked around town until bedtime. Like other newcomers, they were sleepy all of the time because of the mile-high altitude.

Villa thought Albuquerque was the cleanest, most beautiful town she had ever seen. And she was thrilled by the Sandia Mountains.

Christmas

A beautiful snow fell on Christmas Eve, and a friend drove Villa and the children around the streets to see the *luminarias*—little sacks with lit candles glowing from within. Returning home, they found that George and his brother Harvey had arrived cold and hungry. They had driven a one-and-a-half-ton Willys truck loaded with books and tools, including a metal lathe. George had just started to shave and had his face covered with lather, when he delivered the best and wettest kiss that she had ever had. It was to be a most delightful Christmas for them all.

A New Home

Villa had had two jobs and had bought two houses in the three months before George arrived; she had been especially pleased when she sold the first house back to its previous owner for its original price. And George was delighted with their new place—a two-bedroom, modern frame stucco house costing $7,950 and including three good-sized lots, two of them orchards planted with fourteen cherry trees and two each of peach, apricot, and apple. The first summer they allowed customers to pick their own cherries for eight cents a pound, netting $145; they canned and preserved the rest. They planted a garden in the other lot.

She discovered that her vocation was to be a nurse. Teaching jobs were hard to come by, but experienced nurses were always in demand.

They were paying for an irrigation system, but they soon discovered that poor water management—along with alfalfa farmers upstream—kept them from getting it when they needed it. George dug a well and rigged it with an electric pump for irrigation. Several physics majors at the university somehow learned of it, came by to see it, and declared, "It won't work" when he explained it to them—whereupon he started it up to show them that it was indeed pumping water.

He gradually perfected his irrigation system: digging ditches lined with halves of cement blocks, later laying plastic pipe in them with holes drilled about foot apart, making a gauge to determine the amount of moisture in the ground, and installing an automatic switch to turn on the pump. Commercial farmers had yet to employ such modern technology, but George was figuring it out ahead of them.

George took the matriculation examination at the university but never enrolled, as he was too busy inventing. He had started to invent a potato chip machine before he married; and when the cherries ripened and she wished him to help with the seeding, he invented a cherry seeder that worked, but not as efficiently as Villa's fingers.

Ham Radio

George set up a ham radio and learned Morse code; then he joined a radio club that met once a week, where the men discussed equipment and the people whom they had radioed. Villa enjoyed the times he took her. Through it, he got a job helping one of the men start a radio repair shop. Paid sixty cents an hour, he said no one was worth that much. He liked the work because he could do things his way. As their neighbor once explained, "There used to be two ways of doing things: the right way and the army way; now there is also the George Hankins way."

Finances

They had a joint bank account and rarely argued over money. He wanted her to keep a strict account of every cent, as he would do all of his life—even the purchase of a five-cent candy bar was written down. She refused but settled for keeping the bank account straight and paying the household expenses. House payments were forty-five dollars a month, and there were charges for utilities, improvements, and other expenses. They had a fireplace—in Villa's words, she "had bought the fireplace and there just happened to be a house attached." George kept it supplied with wood from their trees that had died of old age.

When they were asked for a loan by their children or friends, they would decide if they could or wanted to give it to them, not expecting to have it repaid. Sometimes it was, sometimes it wasn't; no conflicts. But the one rule that he was adamant about was no credit purchases. Once she bought a record player and six double records of religious music and Bible readings for a hundred dollars, to be paid for in three monthly installments. He was so angry that he wouldn't communicate with her for two weeks. She told him he was acting like a child and ignored him. But she never bought anything else on credit.

The Old Man of the Mountains

George joined the New Mexico Mountain Club and climbed and explored the mountains each weekend and often rescued lost persons. He enjoyed leading groups, especially the Boy Scouts, up the trails. He guided the investigating crew that filmed the 1962 movie *Lonely Are the Brave*, starring Kirk Douglas and Walter Matthau. His boundless energy had earned him the title the Old Man of the Mountains.

Inventions

He enjoyed tinkering in the machine shop in his garage, where he was perfecting the mechanical calculator that he had invented. He later designed and constructed a rescue litter for the Albuquerque Mountain Rescue Council. Fabricated from lightweight aluminum tubing, it was segmented into two parts, each being equipped with its own set of shoulder straps that enabled it to be it to be carried to rescue sites as a pack board. He patented it and sold the rights—apparently to the army—for an undisclosed sum. During a 1963 Associated

Press interview, he described fifteen major rescue operations that he had participated in.

His efforts as an inventor prompted him to begin a diary that meticulously recorded his thoughts and his activities each day—hence his ability to provide the detailed information about the initial Flight 260 search-and-rescue efforts that I have already quoted. His diary consisted of an incredible seventeen thousand index cards, carefully cross-indexed so that entries about important events could be readily accessed.

George became a ground rescue officer and squadron commander for the Civil Air Patrol, in charge of a mobile command center based in a bus that he had converted for the job and usually kept parked in his driveway. George outfitted the bus with a radio system so that ground search teams could be contacted via walkie-talkie.

Hiking with Jo

When he was in his late sixties in May 1964, he and his daughter Jo headed up the La Luz Trail and down the road on the other side of the mountain on a backpacking trek to visit the old homestead and his daughter Ethel's family in Muncie, Indiana. (His third daughter, George Ann, was working in Council Bluffs, Iowa, at the time, but Villa stayed home alone.) Things proceeded well while Jo accompanied him; but after she dropped out in Rolla, Kansas, the police in a nearby town tried to put George in jail because his long hair made him look like a bum. He solved the problem by showing them newspaper clippings about his ventures. Nevertheless, they thought he might frighten the local citizenry and drove him through town to drop him off on the other side. Word of his presence spread rapidly to neighboring towns, where police met him at the town limits and chauffeured him through their territories.

The weather turned bad, and incessant rain soaked George's diary, preventing him from keeping his customary meticulous records of his journey. He wasn't accomplishing what he had set out to do, so he called it quits at Ellinwood, Kansas, and hopped a bus back to Albuquerque.

Paintings done by Jo were featured in the *Albuquerque Journal* upon her return home.

Jo summed up her trip with her father: "All I can say about the walk with Daddy is that it was a private time to be together—we walked silently but with much communication."

George died in Albuquerque in 1974 at the age of seventy-six.

Eugene Szerlip, MD

I first met Dr. Eugene Szerlip atop the wreck pinnacle on the morning following his frigid night upon the mountain after the wreckage was discovered. He later became a critical player in the founding of the Albuquerque Mountain Rescue Council.

Gene was a huge and intimidating, six-foot-four, 220-pound man, but warm, friendly, and exceedingly kind. An orthopedic surgeon, he described himself as a "carpenter of sorts," yet was on call for emergencies at any time of day or night, flying his own plane to such distant New Mexico towns as Tucumcari and Grants to help out local physicians with difficult surgeries. He would land his plane on a road if the community was too small for an airport, and he didn't worry about whether his services would be reimbursed. He served on numerous committees and boards and was board chairman of the Bernalillo County Medical Society.

I once asked him why the frequent cuts and scrapes associated with rock climbing healed rapidly afterward when left untreated; lesser wounds—the consequence of normal activities—lingered far longer, even when carefully treated with antiseptics. He replied that minor cuts and abrasions were best left alone to dry out by themselves. Antiseptics of the 1955 era eradicated bacteria but damaged healthy tissue as well. His sage advice has served me well ever since.

Gene attended the fiftieth anniversary banquet of the New Mexico Mountain Club in 2002, and he died in 2004 at the age of eighty-three.

A. S. "Governor" Rodgers

Bernalillo County Sheriff's Captain A. S. "Governor" Rodgers also weathered that dreadful night upon the mountain, and it was he who recommended that our mountain club team take control of the recovery efforts.

His life was a Horace Greeley rags-to-riches kind of tale. Born in 1928 and raised in Albuquerque, he didn't have to "go west young man," for his grandfather had already done that for him.

"Go west" had been part of Greeley's philosophy, but he disavowed having originating the phrase. It came, instead, from John B. L. Soule's editorial, "Go West Young Man and Grow Up with Your Country," published in the *Terre Haute (Indiana) Express* in 1851. The original wording is especially appropriate here because Captain Rodgers did, indeed, grow up with New Mexico.

Figure 44. Movie actors Fred McMurray (top left) and Bob Hope (middle) with Sheriff's Captain A. S. Rodgers (top right), Mrs. Rodgers, and their sons at their Albuquerque home. Actress June Haver took the picture with the Rodgers family camera. (Courtesy of A. S. Rodgers.)

The twelfth of thirteen children, he was baptized Alfred Smith Rodgers—named for Al Smith, the governor of New York who ran for president against Herbert Hoover in 1928. He was nicknamed Governor accordingly.

When Governor's father died thirteen years later, the boy was left largely on his own, living in a shack behind his mother's house and earning his living with three part-time jobs while attending school. He was married on St. Patrick's Day when he was seventeen and his bride, Marcy, sixteen. They drove twenty-two miles to the next county, Valencia, for their license in a 1931 Model A Ford, and have enjoyed a full and eventful life together for over sixty years.

He bought a piece of land in Albuquerque from his mother (who had by then moved to California) and built a fourteen-by-twenty-eight-foot house entirely by himself. He obtained its lumber free by tearing down three chicken coops for a neighbor in return for the wood. He completed much of the construction after dark by the light of a gas lantern held by Marcy. The place had no electricity, no inside plumbing, and only a wood-coal stove for heat and cooking; outside water came from a hand-operated pitcher pump mounted above a thirty-two-foot well drilled by his brother. Governor shot rabbits and an occasional deer for their meat supply and earned extra cash by cutting and selling Christmas trees.

He worked for Home Delivery and soon branched out with a sideline of potato salads that Marcy prepared for local grocery stores. Dollars were hard to come by in the late 1940s, but the couple began to prosper.

On weekends they found entertainment in the form of dancing at a local dancehall, where he met a police officer who suggested that he might find steady employment in the sheriff's office. In those days of a sparsely populated New Mexico, one district attorney supervised three sheriffs for Bernalillo, Sandoval, and Valencia Counties. Rodgers took the suggestion and was hired on as a deputy. Later he was promoted to sergeant. Eventually he was made captain and became head of the legal division for Bernalillo County.

The New Cadillac

In 1954 Governor Rodgers was pictured in the company of Sheriff Harold Hubbell and convicted murderer Larry Upton in a banner headline story entitled "Killer Sentenced to Die Jan. 12" in the *Albuquerque Journal*. They were shown in a car bound for the state prison in Santa Fe.

Patrolman Rocky Payne—who was to accompany us to the crash scene a few months later—had apprehended Upton in Tijeras Canyon just after his slaying of a young airman who had given him a ride. Upton, having declared that he would never be executed for the crime and would do anything to escape, was placed in shackles in solitary confinement. A short time later he was heard banging on the prison bars with the astonishing announcement: "Here are your handcuffs." He had jammed the heavy-duty shackles between steel sections of his bed so that he could use his own arm as a lever to bend them open. It had required incredible strength—he should have shattered his arm— but he broke free unscathed.

When Upton was sentenced to death for his crime, Rodgers was faced with the unenviable problem of transporting the recalcitrant prisoner from Albuquerque to the penitentiary at Santa Fe.

No problem. Upton asked to see Rodgers: "I won't give you no trouble if you'll promise me a ride in a new Cadillac with the radio playing *Dragnet*." Hence the photo, though the newspaper mentioned nothing about why the party was traveling in style, instead of in a squad car.

It is remarkable that a vicious murderer would—without threat or intimidation—seek out his captor to solve a common problem. And that each man would trust the other to keep his word.

James Larry Upton was the last man to die in the electric chair in New Mexico.

Bob Hope

Governor Rodgers later became chief of security for Bernalillo County, being responsible for, among other things, the welfare of visiting dignitaries to Albuquerque. He chauffeured General Eisenhower when he was starting his run for president and comedian Bob Hope (accompanied by movie stars Fred McMurray and June Haver), who visited the seventy-four-acre ranch Rodgers owned south of town, where he raised cattle and grew all of the food for his table.

When Rodgers asked Hope why he always had others tip luggage carriers, bellmen, and the like for him, the comedian replied that he never carried money because money was dirty, the dirtiest thing that you could touch.

Bob Hope would routinely risk his life entertaining troops in combat zones, but he would never think of risking his health by touching filthy lucre. Perhaps that's why he lasted so long.

Eleanor Roosevelt

Governor Rodgers also met Mrs. Eleanor Roosevelt when she traveled to Albuquerque. He asked her whether she would like a limousine to take her to her hotel, and she replied that she preferred to travel in his squad car. Delighted, he eagerly fetched her meager supply of luggage and discovered that though the suitcases were scant in number, they were filled with books and incredibly heavy. Mrs. Roosevelt enjoyed traveling light—with a ton of baggage.

His duties also entailed the impaneling of coroner juries, including the one for Flight 260 and for the 1958 plane crash near Grants that killed Mike Todd, the husband of Elizabeth Taylor and the producer of the film *Around the World in Eighty Days*. (Bill Lucas, by then a state police corporal, and CAB investigator Phil Goldstein participated in the ensuing investigations.)

Other Ventures

Rodgers was later selected to take a special criminology course at the University of Oklahoma for law enforcement officers from five western states. It was taught by Dr. Lemoyne Snyder, whose work had been featured in the 1957–58 TV documentary *Court of Last Resort*. Dr. Snyder was then nationally recognized for his efforts to alert physicians that they might be failing to diagnose murder as the cause of death: "Approximately 20 percent of all persons die under circumstances that require an official inquiry into the cause of death." He later wrote *Homicide Investigation: Practical Information for Coroners, Police Officers, and Other Investigators*. Rodgers was fascinated by the course and believes that he greatly benefited by it.

He became involved in commercial ventures, founding seven different successful businesses, including insurance and investment brokerage firms and a motel. He was one of the founders of the Fidelity National Bank of Albuquerque. A board member for fourteen years, he served as its chairman at the time that the bank was sold.

Governor and Marcy have bought twenty-two homes in their lifetimes, repairing and reselling them, and living in twelve of them. He also bought and renovated old cars and took up stock car racing—his brother serving as pitman. The competition was keen as the Unser family—who would win seven Indianapolis 500 races between them—lived in town.

Rodgers became undersheriff for Bernalillo County and was later appointed chief investigator for Bernalillo, Sandoval, and Valencia counties by the district attorney. At that time one district attorney served all three counties, and so did Captain Rodgers. These were highly unusual appointments that attested to his abilities, for both the district attorney and the sheriff were Republicans, while he remained a staunch Democrat, loyal to the party of his namesake, Al Smith.

He left Albuquerque for San Diego, California, when his brother offered him a job in his contracting company at double the salary that he was earning as a policeman. He enrolled in psychology classes at San Diego State University and decided to teach criminology in adult education courses for San Diego County. Blocked from teaching because he lacked a high school degree, he earned his diploma at a local high school at the age of fifty-one; his classmates were teenagers. He attributes much of his success to his yearning for a broad education—and hard work came in handy, too.

Captain Rodgers now lives on six acres seven miles outside of Paonia, a town of fifteen hundred in western Colorado. He subscribes to seventeen weekly newspapers and runs a stock brokerage firm with seven different banks and twenty-five companies in the Colorado area as clients. In his leisure time, he enjoys wood (and occasionally clay) sculpture and jewelry crafting.

Entrepreneurship still reigns within the family. Governor and Marcy lived near their son, who had a thriving business in rats and mice—twenty thousand of them—and snakes that he sells to zoos and snake enthusiasts, mostly women. An albino snake recently went for forty-four thousand dollars.

Governor and Marcy begin their days at six o'clock every morning—there are not enough hours in the day as it is. They enjoy people and know that staying active, eating right, and exercise are the keys to a wonderful life.

Bill Lucas

I first met New Mexico State Patrolman Bill Lucas when he gave Sherman Marsh and me a lift down the backside of Sandia Mountain on the day of the crash.

His adventures began in 1944 when he was a turret gunner while serving in Torpedo Squadron Four in the South Pacific during World War II. Turret gunner duty of that day was especially hazardous and required men who were absolutely devoted. They faced backward during torpedo runs while manning a 50-caliber machine gun—seeing where the plane had been, not where it was going, and trusting that the pilot would pull up at the appropriate moment after delivering his torpedoes, but not even sure that he was still alive. And, as the turret wasn't large enough to accommodate a gunner wearing a parachute during operations, he had to be careful not to wear one.

He made it through the war unscathed and married his bride in his sailor's uniform in 1945, then tried out the life of a motorcycle cop on the Clovis, New Mexico, police force.

Figure 45. New Mexico State Police Patrolman Bill Lucas (on the right) arriving at the Los Lunas, New Mexico, railway station with the Pennsylvania Turnpike Phantom and federal marshals in 1953. (Courtesy of Bill Lucas.)

Prison Riot

Learning to fly on the G.I. Bill, Lucas later joined the New Mexico State Police. He made front-page headlines in 1953 by saving the life of Warden Ralph Tahash during a prison riot at the New Mexico State Penitentiary at Santa Fe.

Warden Tahash had broken free from his captors and had fled to an open window in the hospital complex near where Patrolman Lucas and his rookie assistant, Steve Lagomarsino, were standing. When he asked for a weapon, Lucas handed him his own pistol, but Tahash handed it back, saying he wanted Lagomarsino's rifle instead. The warden unleashed several volleys at the inmates and immediately terminated the riot. Warden Tahash credited Lagomarsino and Lucas with saving his life. He estimated that he would have had only fifteen seconds to live otherwise. (A half-century later Lagomarsino would provide me with a multitude of photos of the crash site.)

The Turnpike Phantom

Later that year Bill Lucas volunteered to help some local police officers in Los Lunas track down thieves who had robbed an Albuquerque gas station. The suspect was in the rear of Lucas's police cruiser when Bill received a code alert that he was carrying the infamous Pennsylvania Turnpike Phantom, John W. Wable.

The Phantom had attracted national headlines by robbing and murdering truckers sleeping in their cabs in unlit parking lots along the Pennsylvania Turnpike. As the *New York Daily News* described things in 2007, "Some truckers started to take precautions, arming themselves with clubs and firearms. They traveled with buddies or formed convoys. When it was time to sleep, they swarmed into the parking lots of restaurants and service stations, joking about 'circling the wagons.'

"Fear gripped the turnpike, and troopers patrolled the roads, waking all lone slumbering drivers, sometimes telling them to move along, at other times just making sure they were not dead."

Professional Pilot Adventures

Patrolman Lucas was later promoted to corporal and transferred to Grants, New Mexico—a wild-west uranium-mining town eighty miles west of Albuquerque that earned instant fame during a blizzard in 1958 when the private plane carrying Michael Todd crashed.

After returning to Albuquerque from Grants, he was promoted to sergeant and occasionally flew planes that the state police chartered from Southwest Skyways. When his request for a permanent job as pilot was denied because he was more valued as a police sergeant, Lucas then became a pilot for Southwest Skyways and later for the Carco Air Service, sometimes flying the same Albuquerque to Los Alamos shuttle that had resulted in the discovery of the Flight 260 wreckage.

I flew in that shuttle once myself and found landing at Los Alamos to be a memorable experience—perhaps something like landing on an aircraft carrier, except this landing deck was atop a mesa seven thousand feet above sea level. The pilot landed on a short runway with a yawning chasm at the near end and buildings blocking the other. Prevailing winds helped to slow the landing plane.

Bill explained to me that carriers bounced around a lot in high seas and were far more difficult to land on than stable mesa tops. Takeoffs were a different matter, however. Carriers could be maneuvered so that pilots always took off into a head wind that enabled them to ascend rapidly. Los Alamos takeoffs had prevailing tail and cross winds, from the northwest, and the thin air at seven thousand feet didn't help matters. One of his engines quit on takeoff one time, and he was forced to make an unscheduled landing in Española with passengers on board.

Carco, a company based in Las Vegas, Nevada, had contracts with the Atomic Energy Commission (AEC) to transport nuclear weapon components and personnel to AEC sites. Lucas was scheduled to be promoted to chief pilot when Carco lost its contract with the AEC in 1970. He then became chief pilot for its successor, Ross Aviation, an Albuquerque firm that still exists today. When the police department decided to purchase their own aircraft Lucas sold them a Cessna.

He enjoyed the challenging experiences of flying throughout the Southwest. He spent several weeks flying Senator Ted Kennedy around New Mexico while he was obtaining information concerning Indian water rights legislation. He also flew a photographer who searched for spectacular views of the magnificent landscape, the cabin door removed from the aircraft so that the photographer could take better shots. But when the photographer asked him to shut one of the two engines off because heat waves off the engines were fouling up his exposures, Lucas had other ideas.

Nuclear Flights

He made flights to Panama, where Sandia Labs scientists measured the hole in the ozone layer; flew trips to Aruba and Alaska, where the scientists tested terra-dynamic techniques for implanting telemetry equipment in both jungles and arctic ice fields; and ferried atomic warheads to missile silos in the Midwest as well as fuel rods to nuclear power plants in the Southeast.

And he had one memorable flight that fortunately did not make the history books.

The morning after a RON (remain overnight) stay in Dayton, Ohio, he was flying back to Albuquerque with atomic weapons on board when he noticed that his airspeed dials were off, his autopilot was frozen, and he could not manipulate his ailerons. As it would have been foolhardy to continue, he decided to "rudder it in" to a forced landing at Scott Air Force Base near St. Louis. When he opened the wheel-well door, a large block of ice fell onto the tarmac. The wheels had been wetted by rain during takeoff, and the moisture had pooled and frozen around the aileron cables—literally freezing them solid so that they were inoperable.

He was not well pleased to learn that aircraft maintenance personnel already knew of the potential for the problem and that they could have readily prevented it by drilling a small hole in the fuselage so that residual water from the wheels would drain away before it could collect and freeze around the aileron cables.

One wonders what would have happened had he failed to land the plane safely that day and thereby involved St. Louis with an atomic accident—all because no one had deemed it necessary to drill the small hole in the fuselage.

I am very lucky that I learned to fly.
It's special to spend your days in the sky.

I first flew planes of fabric and wire,
Open cockpits, silk scarves, and a burning desire.

It took several years from first lesson to hiring.
To find a job that paid me for flying.

The next thirty years were a variety, you bet.
I flew all kinds of planes, including a supersonic jet.

We covered the country from Aruba to the North Pole.
There were good RONs; some were a "hole."

We flew in all kinds of weather both day and night.
There were in-flight emergencies; some were a fright.

I've had engines that exploded and wheels that came off.
My controls froze up once; I didn't scoff.

We flew to all the air bases with cargoes so "hot."
Sometimes there was doubt whether we could land or not.

Some of our loads required guards with arms,
We are fortunate to have survived without any harm.

We flew for Sandia when they tested their device.
We dropped them in the jungle, sometimes through the ice.

I had some good captains who helped me to learn.
I dealt with a lot of people who didn't give a durn.

I had good crew members who helped bring us home,
Or I wouldn't be here to write this poem.

If you're too lazy to work or too nervous to steal,
A life as an aviator is a pretty good deal.

Captain Bill E. Lucas (retired)

Maurice Cordova

Maurice Cordova, one of the two state patrolman who accompanied our New Mexico Mountain Club team the first time we visited the crash pinnacle, moved up the ranks to the very top, retiring as chief of the New Mexico State Police in 1985 after thirty-two years' service. I made my second contact with him fifty-five years after the crash, during the copyediting phase of this book preparation. As Diana Rico, my copy editor, had red-inked my spelling of his name (I had written "Murice"), I decided to prove myself right for a change by Googling my spelling in the hopes that I would find someone in Albuquerque named the same way. I got a direct hit on a 2006 *Albuquerque Journal* article, "78-Year-Old State Police Chief Shoots Intruder." Finding him in the phone book, I dialed his number, briefly introduced myself to his wife, and bluntly asked, "Did your husband visit the TWA crash site on the mountain in 1955?" "Yes," she replied, "I'll get him." And we had nice conversation about what we were doing that day fifty-five years ago. Only he spells his name the way Diana does. Seems that I can't lose for winning.

Richard Heim

Dick Heim devoted most of his life to health care—a care for the health of poor people and a healthy care for the wallets of those who footed the bills. He was, of all things, a man who cared about efficiency in governments and corporations and actually managed to put his ideas into practice.

Soon after he served as a member of the mountain club team on the recovery expedition, Dick began moving up the ladder of public sector positions, leaving his position as an administrative staff member at Sandia Labs to become personnel director for the City of Albuquerque in 1957. There he established the first comprehensive personnel program to implement the city's merit system ordinance. He then served as county manager for Bernalillo County, where he started such intergovernmental programs as property tax reappraisal, consolidation of health services, and pooling of computer services. He left that position to become president of the five-year-old Albuquerque American Savings and Loan Association, which earned its first profit during his tenure.

Washington

Then it was on to Washington, D.C., from 1967 to 1970 as administrative assistant to U.S. Senator Clinton Anderson, who had been secretary of agriculture under President Harry S. Truman. In addition to his administrative duties in the senator's office, Heim began learning the intricacies of Congress by serving as Anderson's direct liaison with the staffs of the Senate Finance Committee, the Senate Committee on Aeronautical and Space Sciences, the Joint Committee on Atomic Energy, and the Indian Affairs Subcommittee of the Senate Interior Committee.

He then returned to New Mexico and spent the next five years as executive director of the New Mexico Health and Human Services Department, directing more than twenty-three hundred employees in ninety-five locations around the state. Heim expanded existing programs and constituent benefits while moving the department from a $4.5 million deficit in state funds in 1970 to a $5 million surplus in 1975.

Under Heim, the department also developed an innovative double-whammy program employing welfare mothers to serve elderly and disabled clients in their home communities, thereby reducing both the welfare rolls and the number of clients sent to long-term facilities.

Director of Medicaid

Returning to Washington in 1978 to work in President Jimmy Carter's administration, he was appointed director of the Medicaid bureau in the Health Care Financing Administration—a $20 billion a year federal and state program financing health care for the poor. He made a resolution to make the program work. As the federal government could do little by itself to improve management of this very costly, organizationally complex, and politically sensitive program, he concentrated on developing more effective working relationships with state governments by involving state representatives in the discussion of policy and operational changes.

Accompanied by a single staff member who took notes, he visited all of the ten regional offices to learn about their problems, instead of dictating to them his intentions. He treated them as part of the solution, not part of the problem. He also served as chairman of an interagency task force on Medicaid management information systems.

Following the reorganization of the Health Care Financing Administration, he became the director of its newly formed Office of Intergovernmental Affairs, where he remained until the end of Carter's administration.

New Mexico

Back in Albuquerque, he concentrated his efforts on being a health care management consultant. He assisted the State of Hawaii to restructure its Medicaid program and develop cost-containment measures in all of its health care programs and lobbyied for California and a coalition of seventeen other states against the Reagan administration proposal to impose a federal ceiling on Medicaid expenditures—helping them succeed in their goal to "lose one for the Gipper."

He later served for eight years as senior vice president for corporate affairs for St. Joseph Hospital in Albuquerque and senior vice president for mission effectiveness and corporate affairs for the St. Joseph Healthcare System in Albuquerque. And then more New Mexico State work: cabinet secretary of the Human Services Department, executive director of Community Health Centers, assistant director of the State Land Office.

His mother once jokingly told him, "The trouble with you, Dick, is you can't keep a job." But it was a great life—each job a distinctly different and rewarding challenge that uniquely prepared him for the one that followed. And he loved collaborating with spirited people who were not necessarily the easiest to work with.

"Retirement"

New Mexico Governor Bill Richardson appointed Heim to an unsalaried position on the State Medical Board in 2002. When Heim attempted to resign that appointment at the age of eighty-four in 2008, his resignation was rejected—the board apparently believing that it would have been prejudicial to the health of the State of New Mexico to allow him to do so.

And I almost forgot to mention that Heim was a charter member of the New Mexico Mountain Club in 1950, as well as president of the Albuquerque Ski Club from 1951 to 1953.

Dick's brother, Tom, served as my second man on the ascent of the Shield Ridge in 1962—my last climb in the Sandias. Tragically, Tom died from a climbing accident in Peru a few years later.

Sherman Marsh was a geology student at the University of New Mexico at the time of the crash. A lover of geology, spelunking, climbing, and camping, he became a geologist with the U.S. Geological Service. He experienced a fascinating professional career, traveling all over the world while enjoying his favorite avocations. He is retired and lives near Denver, wintering in Florida. He says that thirty-five years of fieldwork have taken their toll—he now has more metal in him than your average automobile.

Hank Tendall served as president of the New Mexico Mountain Club on numerous occasions and was the first president of the Albuquerque Mountain Rescue Council. He worked as a technical staff member at Sandia Labs. He died in his eighties in Albuquerque.

At the time of the crash, **Paul Stewart** was president of the New Mexico Mountain Club and an engineer working for the U.S. Corps of Engineers. Paul, Sherman, George, and I enjoyed numerous trips together exploring the mountains of Colorado and the back roads of New Mexico.

He moved to Page, Arizona, in the late 1950s to work on the construction of the Glen Canyon Dam. He is in his nineties now, living in Colorado.

Ken Shaw had a genius for conjuring up ideal solutions for potential problems—driving his car rather than hiking to the Crest on the day of the crash, for example, and unexpectedly coming to my aid in later rock climbing exploits.

I remember a climb up the western face of the Shield when another climber and I were inching our way up near the top. It was early evening, we were exhausted after twelve hours on the rock, and I was having considerable difficulty choosing the route, when we were surprised to hear a shout from above. It was Ken, and he helped us negotiate the final hundred feet. Unbeknownst to us, he had decided to drive his car to the crest, hike over to the top of the Shield on the Crest Trail, and help us in some manner. I didn't know where we would top out, as it was a first ascent, and Ken certainly couldn't have known; but he found us anyway. We picked our way back to his car in total darkness.

Ken left the air force several years later and moved away from Albuquerque. I haven't heard from him since.

15
Photo Tales

This book has been wonderfully enhanced by the multitude of photos that populate its pages, many dating from 1955, at the time of the crash.

When I began this narrative I had precisely one photograph: a somewhat blurry image of me and the remains of the airliner tail section. My memory served as the source for much of the account that I wrote fifty years later. The other photographs arrived afterward, illustrating and substantiating many of the details of what I had already written. Some were action shots of the principal characters in my narrative; some depicted unidentified individuals.

This chapter is about those photos and the outstanding people associated with them.

An Unidentified Rescuer Enjoys His Breakfast Out of a Can, The East Mesa in the Background Far Below

Sherman Marsh provided me with the photo for Figure 20—a spectacular shot of a man eating his breakfast out of a can. As Sherman had no idea why he had this photo nor who the man was, I captioned him as "an unidentified rescuer."

I guessed his identity two years later. When browsing the Internet for a good picture of Frank Hibben, I chanced across an incorrectly titled article, "The Crash of Flight 206," from a 1980 issue of the *Albuquerque Journal Magazine.*

The article had great quotes from Frank Hibben and Gene Szerlip that are now part of the book. And it also contained the fantastic tale of the two Albuquerque carpenters—Frank Powers and George Boatman—who were the first to reach the wreckage at the eastern base of the pinnacle the day after the crash. They had been parishioners of Rev. Earl Davis, who was aboard the plane. Powers discovered his pastor with his Bible lying on the ground nearby, its pages flapping in the wind.

I then looked at the online Albuquerque phone book for both Powers and Boatman in the hopes that I might learn more about them. Boatman wasn't there, but—BINGO—Frank Powers was. Only this Frank Powers had never heard of the plane crash.

I browsed the Web for their names, but to no avail. A phone call to the Albuquerque public library yielded the same nonresults, but the helpful librarian said that she had an obituary of a Frank Powers who had died a few months after the newspaper article came out. This seemed promising, as the article had reported that Powers had been recovering from a massive stroke.

She e-mailed me the obituary a few minutes later, and I began searching online phone books for the relatives mentioned. Those from Albuquerque were no longer there, and I couldn't find his sister Lula listed in Hayden, Colorado; but his sister Beulah McCullough might be related to the only McCullough that I could find in the Apache Junction, Arizona, directory—my call there being answered by a gracious lady who explained that her ex-husband had moved to Minneapolis some time ago, but she didn't have his address. As searching that metropolis for the correct McCullough didn't seem worth the effort, I tried another tack.

Rev. Ken George had performed the burial service for Frank Powers. Could I find him? And would he remember anything about Powers? And then I remembered the spectacular photo of the unknown rescuer eating his breakfast. Could Frank Powers have been that man, and might Rev. George be able to identify that photo?

I searched the Internet for the First Assembly of God Church in

Albuquerque where crash victim Rev. Earl F. Davis had been Powers's pastor, but found nothing; then selected the First Family Church as a likely alternative.

The phone receptionist told me that Ken George was no longer at the church, but she had a phone number where I might reach him. That call netted me the information that he was not in his office. Would I care to leave him a message? He would return my call the next day. I gave the receptionist the purpose of my call and said that I would call him back instead, and it had been a great pleasure dealing with such conscientious, efficient, and pleasant people.

The next day, the receptionist put me through to Rev. George, who surprised me by his intimate knowledge about the crash of Flight 260 and the role that Frank Powers had played. He would be pleased to look at the photo if I would e-mail it to him.

I did so and later phoned him.

He corroborated my assumption that the photo could be that of Frank Powers as a younger man—he remembered that Powers had the large hands of a carpenter, like those of the man that are shown in the photo. A friend of his who had also known Powers supported his conclusions. Rev. George had remembered Frank Powers and his story of his remarkable venture to the crash site because of the intensity and obvious sincerity of the man who told it.

As a young evangelist, Ken George was among those who first welcomed Rev. Earl F. Davis to the First Assembly of God Church in late January 1955!

The First Family Church was, indeed, the successor to the First Assembly of God Church, and Rev. George became its pastor nineteen years later, in 1974. He expanded it and moved it to its new location in 1978, renaming it the First Family Church to reflect its emphasis on ministry to the entire family.

Rev. George is now retired from his duties as the New Mexico district superintendent for the Assemblies of God, but I had the good fortune to visit him at his office on the West Mesa in March 2008. It was he who inspired me to call the National Headquarters for the Assemblies of God for the photo and biographical sketch of Rev. Earl Davis that appears in this narrative.

Rev. George has led a fantastic life also, but that's another story.

Serendipity had netted me the right church, the right man, and the right results.

Steve Lagomarsino

The identity of the next unknown person was revealed two days later when my wife and I visited the home of retired New Mexico State Deputy Police Chief Steve Lagomarsino, the man who supplied me with innumerable United Press photos of the crash site.

He was showing us his collection of photos of the crash site when we came across one that I had not seen before—a young man atop the pinnacle, gingerly pointing to the tail below him—prompting me to ask whether he knew the man's identity. Steve replied that he didn't, but recalled that the young man might have lived on the back side of the mountain. I remembered the 1955 newspapers had mentioned that a Jack Hicks lived on the back of the mountain, and that Hicks was the man who was supposed to guide our mountain club team to the crash site on the first day we reached it.

Could this be a photo of Jack Hicks?

Read on, dear reader, read on, till the "WORL" turns round.

Steve Lagomarsino's story was a remarkable one.

Awarded the Bronze Star and the Combat Infantry Badge for his service as a paratrooper in the Rhineland, Ardennes, and central Germany during World War II, he was honorably discharged in 1946. The next year he signed a professional baseball contract as a pitcher for the Boston Braves. He ended his sports career playing for the Albuquerque Dukes, now known as the Isotopes.

Deciding that becoming a state policeman might offer more secure long-term employment, he graduated from the New Mexico State Police Academy in 1952. After he helped save the life of Warden Tahash at the Santa Fe prison riot, however, his new bride took issue with that assumption—telling him that if this was what life would be like as a state patrolman, she would just as soon have him consider another occupation.

He was promoted through the ranks of the New Mexico State Police to become deputy chief with the rank of lieutenant colonel. In 1969 he was chosen to attend the National FBI Academy, where he was elected president of his graduating class. He was elected to serve on the executive board of the National FBI Academy Associates in 1971, becoming its president in 1979.

When he retired from the New Mexico State Police after twelve years as its deputy chief, he received the Citation of Merit Award from Governor Edwin L. Mechem, and the New Mexico State Police Board of Supervisors cited him for "Exemplary Service in the Line of Duty."

After the millennium, the former Albuquerque Dukes player switched gears and pitched in at the nonprofit New Mexico Resources Development Institute to help out-of-work folks find jobs.

He likes keeping busy.

The Horse Camp

Bill Lucas had just bought a facsimile scanner soon after the visit with Steve Lagomarsino in March 2008 and had tried it out by scanning and e-mailing me a faded picture of himself at the horse camp that was established near the foot of the Sandias on the day we recovered the bodies. A mediocre image, it was the only action photo I had of him—and it would provide a story of amateur sleuthing.

As my attempts to enhance its quality on my computer were fruitless, he posted me the original, which arrived in early March 2008. The following sequence of events ensued.

March 3, 2008

10:30 a.m. As I realized that I required professional expertise, I decided on BestPhotoRestoration.com in Atlanta as a likely candidate. The Web site listed a phone number that immediately linked me to Nan Lasher Ball, who told me to come on over. Her studio was in her home.

11:05 a.m. I arrived, and her cheerful voice bid me enter before I had the chance to knock. I waited while she completed business with an obviously highly satisfied customer—a good sign indeed.

I showed her Bill Lucas's horse camp photo, giving her a little of its background, and we entered her studio room, where I glimpsed an image of an aviator displayed on her computer screen. She explained it was her father, a naval aviator in the Pacific during World War II. I responded that the person in my photo had been a turret gunner aboard a naval torpedo bomber in the same Pacific theater—the improbable connection with Bill's wartime ventures enhancing my conclusion that I had selected the right place for my quest.

Nan scanned the photo and brought it up on the screen, commenting that the body at the base of the tree had a wedding ring on its left hand and that Bill was wearing a pistol on his hip—news to me, as I hadn't noticed either the ring or the pistol.

Bit by bit, she enhanced isolated sections of the photo, and new features began to emerge on the screen—a thrilling experience for me, as interesting portions of the old and faded image were being reincarnated before my eyes. She pointed out what she thought was a rifle that seemed to be propped against a tree; but I disagreed, as I knew that Bill would not have been carrying such a cumbrous weapon on a victim recovery expedition.

I explained that I had previously noted the body at the base of the tree, but thought it to be that of an exhausted rescuer resting on the ground. She pointed out that his torso was seriously twisted—it did not appear to be in a particularly restful position. I indicated what appeared to be a western hat—a crash victim that had journeyed downhill in a body bag seemed unlikely to be wearing a hat. She rejoined that perhaps one of the horse-ranch people had used it to cover the person's face—a sensible explanation that I accepted.

Then she astonished me by remarking that the body seemed to be wearing a uniform. Had there been a sailor aboard the plane?

No, there were no sailors aboard, but George Hankins had noted in his diary that one of the passengers at the crash site might have been wearing a uniform. Could this photo be of that man?

As I was leaving the studio, Nan showed me a sample of her expertise: a duplicate of a badly cracked photographic negative of a young bride that had been treasured by her granddaughter as an only keepsake. The restored positive image revealed a lovely woman, to the great comfort of the granddaughter and the delight of everyone who saw it.

She also told me about an elderly man who had eagerly watched her as she restored a faded snapshot of his late wife. He lovingly returned the new copy to its long-accustomed place in his wallet—a remembrance of her that would remain near him always. And there was also a cracked and indistinct collage of photos of the first graduates of the Emory University Medical School, originally a single page in a college yearbook. She had restored it and blown it up to a three-by-five-foot print now prominently displayed at the Crawford Long Hospital in Atlanta.

It was wonderful to learn that my chosen professional areas of research—scanning digitizers, computer graphics, and image processing—had been the source of such unexpected and personally touching benefits to others.

12:06 p.m. Nan e-mailed me her incrementally restored photo of the horse camp, and I forwarded it to Bill Lucas and Ginny Campbell for their independent comments, careful not to prompt them with my own conjectures.

I then began to have second thoughts about the body being the one mentioned in George Hankins's diary. It was more likely that of the copilot—putting me into the considerable quandary of how I should approach Gary Creason with the news that I might have a photo of his father—or perhaps I should never bring up the subject at all.

5:00 p.m. Ginny responded that she was astonished to see a dead body—the face was to the left of Bill Lucas's left arm—but it wasn't at all like one of the pulverized crash victim faces that I had described in my original narrative.

6:17 p.m. Ginny sent me another message asking me what I thought about the things hanging over the horse's head. Were they metal tubes? Were they hung on the tree?

7:37 p.m. Bill Lucas responded to my message by mentioning that he had been searching for newspaper articles about the Santa Fe State Penitentiary riot in 1953. He then addressed my questions: "I believe you improved the photo at the base camp. My time there was very brief. I gave them my report and left."

As Bill had told me that he had noticed nothing special about the photo, I stopped reading his e-mail and turned my thoughts to Ginny's message, which had supplied me with very pertinent facts.

10:41 p.m. I e-mailed Ginny that I had noticed the body also but hadn't spotted the face, and Nan had seen a uniform that I still couldn't make out, and Bill had not mentioned a body at all. I'd get back to Bill to ask him about the things hanging from the tree.

March 4, 2008

9:47 a.m. When I got on the Internet the next morning, I found two messages from Ginny commenting that the hat did not appear to be one that a pilot would wear—it looked more like a civilian's hat.

She had zoomed in on the photo and discovered that the articles by the tree were indeed in front of the horse's head. A white object appeared to be a coat jacket with gloves. None of which made sense. She couldn't imagine what the dark objects with the round metal ends could be—perhaps body bags?

By that time I knew the answer, for I had read the remainder of Bill's e-mail.

He explained that he had been carrying a walkie-talkie radio and had used it to advise the base camp that the recovery party was having trouble with body bags tearing open from being dragged on the rocks. Base camp responded that they would move the horse camp higher up the mountain.

Bill remembered that the horse camp had been composed mostly of the New Mexico Mounted Patrol.

"Just in front of me there is a man leaning against the tree that the horse is tied to. I am probably having a cup of coffee."

I then realized each of the three of us examining the photograph had noticed significant facts about it, but had incorrectly interpreted their meanings.

Three of us were right, and three of us were wrong; and Bill, who didn't notice a body or anything peculiar, was right about everything.

Each of us had looked at the photograph through the eyes of an amateur criminologist searching for forensic evidence of a crime. We reached conclusions based upon our own past experiences or what we expected to see—not the totality of evidence before us.

Nan had seen a contorted body and came to the obvious conclusion that it was associated with the crash that I had just described to her. She also spotted the wedding ring and pistol, which were indeed what they seemed to be. Her discovery of the uniform is mind-boggling— I still can't figure how she saw it. But the uniform was not what we supposed. She also discovered what appeared to be shoes, which may explain what Ginny had seen.

Ginny noticed the same body and also assumed that it was associated with the crash. The metal tubes that she mentioned might, perhaps, be tubing still present at the wreck site—she had placed some at the shrine for crash victims atop the pinnacle. Her discovery of the unpulverized face was right on target. I had looked hard for a head and had not found it.

I also noticed the body, but the western hat told me that it couldn't be a victim; then I changed my mind because Nan had a very logical explanation. The discovery of the uniform by her immediately afterward solidified that belief and triggered my memory of George's notes about a uniformed body. As the notes did not mention a reasonably complete body, I then jumped to the conclusion that the remains in the photo must have been those of Gary Creason's father. After all, the body must have been associated with the crash.

But Bill Lucas hadn't noticed anything peculiar about the photo— his only conjecture being the cup of coffee. I had been elated by the photograph because I now had unposed action photos of all the primary participants that I remembered from my first day at the wreck pinnacle—albeit a poor one of Bill, a horse, and an unseen cup of coffee. I had been expecting a "WOW!" from him because of all the "important" things that the restored photo revealed to us. He saw only the ordinary photograph that he had sent me.

The "body" leaning against the tree was merely a complete-with-hat uniformed member of the New Mexico Mounted Patrol. The clothing that Nan and Ginny discovered was part of his gear. I hadn't realized that the patrol had been there that day and had wrongly concluded that all horses and their keepers were associated with the horse ranch mentioned in the newspapers.

And what about the exhausted rescuer flaked out on the ground whom I had first imagined? The exhausted rescuer wasn't on the ground at all. He was standing up and was the subject of the photo.

Figure 46. New Mexico State Police Patrolman Bill Lucas at the New Mexico Mounted Police horse camp near the base of TWA Canyon, during the final stages of the victim recovery efforts. (Courtesy of Bill Lucas.)

Bill Lucas had endured an appallingly sleepless night upon the mountain in a scanty uniform and twenty-below-zero temperatures; had suffered stab wounds inflicted by cactus and burned trousers inflicted by a campfire; and yet had reported at five o'clock the morning after for a full day's work upon the mountain. He had left the horse camp to return home for a well-earned rest.

But he doesn't look exhausted in Figure 46.

When he arrived at police base camp on the mesa, fellow trooper

C. S. "Mac" McCasland, considered the toughest, most rugged member of the force, approached Lucas to give him the greatest compliment of his life: "I want to shake the hand of a man."

I later redigitized the photo using an "extreme enhancement" setting on my own scanner, which gave me a reasonably clear image that reveals everything in detail.

It's still a lousy photo, but an interesting tale. And I have visual evidence of Bill Lucas in action—albeit probably just drinking coffee.

Harry Moskos

I like to think of Harry Moskos as the alpha and the omega photo man of this saga. He didn't take the photos, but was responsible for my getting a bundle of them.

The alpha part came long before I had first heard of him. He had been part of the Flight 260 photo story from the very beginning, responsible for getting the crash pictures onto the *Albuquerque Tribune* telephoto machine in 1955. The omega part came a half century later, when a large fraction of those photos came into my hands because of the remarkable reader response that he received from his 2006 *Albuquerque Journal* article about the TWA memorial dedication.

Harry's prompt forwarding of pertinent messages to Ginny Campbell—who forwarded them to Hugh Prather and me—netted us the pictures supplied to us by Steve Lagomarsino as well as the rewarding contacts with Governor Rodgers and relatives of Rev. Earl Davis and Lois Dean.

Much of what follows was excerpted from a Scripps News release at the time of Harry's retirement in August 2001.

Harry had begun working in the *Albuquerque Tribune* newsroom in 1953 at the age of sixteen, having just finished his junior year at Albuquerque High. He was already an old hand at news work, as he had started a school weekly paper in the fifth grade. The *Tribune* editor had hired him to operate the paper's telephoto machine, a job that entailed synchronizing the transmission signal with the receiving signal. The superintendent of the Albuquerque Public Schools made a personal visit to the *Tribune* offices to make sure the machine was safe for one of his students to use.

After graduating from the University of New Mexico, Harry left the *Tribune* to become the editor for the *Daily Beacon* in Grants, New Mexico, then joined the Associated Press in 1960 and was appointed state editor for New Mexico the next year. Promoted to bureau chief in 1963 for Associated Press in Honolulu, Hawaii, at age twenty-six he became the youngest bureau chief that AP had ever named.

He covered the 1966 French nuclear tests off the Mururoa Atoll in the South Pacific for AP and was the only print reporter to cover the return of the crew of the USS *Pueblo* at Midway in 1968. (The *Pueblo* had been attacked and hijacked by the North Korean military in January, the crew remaining in captivity for eleven months.)

Returning to the *Tribune* in 1969, he became its managing editor in 1972. Then it was on to El Paso, Texas, to be editor of the *Herald-Post* for nine years. In 1984 he began a seventeen-year stint with the *Knoxville (Tennessee) News-Sentinel*. By the time he retired at age sixty-five in 2001, he was its vice president and editor.

All told, he had served as editor or managing editor of Scripps newspapers for an amazing twenty-nine years.

The Harry Moskos Scholarship for School of Journalism and Electronic Media students at the University of Tennessee was endowed in his name by the Scripps company.

Harry's father was a cobbler, a Greek immigrant from Northern Epirius. His brother Charles was a professor at Northwestern University and was once described by the *Wall Street Journal* as the "most influential military sociologist." Charles authored the U.S. military's "don't ask, don't tell" policy, which governs the conduct and treatment of homosexual service members.

Retirement from Scripps was hardly retirement, for Harry moved back to Albuquerque as a columnist and letters editor for the *Albuquerque Journal*. He took a week's leave to serve as public relations official for Ecumenical Patriarch Bartholomew of Constantinople (Dimitrios Archontonis, spiritual leader of more than 300 million Orthodox Christian faithful worldwide) during Pope Benedict XVI's visit to Istanbul in December 2006.

It's a Small, Small "WORL"

In early 2009, Bill Lucas thoughtfully mailed me a copy of the lurid September 1955 *Stag* magazine article about the crash that had caused considerable anguish among victim family members—especially the widow of pilot Ivan Spong. I had not seen it before and hoped that it might supply me with new facts for the book.

I wasn't surprised to see pictures that were already in my own collection, as Harry Moskos had told me earlier that a few days after he had wired the crash pictures, they had discovered that a severed hand was depicted in one of them. (I hadn't noticed it either until Ginny pointed it out to me.) The photo was the centerpiece for the *Stag* article.

I was surprised, however, that the article was a first-person account by United Press photographer Dick Skrondahl (as told to B. W. von Block)— the main characters being Skrondahl, KOB-TV photographer Dick Kent, State Patrolman Bill Lucas, and forest ranger Jack Hicks.

Thirsting for firsthand knowledge about the crash site, I read on but rapidly became disenchanted. The text proved to be a disjointed jumble of half truths and outright fabrications, mingled with incoherent and confusing misinformation. I could not fathom what the author was describing. He obviously had never visited the crash site.

Going to bed disheartened, appalled, and infuriated, I searched the Web the next day for Dick Skrondahl in hopes that I might find something about him; I learned to my astonishment that he was a notable photographer and author. The *New Mexico Daily Lobo* claimed that he was a member of a long-standing monthly poker club of New Mexico's elite that also included Luther Wilson, director of the University of New Mexico Press—a man who five days prior had assigned his name to the contract for this book!

Surely, something was amiss. So I gave Skrondahl a call to ask whether he had visited the crash scene and whether he was the author of the article. He readily agreed that he had been to the wreck site but denied writing the article, filling the airwaves with the same sentiments that I had about it—it was sheer garbage and an abomination.

He had first learned about the article after it was published, discovering that local newsstands had already sold out. He protested to the editors at *Stag* magazine, who informed him that, as far as they were concerned, he was the author—they had a document to prove it. He had unwittingly signed a byline release when their reporter interviewed him after he had returned to town from the crash site.

Undeterred by this dreadful news, Skrondahl had contacted the pilot's widow to apologize for what had happened.

I could not grasp what he told me about his experiences that day, as they did not mesh well with my own. That afternoon I e-mailed him photos taken atop the pinnacle and asked him whether he could identify them, hoping that he would remember taking some of them and what was occurring at the time.

The next day, I scanned through my file of newspaper clippings for UPI photos of the crash site and was stunned to find Dick Skrondahl credited for having taken the *Albuquerque Tribune* "WORL" photo (Figure 28) that had given me my first insight into how the plane struck the mountain.

I now had solid proof that he had been on the pinnacle at the same time that I was. Surely he would remember someone in our party. Perhaps he had been the one to take our photos.

His answer to my queries was a startling no. He recognized the pictures that had appeared in *Stag* magazine, as well as one of the tail section, and one of the man who had been their guide—but he couldn't his remember his name.

I did. His name was Jack Hicks, and Steve Lagomarsino had the photo that Skrondahl had taken of him.

Dick Skrondahl told me he and his group had been the first to arrive at the wreck site atop the pinnacle, led there from the Crest by his unnamed guide, apparently coming down Echo Canyon on a game trail that I have subsequently learned about. They had taken photos of the crash site, departed the pinnacle, and were descending the mountainside when they met a rescue party laboring its way up the steep slope to the saddle after their exhaustingly frigid night upon the mountain.

When I called Bill Lucas and he corroborated their meeting on the mountainside, I had now established that Dick's party had, indeed, been the first to reach the wreckage atop the pinnacle, having departed before our party arrived at the saddle.

My existing narrative had heretofore been incomplete, missing the significant evidence that Dick Skrondahl had just supplied.

He also named the man in the "WORL" photo as photographer Dick Kent, who was lugging a heavy 16mm camera used in TV news in the old days—thus identifying the last unknown principal in my photos of that first day at the crash site. I reciprocated, in part, by telling him that the name of his guide was Jack Hicks.

Dick Skrondahl, a journalism major at the University of New Mexico at the time of the crash, was a classmate of Harry Moskos and knew Bill Richardson, then bureau chief at AP. He had not seen Frank Hibben at the crash site that day, but knew him well through his hunting and his anthropology classes. He later did photo work for him from time to time.

His helpless position as "author" of the *Stag* magazine article had been a terrible experience for him. It could easily have cost him his profession, but he had learned a great lesson from it. Early in his journalism career, he "was committed to respectfully photographing and writing about any tragedy he was assigned to cover—auto wrecks, murder scenes, train wrecks, plane crashes, and disasters of all kinds."

I have long asserted that the people associated with this saga have been first-rate. And I'm pleased to include Dick Skrondahl among them.

Not so the writer of the *Stag* article. The Wilhelm Gustloft Web site considered vonBlock's 1958 *Battle Cry, 6,000 Victims*—about the sinking of the Wilhelm Gustloft passenger ship in 1945—as "poorly written and terrible with facts—almost purely fiction."

He was notably consistent with his stories of tragic events.

The writer was probably Bela W. Von Block, who also used other pseudonyms.

Thus, Dick Skrondahl, who took the first photo at the crash site, would be the last person whom I would learn about—a fitting ending for this topsy-turvy tale of reality.

It's a small, small "WORL," indeed.

Mary Balk

June 5, 2009. I visited the Georgia State University Library to search for information concerning Frank Busch, vice president of operations for TWA and one of the rescuers who had weathered that terrible night on the mountain after the plane had been spotted. As Busch was reputedly a relative of both cofounders of the Anheuser-Busch Corporation, I wanted verification.

Finding nothing, I asked for advice from a reference librarian and was directed to Library Special Collections to see Traci Drummond, archivist for the Southern Labor Archives. The archives had files concerning Delta Airlines that might include information about other airlines.

Dubious of success, I went anyway, discovering that there was nothing relevant there; Traci Drummond was perplexed that I had no interest in her archives. I then visited the Emory University Library near Decatur, but again found nothing. A fruitless search for information about Busch had undoubtedly been a waste of time.

Unbeknownst to me, Mary Balk, daughter of passenger Robert Balk, had left me a voice-mail message while I was at the archives. I had phoned the Stevens College Alumnae Association the previous day in the faint hope that they had records that might help me get in contact with her. I told them I was writing a book about the plane crash that had killed her father while she was a student there.

They acknowledged knowing of her whereabouts and would provide her with my email address and phone number if I would supply them.

The next day I heard a cheery voice on my answering machine introducing herself and giving me her phone number. It was "hilarious" that I was writing a book about her father, for her late husband, Gary, a history professor, had also taught at Georgia State, and she lived in Decatur (a few minutes from Emory University).

Being uncertain of her last name, I Googled "Gary GSU History" and was astonished by what I found.

His last name was Fink, and he had been chairman of the GSU Department of History and the cofounder of the Southern Labor Archives at GSU, where I had been when she phoned me.

I had never before had reason to consult the GSU Special Collections and had never heard of the Southern Labor Archives. Yet the widow of its cofounder and daughter of crash victim Robert Balk had chosen that very moment to establish contact with me.

When I told Mary about this, she asked me whether I had told Traci Drummond about my connection with her. I explained that I had had no reason to do so—I had known nothing then that could conceivably have connected her with Georgia State or the Southern Labor Archives.

Had I shown Traci my photo of Mary's father, however, it might have been she who could have connected me with Mary, as Mary had recently told Traci about her father and his perishing in the crash while consulting her about ways to donate his professional gear to a museum.

Some might say that this was all mere coincidence, but mere coincidences are all too common in the continuing drama of this half-century-old tale of a plane crash upon Sandia Mountain.

WOW!

I had no photo of TWA flight hostess Sharon Schoening (Figure 14) that would remotely do her justice, and the publication deadline was at hand, when naturally—as is common in this project—something happened. Hugh Prather received a surprise e-mail from a person neither of us knew existed: Nicole Schoening-Von Thies, the niece of the hostess.

"My dad, Shari's little brother, had just found a container of pictures, and I was going through some of them yesterday. I brought home a picture of Shari that I thought was cool and have now noticed it was taken or developed in February of 1955. . . . This may very well be the last photo of Shari."

"WOW!" had been Hugh's instantaneous response—as was mine.

16

ALPHA Critique of CAB Amended Report

A copy of the ALPA Critique of the CAB Amended Report (reproduced in this chapter) was attached to a July 29, 1958, letter addressed to "All TWA pilots" from J. L. DeCelles, chairman, TWA Central Committee. The letter stated that the critique had been presented to the Civil Aeronautics Board along with a request for a conference to discuss the report.

ALPA CRITIQUE OF CAB AMENDED REPORT, TWA MARTIN ACCIDENT AT ALBUQUERQUE, NEW MEXICO

(February 19, 1955)
THE ACCIDENT
ALPA COMMENT:
None
HISTORY OF THE FLIGHT
1) QUOTE FROM CAB REPORT: (Page 1, paragraph 4)
"The tower then requested the flight to report over the Weiler Intersection, and the flight requested information regarding the location

of the Weiler Intersection. The tower operator verified that the Weiler Intersection was formerly the Alameda Intersection and had only been renamed; also, that it was the intersection of the 026 radial from the Albuquerque Omni Range and the back course of the Albuquerque ILS localizer. The flight acknowledged this information."

ALPA COMMENT:

This paragraph should be revised to show that the TWA departure chart for the Albuquerque area did not show the Weiler Intersection.

It should also include a notation to the effect that Flight 260 again asked the tower to verify the definition of the Weiler Intersection at the time of receiving takeoff clearance. This is important because it is a clear indication of intent to check the Weiler Intersection—and, hence, to fly the route by which the flight had been cleared.

2) **QUOTE FROM CAB REPORT:** (Page 1, paragraph 5)

"Flight 260 took off from runway 11 at 0705 on schedule. The time off was not reported, contrary to company practice."

ALPA COMMENT:

TWA policy requires that the time off be reported immediately after takeoff. When ATC requires a check on VHF frequency after departure—as, for example, the Weiler Intersection—it is customary to give the time off to the company on HF frequency. If unable to contact the company on HF—as is frequently the case—it is company and general practice to wait until circumstances permit and then change over briefly to the company VHF frequency, coming back to the ATC frequency as soon as the time off check has been given.

According to CAB Exhibit 27, a radio selector switch box was found in the wreckage with the transmitter selector switch positioned for HF transmission, and according to CAB Exhibit 14-A, the aircraft's VHF frequency selector was found tuned to the company VHF frequency.

It seems entirely probable that Flight 260 delayed giving the time off report due to the necessity to monitor essential traffic which, according to CAB Exhibit 9-B, was encountered northwest of the airport. Undoubtedly, preparations to combat anticipated icing further delayed transmission of the time off report. The fact that the transmitter selector switch was selected to the HF transmitter, coupled with the fact that the VHF frequency selector had been changed from the tower frequency to the company VHF frequency, would seem to indicate that an unsuccessful attempt to contact the company on HF had been made and that the crew was in the process of setting up the radios to give the time off on VHF when the accident occurred.

3) QUOTE FROM CAB REPORT: (Page 2, paragraph 2, line 6)
". . . in a high-speed shallow climb."
ALPA COMMENT:
This statement should be followed by the sentence which immediately precedes it in the testimony of the witness: "The pilot was not
climbing as though intending to cross the ridge at a safe altitude." (See
CAB Exhibit 5-a.)

4) QUOTE FROM CAB REPORT: (Page 2, paragraph 2, lines 6
and 7)
"He noticed that the upper portion of Sandia Ridge was obscured
by clouds."
ALPA COMMENT:
This statement is in direct conflict with other testimony by the same
witness and with the testimony of several other witnesses whose qualifications are unimpeachable. It gives a seriously misleading impression
of the extent to which the mountains might have been visible to the
pilots of Flight 260. The statement should be deleted and the question
of mountain obscuration should be covered in detail under *Investigation*.

The statement is found in slightly different form on the 24th page
of the official transcript of the CAB hearing, and reads as follows, "The
upper third of Sandia Ridge was obscured by clouds."

But, on page 30 of the transcript, the same witness testified that the
altitude of the cloud base adjacent to the to the mountain was *lower
than 7500 feet msl* [mean sea level]. This would mean that the height
of the visible portion of the ridge was approximately 500 feet while the
height of the cloud-covered portion of the ridge was approximately
3,200 feet. In other words, approximately 86% of the ridge was obscured; not just "the upper third," or "the upper portion."

Other witnesses who had observed the extent of mountain obscura-
tion in the direction of the crash site testified as follows:
Witness Dolson—(See page 56, CAB transcript)
"The clouds were right down to where the terrain starts leveling off."
Witness Olson—(See page 83, CAB transcript)
"All you could see was just the little parts of the foothills."
Witness Morrison—(See page 107, CAB transcript)
". . . the Sandia Mountains were completely covered, the base of
the mountains could be seen, the overcast did not extend to the rising
ground of the approaches to the pass . . ."
Witness Marshall—(See page 148, CAB transcript)

"The height of the base at the layer over the mountains was approximately 8,000 feet msl, and it lowered as you went south along the mountain. Around Tijeras Canyon it was nearly to the base and that is approximately 6,000 feet msl."

It is of the utmost importance to note that all of the above estimates of the extent of mountain obscuration were obtained from observers on the ground. It is well known that estimates by ground observers of weather conditions at altitudes differ widely from the actual conditions encountered at those altitudes. The following is an excerpt from the testimony of the crew of Pioneer Air Lines Flight 62 which departed just 11 minutes after TWA Flight 260: (See page 40, CAB transcript)

Q. Now in the vicinity of Albuquerque, during your climb to 10,000 feet, was any part of the Sandia Mountains visible to you?

A. Possibly only just the vicinity around the pass, where the highway goes due east of Albuquerque. However, the biggest peak and all was obscured from the top rightdown to the base.

Q. Clear to the base?

A. Yes.

Q. And that is even from the ground on the ramp at Albuquerque?

A. Well, that was noticed shortly after takeoff and proceeding northbound, just looking dead ahead. We were headed straight for it.

Q. And you couldn't see any portion of the Sandias at any time except to the Southeast?

A. That's about correct. Yes, sir.

5) QUOTE FROM CAB REPORT: (Page 2, paragraph 5, line 3)

"The wreckage was sighted from the air just below the crest of Sandia Mountain."

ALPA COMMENT:

The words "just below" are not properly indicative of the fact which is stated on line 4, paragraph 7, page 2 of the report as follows: "Some 1,439 feet lower than the crest of the ridge . . ."

6) QUOTE FROM CAB REPORT: (Page 2, paragraph 8, lines 5–8)

"Before departure the pilots had been briefed on the weather, which was generally clear and would have permitted visual flight over nearly the entire route, with only short instrument flight probable."

ALPA COMMENT:

At the altitude for which Flight 260 was cleared, the weather over the flight plan route was *not* "generally clear" and certainly would *not* "have permitted visual flight over nearly the entire route, with only short instrument flight probable." On the contrary at 9,000 feet msl, instrument flight would have been necessary over nearly the entire route. Pioneer Flight 62 departed Albuquerque 11 minutes after TWA Flight 260 and climbed to 10,000 feet msl south of the airport before proceeding on course. Approximately 3 to 4 minutes northbound from the airport, Pioneer Flight 62 was skimming, through the tops of a solid overcast which extended over, the entire area of the flight path to a point 10 or 12 miles northeast of the Jemez Intersection. Obviously, at 9,000 msl, TWA 260 would have been on instruments in this solid overcast for nearly the entire route.

7) QUOTE FROM CAB REPORT: (Page 2, paragraph 9)

"The TV towers on the highest point of Sandia Ridge had been visible from the Albuquerque Airport at 0625, approximately 43 minutes before the crash, by official Weather Bureau observation. However, at the time of the crash the upper portion of the ridge was obscured by clouds."

ALPA COMMENT:

This paragraph gives an erroneous impression of the extent to which the Sandia Ridge was obscured at the time of the crash, repeating the same error which is discussed under Section 4 of this ALPA Critique. The paragraph is not pertinent to the report and should be deleted.

8) QUOTE FROM CAB REPORT: (Page 3, paragraph 3)

"This expedition of Investigators reached the site on May 3 and made an exhaustive study of the wreckage after considerable difficulty and hazard, including a rock slide that injured several members, one seriously. The results of their findings, and later study of some of the recovered components of the aircraft, showed no evidence of fire or structural failure prior to impact, nor of malfunctioning of either engine or either propeller. A study of recovered radio components disclosed that No. 1 VOR Navigation Receiver was tuned to the frequency of the Albuquerque Omni Range Station; No. 2 VOR Navigation Receiver was tuned to the frequency of the Albuquerque ILS Localizer. *Other navigational instruments were either not recovered or were so extensively damaged that they could not be tested nor their settings learned.* Both pilots were using safety belts at the time of the crash and had been in their proper respective seats at takeoff."

ALPA COMMENT:

This paragraph contains numerous omissions and one completely false statement. Both the omissions and the false statement are of critical importance. The false statement is all the more remarkable in view of the fact that it is an addition to the original version of the CAB report, and was added in response to the ALPA suggestion that malfunction of navigational instruments might have caused or contributed to the accident.

The Omissions

(1) The Tachometer Indicator for the left (#1) engine was found and indicated that minimum cruise power had been set. (CAB Exhibit 27)

(2) The propeller blades of the left (#1) engine were found to have been set at the angle for minimum cruise power. (CAB Exhibit 22)

(3) The #1 ADF Control was found in the ADF position and was tuned to the Albuquerque ILS Outer Compass Locator. (CAB Exhibit 14a)

(4) The VHF Communications Frequency Selector was found set to the company radio frequency. (CAB Exhibit 14a)

(5) A Radio Transmitter Selector Switch was found to be selected to the position for transmission on the HF band. (CAB Exhibit 27)

(6) The Captain's Omni Bearing Selector was determined to have been set to one of two radials, the "most likely" of which was that of the Weiler Intersection. (CAB Exhibit 27)

(7) One of the two Course Deviation Indicator instruments was found. It was determined that the localizer needle movement was jammed in the full scale right deflection position, although a small round spot of paint was found on the dial which might indicate a 1/2-scale deflection to the left. The localizer warning flag was found to have probably been in the hidden position. The glide slope needle meter movement was found to be nearly centered, and the movement was jammed in that position. (CAB Exhibit 27)

NOTE: If this was the left (#1) instrument, a 1/2-scale deflection to the left would indicate a malfunction, either of the ground or of the airborne equipment; and a full-scale right deflection would either be true or false depending on whether 026 or 206 was selected on the Omni Bearing Selector. On the other hand, if this was the right (#2) instrument, either a 1/2-scale left or a full-scale right deflection would indicate a false reading of the ILS transmitter or receiver equipment.

(8) A Radio Magnetic Indicator Dial was found with the card stopped—at 273 or 274 degree indication. Upon disassembly of the instrument there were no marks to indicate the card was moved on impact. (CAB Exhibit 27.) This represents a fluxgate compass error of approximately 47 degrees in the direction which would have led the flight to the right of its intended heading. The magnitude (and direc-

tion) of this error is precisely that which would have produced the heading which led to the crash site.

The False Statement

The CAB report states that the #1 VOR Navigation Receiver was tuned to the ABQ VOR Station, and the #2 VOR Navigation. Receiver was tuned to the ABQ ILS Localizer, but that other navigational instruments were either not recovered or were so extensively damaged that they could not be tested nor their settings learned. As is evident from "the omissions" listed above, this statement is untrue.

9) QUOTE FROM CAB REPORT. (Page 4, paragraph 1, lines 4–9)

"Tower personnel watched this flight proceed out the back course of the ILS and still had it in sight when it reported over the Weiler Intersection at 9,500 feet msl. Its crew testified that they encountered only approximately one minute of instrument flight near the intersection of the back course of the ILS localizer and the 240 degree radial of the Santa Fe Omni Range."

ALPA COMMENT:

This section of the CAB report is in contradiction to the testimony of the tower operator on which it is based. (See page 110, CAB transcript.)

The flight (Pioneer Air Lines Flight 62) did not report over the Weiler Intersection at 9,500 feet. The flight was cleared to fly at 10,000 feet and there is no reason (or testimony) to suggest that this altitude was not maintained.

Nor does the hearing record or any of its Exhibits contain any basis for the Board's statement that tower personnel still had the Pioneer flight in sight when it reported over the Weiler Intersection. To the contrary, the crew of the Pioneer flight testified that at 10,000 feet they were alternately on instruments in or skimming through the tops of a solid overcast cloud layer from a position 3 or 4 minutes north of the airport to a position 10 or 12 miles northeast of the Jemez Intersection. And the tower operator himself testified that he saw the Pioneer flight when the flight reported at 10,000 feet northbound over the south boundary of the airport and "one more time north of the field. It was a very short time after the report was made and *I don't think he could have been further north than Central Avenue and that is the last time that the aircraft was observed.*"

Finally, a grossly distorted picture of the weather conditions along the flight plan route is given by the statement that the crew (of Pioneer

62) testified "that they encountered only approximately one minute of instrument flight. . . ." The fact is the crew amplified this statement to explain that they were barely on top of the solid overcast from a short distance north of the Albuquerque airport to some 10 or 12 miles northeast of the Jemez Intersection although they were on actual instruments for only about one minute in the vicinity of the Jemez Intersection.

This is one of numerous erroneous passages in the Board's report which contribute to the false impression that TWA Flight 260 would have found VFR weather along the route it was cleared to travel.

10) QUOTE FROM CAB REPORT: (Page 4, paragraph 6, lines 1–2)

"The Board, in an attempt to determine a reason for the pilot's actions in pursuing the course flown, explored all possible evidence and circumstances."

ALPA COMMENT:

The Board did not explore "all possible evidence and circumstances." Had they done so, they would not have failed to comprehend the significance of such arresting facts as:

a) The crew questioned and re-questioned the location and definition of the Weiler Intersection.

b) The aircraft's receivers were found set to the proper frequencies for complying with the flight clearance.

c) The omni bearing selector had been set to check the Weiler Intersection.

d) The aircraft was in cruise power, at the cruising altitude specified in the clearance.

e) This cruising altitude was some three thousand feet below the absolute minimum safe altitude for crossing the ridge.

f) The Sandia Mountains, as viewed from flight altitude, were completely obscured.

g) The Rio Grande valley to the north of Albuquerque, as viewed from flight altitude, was completely obscured.

h) There have been numerous instances of fluxgate compass malfunction. (A graphic file of such malfunction reports was submitted to the Board prior to its writing of the "amended" report.)

i) Some types of fluxgate compass malfunction are extremely difficult to detect. (At the present time several carriers—including TWA—are actively pursuing development of a device to warn pilots of such failures.)

j) The primary heading reference of both the Captain and the First Officer (their respective Radio Magnetic Indicators) were wired to the same fluxgate compass. (See attached ALPA Exhibit 1.)

k) The Radio Magnetic Indicator dial which was recovered from the wreckage was stopped on a heading which was significantly different from the heading on which the aircraft struck the mountain.

l) The magnitude and direction of the error of this Radio Magnetic Indicator were equal to that which would have been required to lead the flight into the crash area.

m) There have been numerous instances of malfunction of VOR navigation receiver components. (A file of such malfunctions was submitted to the Board prior to its writing of the "amended" report.)

n) Several types of VOR navigation receiver malfunction are of such a nature as to have readily contributed to this accident.

o) An incident of simultaneous dual failure of fluxgate and VOR receiver equipment has occurred on at least one occasion and has been made known to the Board.

11) QUOTE FROM CAB REPORT (Page 4, paragraph 6; page 5, paragraph 1)

"The Board, in an attempt to determine a reason for the pilot's actions in pursuing the course flown, explored all possible evidence and circumstances. Consideration was given to a possible misunderstanding in the ATC clearance. It is interesting to note that the 026-degree radial off the Santa Fe Omni Range, which is 206 degrees from that range, is very nearly in line with the Albuquerque Airport and the crash site. This is considered to be a highly remote source of navigational error particularly considering the excellent weather existing along the authorized route.

"As previously stated, the first officer was relatively unfamiliar with the Albuquerque area. In identifying the location of the Weiler Intersection the 026-degree radial of the Albuquerque Omni was mentioned. Had this course been flown with the receiver tuned to the Santa Fe Omni instead of the Albuquerque Omni, the aircraft could conceivably have arrived close to the point of impact. It is impossible to know what changes may have been made in the radio frequencies just prior to the accident. This thought is offered with the full realization that it is entirely un-provable and completely conjectural. The aircraft's receivers were found set to the proper frequencies for using the Albuquerque Localizer and Omni Range in accordance with the flight clearance. However, the flight did not follow this plan."

ALPA COMMENT:

The Board itself admits that the theory offered in these two paragraphs is "entirely un-provable and completely conjectural." The fact is, however, that the theory is ridiculous and fantastic and has no place in a serious attempt to understand this accident.

The theory would require that First Officer Creason (a commercial pilot with nearly 4,000 flying hours and more than 3 years service as an airline copilot, flying a route which he had flown at least 3 times within the previous 6 weeks) would:

a) Tune in the Santa Fe Omni instead of the Albuquerque Omni.

b) Attempt to fly the en route course by means of the intersecting radial rather than the en route radial.

c) Fly a steady northeast heading for four or five minutes out of Albuquerque at 9,000 feet.

d) Fly into an overcast on that heading.

Furthermore, the theory would require that Captain Spong (an air transport pilot of excellent and conservative reputation, with more than 12,000 hours and nearly 13 years experience on the airline, flying a route which he had flown 11 times previously during the preceding 3 week period) would sit idly by and let this fantastic error occur in an area of extremely hazardous terrain.

These 2 paragraphs should be entirely deleted from the Board's report.

12) QUOTE FROM CAB REPORT: (Page 5, paragraph 2)

"It is difficult to conceive of the crew attempting to cross a 10,682-foot ridge at 9,000 feet, especially when the aircraft was capable of climbing to an altitude which would more than clear the ridge. The Martin 404, grossing 40,027 pounds, should, at maximum continuous power, climb at 1,500 feet per minute up to 9,000 feet and slightly less than that thereafter. This rate of climb would have brought the aircraft several thousand feet above the ridge starting from Albuquerque, only 13 miles away. Even with much less power the ridge could have been easily topped. There appears to be no plausible explanation of why the airplane was not climbed, presuming the pilots flew the direct route knowingly."

ALPA COMMENT:

In view of the dramatic immensity of Sandia Ridge and the fact that its elevation is well known to all TWA pilots qualified on the route, it is not only "difficult" to conceive of the crew attempting to cross this 10,682-foot ridge while in cruise power at 9,000 feet, it is *impossible*.

One can only concur with the final sentence of this paragraph of the Board's report—"There appears to be no plausible explanation of why the airplane was not climbed, presuming the pilots flew the direct route knowingly."

It is certainly regrettable that the Board did not take the next logical stop and conclude that therefore it must be presumed that the pilots did *not* fly the direct route knowingly!

13) QUOTE FROM CAB REPORT: (Page 5, paragraph 3, lines 4–8)

"The airways distance between Albuquerque and Santa Fe is 53.5 nautical miles; the direct course is 43 miles. This difference of 10.5 miles would amount to only about 3/4-minute's difference in flying time. However, the flight departed Albuquerque on schedule and if it had been flown according to the flight plan would have arrived at Santa Fe on time."

ALPA COMMENT:

Actually, unless METO power were used, it would take longer to go the direct route than by way of the dog-leg airway. It would be necessary to make a spiral climb in order to top the ridge.

But all the evidence indicates that the crew intended to go by way of the route by which they had been cleared, and they were obviously not attempting to climb over the ridge.

14) QUOTE FROM CAB REPORT: (Page 5, paragraph 5, lines 1–4)

"The captain in command of the flight was well experienced over the route Albuquerque to Santa Fe. In addition the weather was such that visibility along the airway was good for many miles ahead to the north. The *base of the* mountains *was* clearly visible from *the airport although the crest was obscured.*"

ALPA COMMENT:

As previously submitted in this critique, the weather was such that visibility along the airway was *not* good for many miles ahead to the north. In fact, the crew of Pioneer 62 testified (CAB transcript, page 44) that it was not possible to see up the Rio Grande valley because: (CAB transcript, page 43) there was (*as viewed from the air*) a "solid wall" of cloud and "no forward visibility" just a couple of minutes north of Central Avenue.

Although the base of the mountains undoubtedly was clearly visible *from* the airport, it is quite evident, both from the testimony and from common sense, that the base of the mountains was not visible from flight altitude. For the same reasons, it is much less than the whole truth to state that "the *crest* was obscured."

15) QUOTE FROM CAB REPORT: (Page 5, paragraph 5, lines 7–9)

"It was contact during the turn around the airport and for approximately five minutes thereafter before entering the clouds obscuring the top of the mountain."

ALPA COMMENT:

It is highly debatable whether the flight was contact "for approximately five minutes" after completing the turn around the airport before "entering the clouds obscuring the top of the mountain." Not more than four minutes transpired from the completion of the turn until the occurrence of the crash. At least one and probably two of these minutes were flown in cloud, leaving at most three and probably only two minutes of contact flight after the turn. Moreover, testimony indicates that the aircraft entered the clouds while still climbing at an altitude "above 8,000 feet msl." Climb performance charts for the TWA Martin 404 indicate that this would have occurred approximately two minutes after completion of the turn.

It is repetitious, but necessary, to point out the use of the phrase "the clouds obscuring the top of the mountain." Repeated use of such phrases throughout the Board's report show the importance which the Board attached to this erroneous concept.

16) QUOTE FROM CAB REPORT: (Page 5, paragraph 6, lines 1–9)

"The possibility of malfunctioning of navigational instruments having caused or being contributory to this accident was considered at great length. In scrutinizing this possibility it is necessary to keep in mind a number of factors. One is the excellent visibility prevailing from the takeoff to a point where a competent witness saw the aircraft enter an overcast near the area of the crash. Under these VFR conditions crews are required by the CAR to be visually alert. If this crew was, there is no understandable reason why the pilots would not know, by reference to the conspicuous terrain features, that they were not on the planned course."

ALPA COMMENT:

The Board rejects the possibility of navigational instrument malfunction as being involved in this accident. The primary reason for this rejection is the Board's erroneous concept of the weather conditions encountered by the flights. That concept, which is repeated more than

10 times in the body of the CAB report, has already been amply refuted in this critique.

17) QUOTE FROM CAB REPORT: (Page 5, paragraph 6, lines 9–19)

"If we are to believe that undetermined malfunctioning of the aircraft's navigational equipment led the flight into the crash area we must presume a number of instrument failures—failures which would be more or less simultaneous, of similar magnitude, and in the same direction. Furthermore, this extreme unlikelihood would have to be accompanied by the crew not looking beyond the cockpit. And further, all these conditions would have had to prevail continuously from the very start of the flight up until it was within two or three miles of the crash site. This situation is thus based on improbabilities compounded to such an extent that the Board must reject it as being too tenuous to warrant serious consideration as a possible contributing factor of this accident."

ALPA COMMENT:

Flight 260's deviation from flight-plan course was either intentional or it was unintentional. If it was intentional, either the pilots conspired to commit simultaneous suicide and mass murder, or they were mutually ignorant of the facts that:

a) The Sandia Mountains block the direct route.

b) The minimum safe altitude for crossing these mountains is 4,000 feet above the altitude at which the pilots were cruising.

The Board has previously protested that it has never intended to suggest, and does not believe, that the pilots were attempting suicide; and it certainly cannot be seriously suggested that the pilots were unaware of the location and height of the Sandia Mountain range. *Therefore, it can only be concluded that the deviation from course was not intentional.*

But, if the course deviation was not intentional, some explanation must be offered for the facts that:

a) The flight pursued an extremely hazardous heading for an extended length of time, and entered an overcast on that heading.

b) The crew did not detect their departure from the intended course.

It is obvious that, if the course deviation was not intentional, the prolonged *heading* which produced that course deviation was also not intentional. Logically this can only mean that Flight 260 experienced a malfunction of the compass system.

The Board's report contends that "if we are to believe that undetermined malfunctioning of the aircraft's navigational equipment led the flight into the crash area we must presume a number of instrument failures—failures which would be more or less simultaneous, of similar magnitude, and in the same direction."

Presumably the Board has reference to:

a) The fact that the aircraft carried two fluxgate compass systems and a float-type magnetic compass.

b) The fact that the erroneous heading produced an erroneous course which should have manifested itself to the crew.

Let us examine these arguments in the light of facts which were made known to the Board prior to its issuance of the "amended" report.

It is true that the aircraft carried a float-type magnetic compass, but this instrument is so mounted in the cockpit that either pilot must crane his neck in order to read it. Moreover, its indications are neither as precise nor as steady as those of the fluxgate compass, and as a consequence it is used only as means of double-checking the fluxgate compass system when malfunction of the fluxgate system is suspected.

It is true that the aircraft carried two fluxgate compass systems, but this aircraft was so wired that the heading intelligence for the primary heading instrument (the RMI) of both the pilot and the copilot was derived from the copilot's fluxgate compass system.

It is true that the erroneous course should have manifested itself to the crew. The fact that it did not could be adequately explained by any one of the following explanations:

a) The pilot's course deviation indicator was set to receive the Weiler Intersection and could not, therefore, provide any warning of the deviation from the backcourse of the localizer. The copilot's course deviation indicator may have malfunctioned in such a way that the needle bearings would remain nearly centered. (This phenomenon occurs from a variety of causes, such as contamination of the needle bearings, or de-sensitivity of the VOR receivers.) On the other hand, the copilot's course deviation indicator may have malfunctioned in such a way that the needle would stick on the wrong side of the indicator. (The needle is featherweight and is subject to static electric attractions.) Again, it is possible that the copilot's VOR receiver may have malfunctioned for any of several other reasons. (See ALPA Exhibit entitled: Potential causes of VOR Receiver Malfunction.)

b) The Albuquerque ILS localizer transmitter may have malfunctioned or may have been interfered with by some electro-magnetic emission from the government laboratories in the area. Such disorders were actually reported on July 20 and 21, 1957, by two Continental Air Lines pilots. The CAA has been unable to suggest any explanation of the cause of the observed malfunctions and, *as a precaution*, has completely overhauled the Albuquerque localizer antenna system, renewed all RF cables, replaced the co-axial fittings, and repaired the leaky roof of the localizer transmitter shack.

c) The crew may have become confused regarding proper sensing of the deviation indicator needle on a "back course" ILS departure. This, however, seems to be the least likely explanation because it would require simultaneous confusion by both pilots.

18) QUOTE FROM CAB REPORT: (Page 6, paragraph 1, lines 1–2)

"It is difficult to understand why the flight took the heading it did from the airport to Sandia Mountain."

ALPA COMMENT:

It is not difficult to understand this. The flight experienced a malfunction of the fluxgate compass system which was providing heading data to each pilot's RMI. No other conclusion is reasonable. This sentence should be deleted from the report.

19) QUOTE FROM CAB REPORT: (Page 6, paragraph 1, lines 2–8)

"However, there is no question that if the flight had followed the prescribed clearance to the Weiler Intersection the accident would not have occurred. As the Board has previously stated, the evidence is clear that if an instrument malfunction occurred during the VFR portion of the flight it should have become quite evident to the crew and by looking out they would have been sufficiently forewarned that the previously planned and approved course was not being followed."

ALPA COMMENT:

The Board is obviously unaware of the insidious manner in which modern electronic heading and course instruments malfunction. ALPA files, replete with dramatic accounts of such malfunctions, together with a reasoned analysis of the part which such malfunctions could have played in this accident, were presented to the Board many months prior to its issuance of the amended report. But the Board, apparently blinded by its erroneous concept of the weather conditions encountered by the flight, chose to repeat in this section of the amended report the opinion stated more bluntly in the original report: "All the captain had to do was look outside to determine that he was not following the airway."

The type of fluxgate malfunction upon which any intelligible explanation of this accident must necessarily be predicated would probably not have made itself manifest until the final portion of the turn to heading. It is highly probable that the attention of the Captain was distracted during the final part of this turn by a military aircraft which was approaching from the west.

It is standard airline piloting practice to navigate primarily by reference to heading and course instruments; particularly, as in this case, when instrument flight conditions are about to be entered. Of course, the pilot instinctively supplements instrument navigational data by observation of prominent landmarks visible from the cockpit.

Had the mountains been visible from the cockpit as the aircraft rolled out on the northeast heading, they would inescapably have alerted the pilots to the error of their heading. It is most reasonable, therefore, to deduce that the mountains were *not* visible from flight altitude; and this deduction is emphatically substantiated by the testimony of the crew of Pioneer Flight 62.

The portion of the flight from the time when the aircraft assumed the erroneous heading until the time when it flew into the overcast—"the VFR portion of the flight"—was of extremely short duration; probably only two minutes. The aircraft's instruments did not cause the pilots to suspect they were being misled. Confident that their heading and course were secure, the pilots undoubtedly devoted their primary attention to such considerations as preparing the aircraft for flight in the icing conditions into which it was about to fly, checking for traffic, manipulating the controls, reading the instruments, anticipating the Weiler Intersection, putting the engines into cruise power, attempting to give the time off to the company, etc. Apparently they did not find time to supplement their seemingly normal instrument navigational system by deliberate reference to any other landmarks which, if visible, were not sufficiently prominent to attract attention.

20) QUOTE FROM CAB REPORT: (Page 6, Findings)
CAB FINDING #6:
"All ground radio navigational facilities involved in the following this flight plan were functioning normally."
ALPA COMMENT:
This *Finding* should be corrected to read: "6. All ground radio navigational facilities involved in following this flight plan were subsequently

checked and found to be operating normally."

Intermittent false courses of the Albuquerque localizer have been reported by pilots of Continental Air Lines. These false signals, which showed the aircraft to be "on course" when it was actually in the vicinity of the Sandia Mountains, were verified by two ATR pilots, using four different receivers on two different airline aircraft on two successive days. The CAA has been unable to explain these malfunctions, but has—as a precaution—completely overhauled the Albuquerque ILS Localizer system. Obviously, the CAA does not consider it impossible that the transmitter equipment which they found expedient to overhaul may have produced the reported false courses; however, flight checks performed a day or two following these reports found the localizer normal. If it is possible that this equipment could malfunction in the reported instances and yet be subsequently found normal, it is not impossible that a similar intermittent malfunction may have contributed to the subject accident.

CAB FINDING #7:

"The Sandia Mountain area was covered with cloud before and during the flight."

ALPA COMMENT:

This Finding should be corrected to read: "7. The Sandia Mountains were obscured by cloud before and during the flight."

CAB FINDING #9:*"The Flight did not follow the instructions contained in its ATC clearance."

ALPA COMMENT:

This Finding should be changed to read "9. The crew intended to comply with their ATC clearance."

CAB FINDING #10:

"The flight collided with a cloud-shrouded mountain while flying an off-airways course."

ALPA COMMENT:

This Finding should be amended to read: "10. While flying an off-airways course, in cruise power and at the cruising altitude specified in its ATC clearance, the flight crashed 1,500 feet below the summit of a cloud-shrouded mountain."

CAB FINDING #11:

"All major portions of the aircraft were accounted for at the scene of the accident, and no evidence of any malfunction or failure of any of these components was found."

*Author's note: CAB Finding #8 was missing from the critique.

ALPA COMMENT:

This Finding should be corrected to read: "11. Many important components of the aircraft were not recovered. Moreover, many which were recovered were so badly damaged that it was impossible to determine whether they had malfunctioned."

An additional Finding should be listed and should read: "12. Wreckage indicated that the direction of flight at the moment of impact was about 320 degrees magnetic, but the aircraft's Radio Magnetic Indicator dial was found stopped at 273 or 274 degrees indication."

21) QUOTE FROM CAB REPORT: (Page 7)

Probable Cause

The Board determines that the probable cause of this accident was a lack of conformity with prescribed en route procedures and the deviation from airways at an altitude too low to clear obstructions ahead.

ALPA COMMENT:

This section of the Board's report should read as follows:

Probable Cause

The Board determines that the probable cause of this accident was a malfunction of the aircraft's fluxgate compass system, which resulted in a deviation from airways at an altitude too low to clear the mountains. Failure to detect departure from the prescribed course can probably be attributed to one of the following causes:

1) Possible malfunction of the airborne ILS Localizer receiver.

2) Possible malfunction of the Albuquerque ILS transmitting system.

3) Possible confusion by the crew with respect to proper sensing of the Course Deviation Indicator during a back course ILS departure.

BY THE AIR LINE PILOTS ASSOCIATION
J. L. DeCelles, Chairman TWA
Central Air Safety Committee

Notes

CHAPTER 1

1   Robert Buck, *North Star over My Shoulder* (New York: Simon & Schuster, 2002).

3   Derek Dunn-Rankin, "Perfect Hopes and Loving Trust," *Desoto (FL) Sun Herald*, June 18, 2006.

5   Ernest Cloos, "Memorial to Robert Balk (1899–1955)," *Proceedings Volume of the Geological Society of America Annual Report* (1955), pp. 99–100.

5   Edwin B. Eckel, *The Geological Society of America: Life History of a Learned Society*, Geological Society of America (ca. 1982), p. 38.

6   "Robert Tips," TWA Flight 260 Memorial Collection in the Sandia Vista Room, Albuquerque Sunport, NM.

6   C. Austin Miles, "In the Garden," 1912.

8   *New Mexico District News*, New Mexico District Council of the Assemblies of God, March 1955.

8   Leroy Doyel, "Lois Dean," TWA Flight 260 Memorial Collection in the Sandia Vista Room, Albuquerque Sunport, NM.

9 "Dan A. Collier," TWA Flight 260 Memorial Collection in the Sandia Vista Room, Albuquerque Sunport, NM.

12 "Ivan Spong," TWA Flight 260 Memorial Collection in the Sandia Vista Room, Albuquerque Sunport, NM.

13 "J. J. Creason," TWA Flight 260 Memorial Collection in the Sandia Vista Room, Albuquerque Sunport, NM.

13 J. L. DeCelles, letter to Robert Serling, August 30, 1959.

16 Robert Serling, *The Probable Cause* (New York: Ballantine, 1960).

23 C. Austin Miles, "In the Garden." 1912.

23 Michael Kimball, "Victim's Son Finds 'Missing Link,'" NewsOK, February 19, 2008.

23 Charles M. Williams, "Attendee Biographies, TWA Flight 260 Memorial Dedication," TWA Flight 260 Memorial Collection in the Sandia Vista Room. Albuquerque Sunport, NM.

CHAPTER 2

25 "Albuquerque's Environmental Story," Friends of Albuquerque's Environmental Story and the City of Albuquerque, 2008.

25 Robert Julyan, *The Mountains of New Mexico* (Albuquerque: University of New Mexico Press, 2006).

25 Robert Julyan and Mary Stuever (eds.), *Field Guide to the Sandia Mountains* (Albuquerque: University of New Mexico Press, 2005).

27 Charles M. Williams, *Adventures on a Watermelon*, unpublished manuscript, TWA Flight 260 Memorial Collection in the Sandia Vista Room, Albuquerque Sunport, NM.

28 Toby Smith, "The Crash of Flight 206," *Albuquerque Journal Magazine*, May 27, 1980, pp. 8–10.

CHAPTER 3

48 Toby Smith, "The Crash of Flight 206," *Albuquerque Journal Magazine*, May 27, 1980, pp. 8–10.

49 George D. Hankins, personal diary, February 21, 1955.

CHAPTER 4

60 George D. Hankins, personal diary, March 5, 1955.

CHAPTER 5

73 Jane C. Love, "In Memory of Christina Lochman-Balk, 1907–2006," *New Mexico Geology*, vol. 28, August 2006.

73 J. L. DeCelles, letter to Robert Serling, August 30, 1959.

CHAPTER 6

78 Civil Aeronautics Board, *Accident Investigation Report: Trans World Airlines, Inc., Sandia Mountain, Near Albuquerque, New Mexico (February 19, 1955)*, October 12, 1955.

80 O. L. Hanson, letter to David Halperin, May 25, 1956.

82 J. L. DeCelles, letter to Robert Serling, August 30, 1959.

100 J. L. DeCelles, letter to T. G. Linnert, November 26, 1958.

102 Edgar A. Haine, *Disaster in the Air*, (Cranbury, NJ: Associated University Presses, 2000), p. 196.

102 Civil Aeronautics Board, *Amended Report: TWA Martin Accident at Albuquerque, New Mexico (February 19, 1955)*, October 12, 1955.

102 Air Line Pilots Association, *Critique of Amended CAB Accident Report*, July 29, 1958.

CHAPTER 7

116 Toby Smith, "Remembering TWA 260," *Albuquerque Journal*, February 13, 2005.

118 "Lost . . . and Found," Cibola Search and Rescue Team newsletter, January 2000.

CHAPTER 10

149 Harry Moskos, "Remembering TWA 260," *Albuquerque Journal*, September 15, 2006.

CHAPTER 11

162 Steve Rock, "Crusade to Clear Pilots Names Brings Healing," *Kansas City Star*, September 22, 2006.

CHAPTER 13

172 Carolyn V. Coarsey, "Psychological Aftermath of Air Disaster: What Can Be Learned for Training," PhD dissertation, University of New Mexico, 1992.

172 Carolyn V. Coarsey, *Handbook for Human Services Response* (Blairsville, GA: Higher Resources, 2004).

172 Carolyn V. Coarsey-Rader, "Survivors of U.S. Airline Accidents Shed Light on Post-accident Trauma," *Flight Safety Digest*, October 1993.

182 *Aviation Disaster Family Assistance Act*, Public Law 264, 104th Congress, *U.S. Statutes at Large*, 49 USCA Section 4010, October 9, 1996.

182 *National Air Disaster Alliance/Foundation Annual Report*, 2003.

187 George Bibel, *Beyond the Black Box: The Forensics of Airplane Crashes* (Baltimore: Johns Hopkins University Press, 2007), pp. 5, 373.

CHAPTER 14

189 Adams Guns, "Frank C. Hibben, 1910–2002," http:// *www.adams-guns.com/hibben.htm* (accessed January 28, 2010).

192 Villa Hankins, *Memoirs*, unpublished manuscript.

198 Paul Logan, "Orthopedic Surgeon Gene Szerlip Made His Mark," *Albuquerque Journal*, March 13, 2004.

200 "Killer Sentenced to Die Jan. 12," *Albuquerque Journal*, October 13, 1954.

CHAPTER 15

205 Mara Bovsun, "The Turnpike Phantom," *New York Daily News*, Sept. 23, 2007.

205 Dan Cupper, "How the Fear of Crime Affects Behavior: John W. Wable, the Pennsylvania Turnpike Murderer," in *The Pennsylvania Turnpike: A History* (Lebanon, PA: Applied Arts Publishers, 1990).

214 Toby Smith, "The Crash of TWA Flight 206," *Albuquerque Journal Magazine*, May 27, 1980, pp. 8–10.

216 Randy W. Baumgardner, *FBI National Academy*, (Nashville: Turner Publishing, 2000), p. 31.

222 E. W. Scripps Company, "Veteran Newsman Harry Moskos Retiring as Editor of the *Knoxville News-Sentinel*," news release, August 2, 2001.

224 Eva Dameron, "Dealing a Hand to NM's Elite," *New Mexico Daily Lobo*, January 25, 2007.